Romanticism in Perspective: Texts, Cultures, Histories

General Editors: **Marilyn Gaull**, Professor of English, Temple University/New York University; **Stephen Prickett**, Regius Professor of English Language and Literature, University of Glasgow

This series aims to offer a fresh assessment of Romanticism by looking at it from a wide variety of perspectives. Both comparative and interdisciplinary, it will bring together cognate themes from architecture, art history, landscape gardening, linguistics, literature, philosophy, politics, science, social and political history and theology to deal with original, contentious or as yet unexplored aspects of Romanticism as a Europe-wide phenomenon.

Titles include:

Toby R. Benis
ROMANTICISM ON THE ROAD
The Marginal Gains of Wordsworth's Homeless

Richard Cronin (*editor*)
1798: THE YEAR OF THE *LYRICAL BALLADS*

Péter Dávidházi
THE ROMANTIC CULT OF SHAKESPEARE
Literary Reception in Anthropological Perspective

Charles Donelan
ROMANTICISM AND MALE FANTASY IN BYRON'S DON JUAN
A Marketable Vice

Tim Fulford
ROMANTICISM AND MASCULINITY
Gender, Politics and Poetics in the Writings of Burke, Coleridge, Cobbett, Wordsworth, De Quincey and Hazlitt

David Jasper
THE SACRED AND SECULAR CANON IN ROMANTICISM
Preserving the Sacred Truths

Malcolm Kelsall
JEFFERSON AND THE ICONOGRAPHY OF ROMANTICISM
Folk, Land, Culture and the Romantic Nation

Mark S. Lussier
ROMANTIC DYNAMICS
The Poetics of Physicality

Andrew McCann
CULTURAL POLITICS IN THE 1790s
Literature, Radicalism and the Public Sphere

Ashton Nichols
THE REVOLUTIONARY 'I'
Wordsworth and the Politics of Self-Presentation

Jeffrey C. Robinson
RECEPTION AND POETICS IN KEATS
'My Ended Poet'

Anya Taylor
BACCHUS IN ROMANTIC ENGLAND
Writers and Drink, 1780–1830

Michael Wiley
ROMANTIC GEOGRAPHY
Wordsworth and Anglo-European Spaces

Eric Wilson
EMERSON'S SUBLIME SCIENCE

John Wyatt
WORDSWORTH'S POEMS OF TRAVEL, 1819–42
'Such Sweet Wayfaring'

Romanticism in Perspective
Series Standing Order ISBN 0–333–71490–3
(*outside North America only*)

You can receive future titles in this series as they are published by placing a standing order. Please contact your bookseller or, in case of difficulty, write to us at the address below with your name and address, the title of the series and the ISBN quoted above.

Customer Services Department, Macmillan Distribution Ltd, Houndmills, Basingstoke, Hampshire RG21 6XS, England

The Politics of Romantic Poetry

In Search of the Pure Commonwealth

Richard Cronin
Reader in English Literature
University of Glasgow

First published in Great Britain 2000 by
MACMILLAN PRESS LTD
Houndmills, Basingstoke, Hampshire RG21 6XS and London
Companies and representatives throughout the world

A catalogue record for this book is available from the British Library.

ISBN 0–333–76106–5

 First published in the United States of America 2000 by
ST. MARTIN'S PRESS, INC.,
Scholarly and Reference Division,
175 Fifth Avenue, New York, N.Y. 10010

ISBN 0–312–22749–3

Library of Congress Cataloging-in-Publication Data
Cronin, Richard.
The politics of romantic poetry : in search of the pure commonwealth / Richard Cronin.
p. cm. — (Romanticism in perspective)
Includes bibliographical references (p.   ) and index.
ISBN 0–312–22749–3 (cloth)
1. English poetry—19th century—History and criticism.
2. Politics and literature—Great Britain—History—19th century.
3. Politics and literature—Great Britain—History—18th century.
4. English poetry—18th century—History and criticism.
5. Political poetry, English—History and criticism.   6. France–
–History—Revolution, 1789–1799—Influence.   7. Romanticism—Great Britain.   8. State, The, in literature.   I. Title.   II. Series.
PR585.H5C76   1999
821'.709358—dc21   99–36364
                                                                          CIP

© Richard Cronin 2000

All rights reserved. No reproduction, copy or transmission of this publication may be made without written permission.

No paragraph of this publication may be reproduced, copied or transmitted save with written permission or in accordance with the provisions of the Copyright, Designs and Patents Act 1988, or under the terms of any licence permitting limited copying issued by the Copyright Licensing Agency, 90 Tottenham Court Road, London W1P 0LP.

Any person who does any unauthorised act in relation to this publication may be liable to criminal prosecution and civil claims for damages.

The author has asserted his right to be identified as the author of this work in accordance with the Copyright, Designs and Patents Act 1988.

This book is printed on paper suitable for recycling and made from fully managed and sustained forest sources.

10 9   8   7   6   5   4   3   2   1
09 08 07 06 05 04 03 02 01 00

Printed and bound in Great Britain by
Antony Rowe Ltd, Chippenham, Wiltshire

To Dorothy and John

Contents

Acknowledgements	viii
Introduction	1
Part One: The Revolutionary Years	19
Introduction – *Religious Musings*	21
1 Erasmus Darwin: from the Bastille to Birmingham	29
2 William Blake and Revolutionary Prophecy	48
3 The English Jacobins	61
Part Two: The War against Napoleon	83
Introduction – *The Poet's Pilgrimage to Waterloo*	85
4 Walter Scott and Anti-Gallican Minstrelsy	92
5 Wordsworth at War	110
6 Mapping *Childe Harold I and II*	128
Part Three: England in 1819	145
Introduction – *Peter Bell the Third*	147
7 Asleep in Italy: Byron and Shelley in 1819	156
8 Leigh Hunt, Keats and the Politics of Cockney Poetry	181
Notes	200
Index	221

Acknowledgements

Versions of parts of this book have appeared as articles in *The Byron Journal*, *ELH*, *Essays and Studies*, *The Keats-Shelley Review*, *Review of English Studies*, and *SEL*, and I am grateful to the editors of these journals for permission to reuse the material. I am grateful to the many Romantic scholars with whom I have discussed this material over the years, especially to Jack Donovan, Marilyn Gaull, Michael O'Neill, Clifford Siskin and Timothy Webb. I have the great good fortune to be a member of a Department in which it is both a pleasure and an education to work. Amongst my colleagues I am, as always, particularly indebted to Dorothy McMillan and to Robert Cummings. I am also fortunate in having as my colleagues so many who share my interest in Romanticism. I have learnt much from all of them, and I would like to record here not only my debt to but my admiration for Drummond Bone, David Jasper, Alice Jenkins, Seamus Perry, Stephen Prickett, Nicola Trott and Duncan Wu. I have also learnt much from those who have been students at Glasgow both as undergraduates and postgraduates. Amongst many I would mention Alison Chapman, Thomas Docherty, Chankil Park, Jane Stabler and Ya-Feng Wu. Finally, I would like to record my debt to three colleagues who, by making the administrative burdens placed on me in recent years so much easier to bear, have greatly assisted me in completing this book; Pat Devlin, Anna MacMillan and Ingrid Swanson.

Introduction

This is a book on the politics of English Romantic poetry. It is a well established field. Carl Woodring's *Politics in English Romantic Poetry* gave in 1970 a commanding survey of the topic that was already able to draw on a large number of more specialized studies; Todd on Wordsworth's politics, K. N. Cameron on Shelley's, Erdman's work on Blake and Byron.[1] There has been much more since: an extraordinary outpouring of books on Wordsworth;[2] Kelvin Everest and Nigel Leask on Coleridge; Malcolm Kelsall and Jerome Christensen on Byron; Dawson, and Scrivener on Shelley,[3] and a more recent interest in Keats's politics, initiated by Jerome McGann and developed by critics such as Daniel Watkins, Marjorie Levinson, and Nicholas Roe.[4] There is little evidence that interest in this kind of approach to the literature of the period is slackening. In 1998 there were important contributions to the field by James Chandler, Kenneth Johnston and Clifford Siskin.[5]

It has all been part of a more general critical movement, of course, most easily explained as a reaction against the 'new criticism' of the 1950s and 60s, which has been thought to prize poetry precisely insofar as it escapes the partiality of merely political commitment by occupying an aesthetic realm in which the ideological quarrels that beset less elevated kingdoms no longer obtain. In the narrower field of Romantic studies the principal target of attack has been not Cleanth Brooks but M. H. Abrams, who is widely represented as the last of a long critical tradition that described the great Romantics as winning their poetic maturity by surrendering the political commitments that marked their youth in favour of a more dignified commitment to the life of the imagination. But this, one might think, is a point that has been made often enough. It might seem more timely to attempt a rehabilitation of Brooks and Abrams of the kind so elegantly undertaken by

Susan Wolfson in her recent *Formal Charges: The Shaping of Poetry in British Romanticism* than to repeat objections to their work that have by now been so well aired. Anyone offering yet another book on the politics of Romantic poetry might reasonably be asked to present a fairly convincing excuse.

It is a field, then, that is in some danger of being overworked, but it remains a divided field. Malcolm Kelsall, to take a single example, continues Woodring's project. The task he sets himself is to elucidate Byron's poems by mapping the political context within which they were produced and that they addressed. Kelsall assumes distinctions between text and context, between literary fiction and historical fact, between poetic power and critical knowledge. The century and a half that separates him from Byron allows him to see clearly the differences between the world as Byron described it and the world as it was, and allows him to survey the political conflicts of Byron's day and to place Byron within them with a disinterested detachment that is akin to objectivity. For Marjorie Levinson, on the other hand, the distinctions that Kelsall assumes are vertiginously problematic. Both of them practise historical criticism – indeed the major achievement of Romantic studies in the last twenty years is to have transferred to 'history' the glamour that was once routinely attached to the word 'imagination' – but they understand that practice quite differently. One is an old, one a new historicist, we say, but both labels are too general to be useful: each embraces a range of divergent, even inconsistent critical methods. Nevertheless, the distinction retains point. If it does not mark any very clear theoretical division, it at least points to a rather emphatic difference of critical style. There is an occasion, perhaps, for a book that examines this division, and asks what it portends. But there is some reason for supposing that it does not portend very much. Consider, for example, the two most influential historicist accounts of Romantic poetry to have been published in the 1980s.

It is, at first sight, odd that Marilyn Butler's *Romantics, Rebels, and Reactionaries*[6] should be claimed by Levinson as a decisive influence on her own work, because the book seems resolutely old historicist in its method. Butler's ambition is to save the writers she discusses from the falsifications of 'hindsight' by placing them within a historical context that is represented as real rather than textual. She examines texts for their political implications, much as Malcolm Kelsall does, but insists still more emphatically on a distinction between art and ideology, or between literature and propaganda. Her stance is anti-theoretical: if she asks her readers to 'shed their preconceptions' about Romanticism, it is for pragmatic rather than theoretical reasons, because those preconceptions 'interfere with so much good reading'. Her apparent lack of interest in theory is a scandal that has provoked in her more theoretically disposed admirers protective gestures that, though evidently well-meaning, seem somewhat unconvincing, as when Levinson represents the 'absence of theory' in Butler's work as an 'act of sabotage' that works to undermine the authority of 'the groups in power'.[7]

Given this, it is worth enquiring why her book has proved so influential. Partly, perhaps, it is because she condenses within its short space a density of reference to the writing of the period that none of the more theoretically sophisticated proponents of historicism can match – the big six dominate the book, but they have to jostle their way through a rich crowd of minor actors: Robert Bage and 'Barry Cornwall', Erasmus Darwin and Charles Dupuis, Josiah Wedgwood and John Scott. Her successors are, in theory, a good deal more suspicious than she is herself of the mechanisms that have allowed six male poets to circumscribe a literary period, but in their own work they confine themselves much more closely than Butler to the canonical figures.[8] But it is not just the width of Butler's knowledge that has won the admiration of critics who, one would have thought, differ so widely from her in their methods. Her successors have found, I suspect, her cast of mind congenial.

In Butler's book 'Romanticism' vies as a period label with two other terms, 'Enlightenment' and 'Neoclassicism'. At times Butler writes as if she wishes to confine the term Romanticism to the central phase of a history in three parts, the period extending from about 1798 to about 1812, the period dominated by what she calls the literature of counter-revolution. Before 1798, she prefers her other terms, and after 1812, she argues, the second generation of Romantic poets made a brave effort to restore neoclassicist and enlightenment modes. Romanticism, in this narrow definition, is represented as distinctively reactionary, but it is flanked by two brief periods in which literature allies itself, not exactly with rebellion, but at any rate with a set of progressive social and political values. Neoclassicism is essentially social, cheerful and outward-looking; Romanticism, on the contrary, is marked by a gloomy, egotistical inwardness. True to this analysis, Butler identifies a 'great decade', but it is a decade split in the middle, and a great decade that, surely not by coincidence, all but excludes Wordsworth's. It extends from 1793–8 and from 1817 to 1822.

There seem obvious problems here. The earlier of the two five-year periods seems, even in Butler's version, thinly populated. Blake seems to be its only major poet, or he would have been had not Butler chosen to close the period at a date which contrives at once to include and to exclude Wordsworth; to admit the first but exclude the second edition of *Lyrical Ballads*. The second period seems richer, but it proves difficult to describe the major work of Byron, Shelley and Keats as characterized by cheerful sociability. Jerome McGann seems at least as persuasive when he represents the poetry of these years as tending characteristically towards a nihilistic despair. Butler recognizes this, and responds by suggesting, somewhat diffidently, that the great Romantic works might be the products of the two brief periods when Neoclassicism and Romanticism, the outward and the inward, achieved some kind of balance. But the suggestion never seems more than half-hearted. Her own preference remains clear. It is evident in her own critical style, in the sharp, even brusque, accounts she offers of a novel or a poem, accounts which are apt to find, for example, 'a direct rendering of current political tension' in *The Marriage of Heaven and Hell*, and in *Alastor* an uncomplicated rebuke of Wordsworthian introversion. It is evident too in her manner of tracing a writer's career, as when Blake is seen to lapse from 'the critique of institutions' that had energized his early work so far that he could bring himself at the last to produce woodcuts from Virgil that appealed to the 'piety' of Samuel Palmer.

Butler's literary judgements, and the terse analyses that support them, can seem distressingly blunt when read independently, but they seem much less so within the book as a whole, and not only because one admires a talent that allows Butler to condense so much into so short a space. Her judgements are strengthened by being so clearly the expression of a distinctive ethical code, a belief that cultural and social advantage confers obligation, which takes the form of an insistence on the duties of citizenship and the virtues of the civic life. It is an admirable, perhaps somewhat old-fashioned, code, and it is also distinctively British. But it was in America that Butler's book exerted its strongest influence, and the reason is clear enough. Much more quietly than her successors were to do, Butler had reversed the understanding of Romanticism that had held sway from Arnold to Abrams, a critical tradition that prized above all else the movement from public engagement to the meditative inwardness that it represented, in its study of each of the five major poets (for in this school of thought Byron's was always an uneasy presence, his work largely ignored), as a development towards spiritual and aesthetic maturity. In other words, Butler opened up what had seemed to all those critics who had been educated under Abrams's influence a forbiddingly closed critical consensus.

After a brief regency in which the realm was governed by Paul de Man, Jerome McGann has succeeded M. H. Abrams as the most influential critic of Romanticism, and *The Romantic Ideology* is his most influential book.[9] This is unfortunate, because although McGann is severe on 'confusion of thought', 'the mortal sin of every form of criticism', it is a sin from which *The Romantic Ideology* does not seem exempt. McGann's book is clear enough in its drift. Criticism has traditionally sought to criticize Romanticism from within, and this, for McGann, is a contradiction in terms, for the act of criticism demands that critics maintain a distance from their object. Traditional critics have acted as if Romantic criticism and criticism of Romanticism were synonymous, whereas in fact they are logically inconsistent. McGann's project and Butler's seem starkly opposed. Butler writes to preserve us from the errors of hindsight, McGann to insist that only hindsight can preserve us from error.

But McGann does not insist that critics must firmly establish their difference from their field of study simply as a logical imperative. For him it is more by way of a moral duty. We are not recommended to recognize our own difference from the Romantics in order to 'debunk or deconstruct' (an odd but revealing conjunction) the Romantic achievement, but rather because the recognition that 'our present culture has advanced, for better and for worse, well beyond those forms of consciousness that came to dominance in the Romantic Period' is essential if the literature of the past is to do its proper job, that is 'to force a critical engagement' with present forms of thought. We must recognize our separation from Romantic 'forms of consciousness' so that the forms of our own consciousness may be subjected to the 'critical power' of the Romantic poems that we read. Criticism must work to expose the fact that Romantic poems are the products of a Romantic ideology, a set of illusory values that generates the 'false consciousness' of Romantic poetry, but such criticism arrives at its proper end only when it allows the Romantic poems to turn on their critics, and expose their own unquestioned assumptions, their own ideology, their own false consciousness. This is a programme generous enough to secure for McGann's book its lasting popularity, and to persuade its readers to overlook the somewhat suspect manoeuvres that McGann undertakes when he tries to work his programme out.

A small example to begin with. McGann quotes Morse Peckham rather alarmingly advising 'all students of Romanticism' that they should read Hegel's *Phenomenology* 'repeatedly'. They should do so, according to Peckham, because no response to the cultural crisis that precipitated Romanticism was 'so pure, so free of non-Romantic notions'. Peckham wants us to share Hegel's manner of thought, and McGann retorts, as one would expect, that we should instead adopt towards Hegel 'the critical posture that history expects': Hegel's

> is a document so absorbed by its own subject that, from a critical vantage, we can only follow its procedures to our peril. Today no criticism of the Romantic movement can seek to be 'free of non-Romantic notions' if it means to be taken seriously as criticism.

This is roundly stated, but seems clear enough, until we read, only ten pages later: 'Hegel's theory of Romantic Art is important, then, precisely because it is a non-Romantic theory of its subject.' It may be that McGann is making an unusually emphatic distinction between the *Phenomenology*, a document entirely free from non-Romantic notions, and the resolutely non-Romantic 'Introduction to the Philosophy of Art', but this seems unlikely. It seems rather to be the case that in the first instance McGann was interested in the difference between Hegel, on the one hand, and Heine and Marx on the other, from which point of view Hegel seems quintessentially Romantic. Ten pages later, he is comparing the 'completeness' of Hegel's thought, its comprehensive, systematic character, with the fragmentariness of Coleridge's aesthetic pronouncements, and from this new point of view Coleridge is Romantic, and Hegel quite the opposite.

Throughout *The Romantic Ideology* the word 'Romantic' changes its meaning with a rapidity and an unpredictability rare even in the traditional critics whose confusion of mind is McGann's principal target. McGann dismisses contemptuously the view that Romantic is simply a description of all work produced within a particular period. To describe Jane Austen, for example, as a Romantic is 'to misuse words shamelessly', but for M. H. Abrams to deny that Byron is a Romantic is to expose his notion of Romanticism as unable to 'account for all the available data'. Such positions could be rendered consistent only by an unusually precise definition of Romanticism, but the definitions McGann offers seem unusual only for the violence with which they contradict each other.

It is true that a single definition seems dominant: 'Amidst the tottering structures of early nineteenth century Europe, poetry asserted the integrity of the biosphere and the inner, spiritual self both of which were believed to transcend the age's troubling doctrinal conflicts and ideological shifts.' Nature and consciousness, then, are represented in Romantic poetry as transcending history, or, in another formulation: 'The idea that poetry, or even consciousness, can set one free of the ruins of history and culture is the grand illusion of every Romantic poet.' This is a clearly defined position, but its relation with another often repeated observation is unclear: 'Romantic imagination emerges with the birth of an historical sense.' Keats's 'La Belle Dame Sans Merci', for example, is distinguished from traditional ballads because 'Keats's poetic materials are self-consciously recognized to be socially and historically defined'. For McGann, Keats's poem inhabits 'the ruins of history and culture', and, far from identifying it as non-Romantic, this serves only to show 'the extremity of the poem's Romanticism'. Romantic poetry, it seems, insists that art transcends history, except in its extreme forms, when it denies it.

McGann tries to clarify his position in a chapter entitled 'Phases of English Romanticism'. There are three phases: an early phase corresponding to the early years of the French Revolution, a middle phase dominated by the Terror and the Napoleonic wars, and a third phase, which begins with the outbreak of the Peninsular campaign and includes the post-war years. This would be clear enough, except that McGann posits, in addition to the three phases, two kinds of Romanticism: 'primary' and 'secondary', or, with a nod to Harold Bloom, 'revisionist', and throughout the chapter phases and kinds become puzzlingly entangled. Primary Romanticism is confidently exuberant, untouched by anxiety about the status of its own critical methods. Butler describes this as enlightenment or neoclassical Romanticism, and for McGann as for Butler its chief exponent is Blake. *The Marriage of Heaven and Hell* is McGann's preferred example. Secondary Romanticism, by contrast, is so 'deeply self-critical' that it tends to despair. McGann sometimes writes as if 'primary Romanticism' were the same as Romanticism of the first phase. Primary works, he says, are rare in the period, which would be unsurprising if these were works written before 1793, because Blake is the only one of the six poets McGann is concerned with who wrote important poems before that date. But elsewhere McGann writes as if the transition between primary and secondary works was a rite of passage that all six poets had to undergo, so that, for example, *Queen Mab* might be a primary work, and *The Triumph of Life* secondary or revisionist. The confusing effect of superimposing the one scheme on the other is most marked in the comments on Wordsworth. From the time of *Lyrical Ballads* Wordsworth's poems differ from Blake's early work in that 'they are already laden with self-critical and revisionist elements'. They are products of the 'second phase' of Romanticism, and McGann seems to suggest that they are also 'secondary' in kind. But then we read that Wordsworth's 'secondary' period is 'brief to the point of non-existence', because, at the date when Wordsworth ought to have begun writing secondary poems, 1808, he started to write bad poems instead. The third phase of Romanticism is dominated by Byron, who, from the very first, produced work 'so deeply self-critical and revisionist' that it 'has to be defined in negative terms'. This seems a spectacularly secondary achievement, until McGann goes on to describe the period in which Byron wrote the first two cantos of *Childe Harold* as his 'primary phase'. By this point it is hard to see that McGann's scheme is serving any useful purpose.

The lack of clarity in McGann's definition of Romanticism is matched by a similar fuzziness in his notion of ideology. He begins by denying himself Althusser's willingness to allow a distinction between the aesthetic and the ideological. To separate poetry from ideology is to be guilty of a 'false idealism'. Romantic poems, he insists, are constituted by their ideology, and to read them critically is to expose the contradictions of that ideology. But elsewhere he writes as if poetry and ideology were rather easily separable, as if one must 'see the place that doctrine and ideology occupy' in a poem in order to discount them. A Sidney sonnet, for example, may contain 'ideas' that 'seem dated or even, perhaps, wrong', but, once we recognize that, we are freed to appreciate in the poem a 'human drama' that is 'complete and true', and 'must surely seem as fresh today as it was for Sidney at the end of the sixteenth century'. The critic's task, as McGann puts it elsewhere, finding a somewhat lurid metaphor in Trelawney's behaviour at Shelley's cremation, is to 'reach for the unconsumed heart of the poem'. From outdoing Althusser McGann seems to have withdrawn into a kind of enthusiastically untheoretical humanism that differs from Abrams's only in seeming so very much more old-fashioned. But McGann assumes these wildly divergent positions only by the way. He places himself most often in a rather undefined middle ground.

'Romantic poetry', we are told, 'incorporates Romantic Ideology as a drama of the contradictions which are inherent to that ideology.' This is a tricky sentence that carefully glides between two rather different claims: that Romantic poetry reproduces the contradictions of the ideology that it incorporates, and that Romantic poetry represents those contradictions, displays them to us for our better understanding. McGann's more extravagant metaphorical flights are often prompted by the need to conflate these two positions:

> The works of the Romantic poets are not in bondage to themselves: they survive in the valley of their saying, where they speak their truths (including the error of their truths).

It might seem an unnecessary truism to insist that a thing cannot be bound to itself, but McGann says this in order to suggest the odd possibility that a thing might be independent of itself, an extreme paradox (some would say self-contradiction) which is at the centre of McGann's book. He wants to argue simultaneously that Romantic poems reproduce an erroneous ideology, and also that Romantic poetry 'assumes' the 'dominant cultural illusions' of its age 'only to weigh them out and find them wanting'.

So it is that a book that begins with a ringing declaration – 'Today no criticism of the Romantic Movement can seek to be "free of non-Romantic notions" if it means to be taken seriously as criticism' – can end by flatly contradicting itself: 'The literary criticism of Romantic works will justify itself, therefore, when it is seen to have followed the example of the poetry itself.' McGann brings to bear on Romantic poetry a 'critical' method that exposes the errors of that poetry's ideology, but goes on to argue that the poems themselves have anticipated him, and that they use against 'themselves' the very critical methods that he uses against them. He begins by accusing Abrams of being trapped in the belief that the best guides to reading Romantic poems are the Romantic poets themselves, and ends by confessing that he remains a proponent of much the same point of view.

Butler and McGann share an ambition to 'historicize' Romanticism, and both assume that to historicize is also to politicize. Butler's account is admirable in its directness and clarity, but its virtues are expensively purchased by maintaining a system of values which, if consistently applied, would support the view that Erasmus Darwin is a better poet than Wordsworth. McGann, by comparison, adopts values which are certainly flexible enough to avoid any such uncomfortable consequence, but he achieves his flexibility only at the risk of inconsistency.

Butler's and McGann's accounts have been challenged, most incisively perhaps by Clifford Siskin in his *The Historicity of Romantic Discourse*.[10] On the face of it, his is a project much like McGann's: to 'historicize' Romanticism, that is, to argue that all those characteristics that the Romantics and their critics (Arnold through to Abrams and Hartman) have described as 'natural', as features of 'reality' (psychological depth, self-development, imaginative truth) are, in truth, historically constructed. It is a project that requires Siskin to develop a new kind of literary history, a kind that he terms 'generic history', by which he means not a history of literary genres, but rather a method that uses genre to construct history. Romanticism is defined by 'the lyric turn', that is, the turn by which the self is established at the centre of the text. The defining device of eighteenth-century poetry is personification of abstract qualities such as Fear. Qualities are personified so that they may be presented as the properties not of individuals but of the whole community. The possibility of action is displaced from the human speaker to the figure of speech. Hence the apparent self-effacement of these texts, in which the poet passively observes an action in which the agent is not the poet, nor indeed any human being, but a train of personified abstractions. It is by this means that the eighteenth-century speaker gains his special authority, for it is an authority that he accrues by virtue of his appearing to be absent. His invisibility allows him to function within the poem as a representative observer, a purveyor of thoughts sanctioned by their general truth. The reader passively accepts a voice that he recognizes through community to be his own. But, in truth, such personifications are available to be 'read' only by a cultural elite, they are not available to the mob, and they are not commonly available to women. Hence they figure both a universal human community and an exclusive literary community 'grafted upon it'. Siskin's metaphor here seems to reverse priorities. His argument would better support the view that the practice of personification in eighteenth-century poems figures a universal community which is represented as the possession of an exclusive literary community.

Romanticism begins when Wordsworth turns against personification in an effort to return the language of poetry to that of real speech, to abandon artificial elevation. It must have seemed a simple enough reform, but the consequences were far-reaching. In eighteenth-century poetry personifications act; they tremble, threaten, administer punishment and offer reward. When Wordsworth banished the figure, he was forced to transfer the possibility of action elsewhere, to the poet himself, and the effect was to instigate a different reality, the reality of 'the privatised active self'. Personifications act but they do not change. The new reality, on the other hand, the active self, was represented as 'developing'. Indeed, its development became the central poetic theme, and not by accident. It was a necessary response to a simultaneous recognition of rapid social change and a desire for continuity.

The 'lyric turn' seems to indicate a generic history that operates on the most general of levels, a level at which the lyric is distinguished from the narrative and the dramatic, but Siskin goes on to suggest the paradigmatic importance in the period of a single lyric form, the sonnet. The sonnet takes apparent division, the formal gap that separates octave from sestet, and makes of that division the ground of a higher unity. It is through this procedure that the sonnet establishes itself as the defining form of Romanticism. Siskin does not mean simply that

Romanticism as a literary movement began when Coleridge read the sonnets of William Lisle Bowles. For him the sonnet is a genre rewritten in texts as apparently unlike one another, and as unlike sonnets, as *The Prelude* and *Pride and Prejudice*. Such texts console as the sonnet consoles, by making loss the sign of imaginative gain; by making difference in social status, economic and temperamental difference the ground of a harmonious marriage; by making the fact of change the proof not that we are separated from our former selves, but that we are bound to what we have been by a process of personal development. Such texts offer the consolation Mill, Arnold, Abrams and Hartman recognize as defining the category 'Literature'. Literature is writing which takes the fact of social division, the fact of historical change, and reveals that both, like the division between the octave and the sestet of a sonnet, serve only 'as discords do / In sweetest music'. They are the condition of, not a threat to, the music's harmony.

Siskin's account has the clarity of Butler's, and shares with McGann the virtue of constructing an argument that does not require him to categorize the central years of the Romantic period as an unfortunate, reactionary aberration. But it is not without its own problems. It could be said, for example, that Siskin establishes the 'historicity' of Romantic discourse only by denying it a history. Butler and McGann are both happy to accept that Romantic writing changes over the years, but Siskin seems unwilling to concede this. He finds ridiculous Butler's readiness to locate 'three more or less chronological *phases* in the period 1814–19'. He italicizes 'phases' as if his concern was with the vagueness of the word, but it seems clear that his real objection is to any attempt to dissipate the monolithic authority of the term Romanticism. He retains a Foucauldian confidence that 'at the end of the eighteenth century man re-constituted himself', and it functions to convince him that, although he recognizes the danger of the 'elision of historical differences', within Romanticism there are no differences to elide. He turns easily from 'Tintern Abbey' to 'Mont Blanc' as though they were contemporary texts. For him, the concept of literary period is something like a Kantian category, one of 'the enabling acts of historical knowledge', and he resists any attempt to make historical distinctions within periods as threats to the authority of the period concept.

There remains room, then, for an alternative account of the politics of Romantic poetry. But any such account had best begin by indicating what it takes political poetry to be, and this is no easy matter. It would not, I think, be helpful to return to the clear but narrow view that once obtained, according to which political poetry is poetry concerned with the principles or the practice of government, for that view would lead necessarily to the conclusion that *The Prelude*, to take just one example, is an emphatically and explicitly non-political poem. But the obvious alternative, to which Butler, McGann and Siskin are all inclined, seems even less attractive. They tend to the view that all poetry is political, because, to put it more crudely than any of the three would agree to, to write a non-political poem is itself a political act, something like abstaining in a General Election. On the face of it, this could be true only if the field of politics were coextensive with reality, and there are some who have argued quite persuasively that this is indeed effectively the case, for in writing reality cannot be encountered, but only represented, and any representation of reality might be said to serve political ends. The strongest objection to this argument seems to me not logical but pragmatic. It is an argument that seems to accept the centrality of politics in literature, but only by identifying centre and circumference. To argue that all literature is political, and to define the literary as that which escapes the merely political are ostensibly opposite, but practically equivalent positions. The same is true, I think, of the practice of designating as political any relationship that can be described as an exercise of power by one individual or group over another. This seems to be the practice that has resulted in the production of scores of books entitled, 'The Politics of —', in which the blank may be supplied by almost any noun from pcs to penguins. My subtitle, of course, identifies my own book as a contribution to this flourishing critical genre, but I remain suspicious of its more grandiose claims. It is perfectly true that any relationship between two animate parties may be described as an exercise of power, but this is a sufficient description only for those who concede that to exercise power or to submit to it exhausts the possibilities of human behaviour, a bleak thought and also surely improbable.

I prefer to define the kind of political poetry with which I am concerned by quoting the resonant words of Geoffrey Hill, who holds that poetry memorializes a lost kingdom: 'I think there's a real sense in which every fine and moving poem bears witness to this lost kingdom of innocence and original justice.'[11] The sense is perhaps too tenuous in which this holds good of 'every' fine poem; there are poets for whom the 'kingdom' of which Hill speaks is more properly a republic; and there are poets for whom the kingdom was not lost in some undatable past but is to be won in an as yet unapprehended future, poets whose idiom is prophetic rather than nostalgic. Nevertheless,

Hill's terse sentence serves to define the kind of political poetry with which I will be concerned, poetry that speaks to a divided society in an attempt to constitute its readers as citizens of what Hill calls, remembering a passage from Hopkins, the just kingdom, and that I prefer to nominate in an echo of Wordsworth 'the pure commonwealth'. For Wordsworth the primary sign and the one effective guarantee of the purity of the commonwealth is the purity of its language, and I cite Hill here because he is as insistent on this point as Wordsworth himself: 'The history of the creation and debasement of words is a paradigm for the loss of the kingdom of innocence and original justice.' This will be a book committed to the notion that the political import of a poem is a function of its style quite as much as of its sentiments, and that a poet's most effective political act is the forging of a new language.

It is this commitment that will, I hope, lend a certain distinctiveness to the chapters that follow, or, at any rate, secure for better or worse a distinction between my approach and that of the admirable critics that I have cited, for, like most of them, I was trained in a school of criticism in which a studied refusal to place a poem within its historical context was prized as an indication that the critic's proper concern was with questions of literary value, but, unlike them, I am not in open rebellion against my teachers. Historicist criticism may have dominated academic studies of Romantic poetry for the past twenty years, but it has not monopolized that study. There has been distinguished work that has defiantly maintained the interest in the formal qualities of the poem that characterized the new criticism of the 1950s and 60s. It was, after all, just one year after Marilyn Butler published her groundbreaking study that Helen Vendler published *The Odes of John Keats*, and just a year before the appearance of the most recent of the monumental works of historicist criticism, James Chandler's *England in 1819*, that Michael O'Neill published his *Romanticism and the Self-Conscious Poem*, and in the criticism of Vendler and O'Neill poems are examined with a tender vigilance that is both the index of the delight that they take in the poems, and the means by which they share it with their readers. It is not just that Vendler and O'Neill do not practise historical criticism: they are openly hostile towards it. For them, such criticism, at any rate as it is written by its most influential modern practitioners, offers a knowledge of the text purchased at the ruinous cost of wilfully refusing the kind of pleasure in language, its sounds and its rhythms, that it is the peculiar function of poetry to offer. The urgent task for the critic of Romantic poetry is not, it seems to me, to choose between these two apparently antithetical approaches, for both remain too valuable to be rejected. The need is rather to find a critical manner through which the two may be reconciled. It has been my primary concern in working on this book to suggest that a criticism of Romantic poets is possible that does not choose between attention to the language of a poem or attention to its historical context, but seeks rather to show that it is through their language that poems most fully engage with their historical moment.

This brings me to another, and rather delicate, point of contention between my work and that of many of my predecessors in this field. In the title of her seminal book Marilyn Butler classifies the Romantics into two groups 'rebels and reactionaries'. Her phrasing is jauntily journalistic, and in the book itself she does much to resist its implications, implications which serve, surely, to confer a dynamic glamour on one group of writers whilst representing another as crustily antiquated. Many of us remain very willing to confess that we are distinguished by a rebellious individualism, a fierce refusal to truckle to authority, whereas rather few – I can think only of Evelyn Waugh – would be happy to think of ourselves as reactionary. There is a great deal of Romantic criticism, including almost all recent work on the politics of Romantic literature, that is written from an emphatic political perspective, marked, for example, by the use of the word 'radical' as approbatory, and the word 'conservative' as derogatory. Everyone would acknowledge as a right, and some would require as an obligation, that criticism should express the values of the critic, and it may well be that Romantic criticism is generally undertaken by academics who maintain uncompromising traditional left-wing values of a kind rarely encountered these days amongst the general or even the student populace. If so, one could only suggest that they are an oddly unrepresentative bunch, given that, at the time of writing, almost all of them live and work either under an administration led by President Clinton or under an administration led by Prime Minister Blair, neither of which is remarkable for the clarity or the vigour of its ideological commitments, and both of which were elected by overwhelming majorities.

It is an unproductive and impertinent tactic to doubt the sincerity of those with whom one takes issue, and I do not wish to seem to do so. Nevertheless, it has to be asked whether there is not some risk of an unfortunate discrepancy developing between the values that have come almost conventionally to inform Romantic criticism and those that inform the practice of these same critics in other areas of their life. For example, evidence that some poet, whether Wordsworth or Coleridge or Byron or Shelley, succumbed to his fear of mob violence is standardly used to convict that poet of complicity in a bourgeois code of ethics by critics that one scarcely suspects of bringing a similar analysis to bear on events in Bosnia, or Northern Ireland. It is strange to find critics who live to all appearances sedate and deservedly successful professional lives espouse in their criticism a demand for revolutionary integrity that in its uncompromising rigour would not disgrace Saint-Just. But the substantial objection to this critical mode is that it obstructs attentive criticism by encouraging a procedure in which the critic's only obligation is to demonstrate how far and in what way a poet or a poem fails to achieve the alarmingly high standard of radical purity demanded by the critic.

This kind of criticism is constrictive, too, insofar as it encourages the attempt to place the literary text at a certain point on a linear axis, extending, it may be, from Paine or Cobbett to Burke or the later Southey, and this is a procedure likely to mislead. I cited Geoffrey Hill earlier partly with the intention of disputing the appropriateness of this tactic, for Geoffrey Hill is himself a political poet, but the political stance that his poems announce, though disturbing in its extremism, is not easily placeable within the conventional political spectrum. There is, for example, an apparently simple connection between a poem's politics and the readership that it addresses. Radicals throughout this period tended to favour democratic forms of government, whereas their opponents favoured a restricted electorate, and it might seem to follow that radical poets, like Paine and Cobbett in prose, could be easily identified by their use of a poetic language and a subject matter that made their work available to as wide a readership as possible. It was just such a notion after all that prompted Hazlitt's ringing praise of Wordsworth:

> His Muse (it cannot be denied, and without this we cannot explain its character at all) is a levelling one. It proceeds on a principle of equality, and strives to reduce all things to the same standard.[12]

A large number of modern critics have joined in gainsaying what Hazlitt insists 'cannot be denied', but the principle he adduces remains influential: that a radical poetry demands a particular style and subject matter, and that it addresses itself not to a single class but to all, and in doing so assumes the equality of all of humankind. David Simpson, for example, in his fine study of this period traces Coleridge's hardening conservatism in his willingness to exclude from knowledge of the true language of poetry 'the ordinary...men and women who lack, for

Coleridge, the balance of education and intuition necessary to see things steadily and see them whole'.[13] But there are difficulties in any such argument. It may be that Wordsworth in *Lyrical Ballads* affiliates his own verse with the oral tradition of popular ballads that might seem the best recourse for a poet dedicated to the 'principle of equality', but it would be hard to claim that Wordsworth's poems show a knowledge of that tradition equal to Walter Scott's, nor that they were so deeply influenced by it, nor that they succeeded in addressing so wide an audience, and no one would claim either that Scott's Muse was a levelling one, or that Scott developed a poetic style, whatever the claims that Lukacs has made for the novels, that expressed the principles of the French Revolution. There is no simple equivalence that allows us to judge the relative radicalism of a text by the width of the readership that it addresses, a point that one might have expected to obtrude itself rather forcibly on literary critics. Simpson's book, for example, is lucid, vigorously written, and free from forbidding jargon, but one would have to accept, surely, that its idiom excluded from its readership the great bulk of 'ordinary men and women', and it does not follow from this that Simpson's politics are latently conservative.

Like Butler and McGann, I will divide the Romantic period into three phases: the early period dominated by the Revolution and the Revolutionary war, the time when, as Wordsworth recalled, he and many of his fellow poets found themselves in support of their country's 'nominal enemies'; the period of the Napoleonic wars when Britain was in danger of defeat, even invasion; and the immediately post-war period, dominated in Britain by popular unrest. In each case my purpose will be, not to offer a survey of poetry written in the period, but to identify a dominant discourse, and to analyse its limitations.

The first period is characterized by an attempt to frame a universal language, a language in which it might be possible to address all of humanity. The most powerful of the languages available in the 1790s that could plausibly claim universal status was the language of science, and hence it is appropriate that the most celebrated poet of these years, Erasmus Darwin, was concerned 'to inlist Imagination under the banner of Science'. The language framed by Darwin justifies its claim to universality, in part, by rejecting supernatural in favour of natural explanations of phenomena, that is, by excluding religion. Given that differences of religious belief were among the most powerful forces of division in his world, his tactic is entirely logical, but it results in a paradox. Darwin framed a language that addresses all of humanity only by rigorously excluding the large majority of human individuals who were united in their possession of a religious faith, however much they may have been divided by the faiths that they professed. Darwin's poetry forces one to the conclusion that a universal language may be among the more exclusive idioms available to a poet. I turn then, as a counter to Darwin, to his most talented illustrator, William Blake, who in *The Marriage of Heaven and Hell* framed a language designed to reconcile the kind of intellectual radicalism shared by Darwin, Priestley and the rest of the literary set that gathered around the publisher Joseph Johnson with the radicalism of the streets, which was apt to express itself in the mode of Biblical prophecy, and to flaunt its own outrageous credulity as a flamboyant rejection of godless common sense. In *The Marriage of Heaven and Hell* the attempt to produce a work that could be read by all of Blake's fellow-radicals results, and could only result, in a text remarkable for its massive idiosyncracy. Finally, I turn to Southey and Landor, who courageously continued to write an international poetry at a time when the nations were at war. In them, the attempt to devise a universal language assumes its latest guise: it becomes the mark of the traitor.

The book's second part begins with Walter Scott, for Scott, like Erasmus Darwin before him, framed most powerfully the language of the new period, which was not a language designed to unite all mankind but to unite the nation in its war against the French. But Scott's poems are set in the past. Modern Britain is produced as a unified state only proleptically, and it could not well be otherwise, for no description of Scott's Britain could avoid encountering the economic, geographical and political differences that divided the kingdom, a fact which emerges with some clarity when I turn to Wordsworth's *Poems in Two Volumes*, a collection which attempted to resolve the differences of his fellow citizens, and succeeded only in provoking a hostility so intense that Wordsworth was deterred from publishing his poems for some years. This section ends with another paradox, the emergence at the very end of the war years of a new poet to usurp Scott's place as the 'Monarch of Parnassus', the chief poet of the nation. It was a station that Byron earned by systematically and flamboyantly refusing any suprapersonal loyalty.

The book's third part is concerned with the post-war years, when the conflict between nations was supplanted by an internal conflict between classes. In the work by Byron and Shelley discussed there the poetic identity that the two poets had chosen as 'genteel reformers' becomes itself problematic, with the consequence that, as both recognize, poetic style could no longer disengage itself from class conflict. The book ends with the Cockney poets, with Leigh Hunt and Keats, who cannot find, any more than Byron or Shelley, a poetic language that subsumes class differences, but who devise a language in which those differences may be uncomfortably contained.

In his great preface Wordsworth defines the poet as 'a man speaking to men'. It is the project that unites all the poets that appear in this book, and it is a project in which all of them failed, and not simply because they neglected to address women. They failed because they wrote at a time when there was no language available that could address itself to the 'one human heart' that they were confident all of us share. This book charts that failure in each of its three phases, each of them presided over, perhaps, by a single iconic figure. Presiding over the first phase is Anarcharsis Cloots, so touchingly dedicated to universal revolution that he once confessed his ambition to establish a republic on the moon, and so confident of the universal power of his own rhetoric that he designated himself 'Orator of the Human Race'. Nelson presides over the second phase, at the moment when he orders the signal flags raised before the Battle of Trafalgar, conscious that, despite all his personal peculiarities, at this moment he speaks for 'England'. The characteristic figure of the third phase is 'Orator' Hunt, 'Bristol' Hunt, or simply Henry, ascending the platform to make his speech to the thousands gathered at St Peter's Field in Manchester, recognizable to everyone by virtue of his trademark white top hat. That speech was never made, but was forestalled by a cavalry charge by the local militia, a graphic enough demonstration that in 1819 the language that spoke to one section of the population instilled in another only a fierce desire that it should be silenced.

Part One
The Revolutionary Years

Introduction
Religious Musings

In 1796 Coleridge was happy to 'rest all [his] poetical credit on the *Religious Musings*'.[1] For all that the poem may end with Coleridge dismissing it as an example of 'young and novice thought', it was much the most ambitious poem that he had yet attempted – in some respects the most ambitious poem he was ever to write – and yet for all its ambition it remains, as Coleridge confesses in his subtitle, 'a desultory poem'.[2]

Burke opposes writing 'in a desultory and occasional manner' to writing 'systematically',[3] but it is the defining characteristic of Coleridge's poem that it is both desultory and systematical. It skips about from topic to topic, and yet the topics it favours are often in themselves systematically totalizing theological, psychological or historical theories. Repeatedly the poem recurs to a vision in which all things are recognized as parts of some one stupendous unity:

> 'Tis the sublime of man,
> Our noontide majesty to know ourselves
> Parts and proportions of one wondrous whole!
> (126–8)[4]

But the poem, as its subtitle acknowledges, signally fails to embody in itself the kind of whole that it celebrates. It remains a fragmentary poem that lauds the process by which fragments collapse into unity. It is a poem heralding an apocalypse in which 'unimaginable day / Wraps in one blaze earth, heaven, and deepest hell', but its own lights are fitful.

The poem's desultory character is most easily explained by the circumstances of its composition. The subtitle announces it as written on 'the Christmas Eve of 1794'. The date is obviously symbolic, but also seems not far from the truth.[5] In October 1795 he recorded in a letter to Cottle that the poem was complete at 'not quite three hundred lines'.[6] It ended in a confident vision of a world that at last had come to coincide with the world that the poet had always imagined. But in February 1796 Coleridge began writing an additional section of the poem, which was published on 9 March of that year in *The Watchman*, under the title 'The Present State of Society'. Society has become 'a sun-scorched waste', a metaphor uncomfortably at odds with the earlier association of the sun with divine illumination, 'noontide majesty'. Human ills in this section are no longer abstractly conceived as the 'misery' that must soon be expelled from 'a world so fair' because they are incongruous with it (159). Rather, they are presented with graphic bitterness: poverty-impelled crime and prostitution, the suffering of those refused treatment for their diseases, and the suffering of soldiers and their widows. These are not the 'Wide-wasting ills' that can be calmly contemplated by the sage who understands that each is 'the immediate source/Of mightier good' (217–18), but offences that demand a retribution to be visited on 'the great, the rich, the mighty Men,/The Kings and the chief Captains of the World' (309–10). This section, like the original poem, ends in a vision of bliss, but it is a rather different vision. The original poem had ended by confidently proclaiming the power of the poet and sage to 'tame the outrageous mass', attributing to them a 'plastic might' capable of moulding the world into conformity with their own imaginations (246–7). But in March 1796 the vision of bliss functions only as a consolation enjoyed by the 'favoured good man in his lonely walk' (352). He no longer seems granted the power to compel into existence the future he glimpses, but only to muse 'expectant on these promised years' (376).

Once again Coleridge thought the poem complete, but in April 1796, when the volume that *Religious Musings* was to end was already set, Coleridge added yet another section.[7] There is yet another apocalypse, and, as before, it culminates in the collapse of the many into the one:

> And lo! the throne of the redeeming God
> Forth flashing unimaginable day
> Wraps in one blaze earth, heaven, and deepest hell.
> (399–401)

But once again the repetition masks difference. It is not just that the destruction of 'the black-visaged, red-eyed Fiend' (388) is no longer explicitly identified with the overthrow of the 'Kings and the chief

Captains of the World', but that the poem quite suddenly jettisons its metaphysical underpinnings in favour of a quite different and inconsistent set. Once again the manoeuvre is disguised, for it is at this point in the poem that Coleridge chooses to celebrate his philosophical forebears: Newton, Hartley who first 'marked the ideal tribes/Up the fine fibres though the sentient brain', and Priestley. Newton, Hartley and Priestley constitute for Coleridge the tradition of religious philosophical materialism within which he has firmly placed his own poem, but he celebrates them just at the point that he is about to repudiate their authority in favour of a rival tradition, neoplatonic and Berkeleyan, which represents the material world as no more than 'a vision shadowy of Truth' (396), and apocalypse as the moment of escape from shadows into the light of 'unimaginable day' (400).[8] From this new perspective apocalypse is not an event being currently enacted in the history of Europe, nor even a political rearrangement to be expected at some time in the future. It is more by way of an imaginative perception, available now to 'Contemplant Spirits' as it always has been, and always will be.

The poem, one might say, is 'desultory', it hops about, because Coleridge did not stay still during the sixteen months of its composition. He began the poem a disciple of Hartley and Priestley and ended it a Berkeleyan, already half-convinced that the mistake Hartley and Priestley shared with Newton was to represent the mind as passive, 'a lazy Looker-on on an external World',[9] rather than itself constituting that world in the act of its perception. Coleridge's shift from one position to another was impelled, at least in part, by circumstances. In the ten weeks before the Christmas of 1794, three members of the London Corresponding Society, first Hardy, then Horne Tooke, and then John Thelwall, had been acquitted of high treason. They had been supported outside the courtroom by mass demonstrations, and inside it by the verdicts of English juries. Coleridge began to write his poem at a time when he had every reason to believe that his own hatred of the war with France, and his own ambition for a radical reform of the British political system, were popular sentiments opposed only by the tiny minority of the Government and its supporters. He imagined an 'Elect' made up of 'Philosophers and Bards', whose teachings would 'Spread in concentric circles' (226–7), directing the activities of those who had been incited into action by political agitators, men like Hardy and Thelwall, 'eloquent men' who have the power to rouse 'the unnumbered tribes/That toil and groan and bleed, hungry and blind' (240–2). A year later Pitt had passed his Gagging Acts, and it became treason to speak or write against the King, the Government or the Constitution, or to hold a meeting of more than fifty people without the consent of a magistrate. In *The Plot Discovered* Coleridge explained the implications:

> By the operation of Lord Grenville's Bill, the Press is made useless. Every town is insulated: the vast conductors are destroyed by which the electric fluid of truth was conveyed from man to man, and nation to nation.[10]

Pitt had effectively destroyed the mechanism that Coleridge had trusted when he began his poem to achieve social and political renovation. It might seem an inevitable consequence that the new world that the poem celebrates should by its conclusion be reduced to a private vision, consoling the sage as he inhabits the 'sun-scorched waste' of 'Society'.

But it would be wrong simply to claim that the original poem was overtaken by political events, for from the very first the poem is doubtful of the relationship between the Elect, the 'Philosophers and Bards', and the 'tribes/That toil and groan and bleed, hungry and blind'. The tribes are valued only for their destructive power to reduce the nation to 'chaos'. They serve the Elect as the Great Fire served Wren, reducing the nation to a rubble, an 'outrageous mass', that the Elect have the 'plastic might' to 'tame'. But because they have been 'Rudely disbranched' from 'the tree/Of Knowledge' (264–6), their destructive activity is mindless, 'blind', as likely to be visited on the Elect themselves as on the 'Kings and the chief Captains of the World'. On 29 October 1795 the tribes pelted the King as he went to open Parliament, and one tribesman broke his coach window with a pebble, or possibly a bullet, but, as Priestley had discovered in 1791 when a Birmingham mob burned down his library and laboratory, and as Coleridge himself had reason to know, 'the blind multitude' was as likely to be aroused by the 'dark lies' of 'Statesmen blood-stained and priests idolatrous' (373–4) as by the truths communicated by 'eloquent men' such as John Thelwall and Coleridge himself.

One consequence is that the poem never seems confident of whom it is addressing, of whether it is a poem written by one of the 'Elect' to his peers, or by one of the 'eloquent men' addressing 'the unnumbered tribes'. The difficulty of the poem, its compressed Miltonic syntax and its daunting range of intellectual reference, suggests the former possibility. Coleridge responded loftily when accused by Poole of obscurity: 'the Poem was not written for common Readers'.[11] But he scribbled on his manuscript a direction to his printer, suggesting that copies of the volume be distributed in the Midlands and Northern centres of radical dissent: '250 Birmingham – 150 Manchester – 80 Liverpool'.[12] The figures seem optimistically inflated, as if Coleridge had not always been so confident that the poem was beyond the capacity of 'common Readers'. It is an indecision that enters into the texture of the poem. The poem assumes a readership familiar with Hartley's *Observations*, with Spinoza, and with Priestley's rigorously materialist version of Unitarianism. A note added for the 1797 edition aptly encapsulates the lofty exclusiveness, if not the philosophical bent, that characterizes this aspect of the poem: 'This paragraph is intelligible to those who, like the Author, believe and feel the sublime system of Berkley.' And yet Coleridge was able, quite appropriately, to publish one lengthy section of the poem in *The Watchman*, a journal that he clearly intended to reach a wide readership. He feels able to incorporate a figure drawn from the most popular kind of Protestant iconography, the Whore of Babylon (323–7), and also to wonder whether the Elect might be 'Monads of the infinite mind' (408). Among the many desultory qualities of the poem is the desultory manner in which it defines its readership.

When Coleridge first mentioned his poem, he described it to Southey as 'in blank verse on the Nativity',[13] and most commentators on the poem have noted the borrowings from Milton's nativity poem, begun like Coleridge's on the night before Christmas, but 165 years earlier. Milton's poem begins by indicating the date of its composition, 'This is the month, and this the happy morn', and Coleridge follows him, 'This is the time.' Both poets write at the moment when Christ is about to be born, and both commemorate an event that happened many centuries ago. Milton playfully calls attention to the paradox by describing his hurry to finish his poem in time to present his 'humble ode', his shepherd's gift, to the new-born baby before the 'star-led wizards' arrive with their more splendid offerings. So, Milton writes as a rapt witness to the birth of Christ, and the inauguration of 'His reign of peace', but also as a poet in a troubled and divided kingdom just four years into a reign that will be anything but peaceful. He can accept the discrepancy serenely, because, as Don Cameron Allen puts it, 'the discord between the past and the present' is transformed into the 'concord of eternity'.[14] Milton speaks as a seventeenth-century poet who imagines himself the witness of a long-ago event, but the fact and the fiction are resolved because, as a Christian, the full cycle of time has been revealed to him, making it possible for the music of his ode humbly to assimilate itself to the divine harmony, 'the base of heaven's deep organ'. Coleridge ends his poem, very beautifully, making a similar claim. The meditative man rises to a vision of 'Love, omnific, omnipresent Love', and it acts on his soul like the warmth of the sun on an iced-up river:

> when he his influence
> Sheds on the frost-bound waters – The glad stream
> Flows to the ray and warbles as it flows.
> (417–19)

But this can only be an incongruous postscript to a poem that could not conceivably be thought of either as flowing or as warbling.

Milton's ode depends, of course, on his trust that secular history, the history of Kings and Parliaments and taxes and wars, will and must 'melt' into the grandly simple pattern of providential history. Coleridge claims a similar confidence, but unconvincingly. He never succeeds in making providence and history flow together in his poem. *Religious Musings* is at once a poem about the Apocalypse and a poem about the Revolution, but the two terms never quite become synonymous.[15]

At Christmas in 1794 Coleridge began a poem about the nativity, the beginning of the Christian era, the moment when, as the calendar records, one time ended, and another began. He was writing only eighteen months after the French Convention had voted to abandon the Christian calendar and begin time anew, substituting for the seven days of the Christian week a ten-day unit ending not with a sabbath but with a rest day to be known as a *decadi*. Each of the twelve months was to be of thirty days, and the remaining five days of the year, substituting for Christmas and the other Christian festivals, were nominated *sans-culottides*. In voting for the new calendar the Convention accepted its responsibility to govern what Fabre, its chief architect, called 'the empire of signs'. Instead of saint's days agricultural items were suggested for daily contemplation, instead of St Anthony hops, instead of St Valentine a crayfish.[16] The new calendar was an integral part of the Jacobin programme of aggressive dechristianization, though it survived for twelve years the fall of Robespierre, and it provides one of the obvious, though neglected, contexts for *Religious Musings*. Coleridge's nativity poem rejects the Jacobin attempt to demystify the calendar: it re-inscribes the notion that time is divinely ordained rather than an instrument of state policy, and this is part of a larger attempt to redefine the French Revolution as an unfolding of God's providential purpose rather than what it was for the Jacobins, an affirmation that history was determined not by God but by human and natural agencies.

In Coleridge's poem revolution becomes apocalypse: Coleridge reverts from the 'natural' conception of time inscribed in the revolutionary calendar, its months named from the weather or the agricultural cycle, to the supernatural conception that unites him with Milton and with the whole of the Christian tradition that the Jacobins rejected. And yet this is not consistently so, for there are passages in *Religious Musings* that seem to modify the Christian God into a figure very like the God of Nature or the God of Reason proposed by the Jacobins. Robespierre himself could scarcely have quarrelled with a definition of God as 'Nature's essence, mind, and energy!' (49), a point that many years later troubled Coleridge, when he acknowledged that certain expressions in the poem 'may easily be construed into Spinosism'.[17]

Like Milton in his nativity poem Coleridge presses towards the moment when history is dissolved into eternity, when 'Time is no more!', but he was forced to complete the poem because, in a rather different sense, he had run out of time. As Joseph Cottle recalls: 'A part of the poem was even written after all before in the volume was printed; the press being suspended till he had progressively completed it.'[18] There is no better clue to the oddity of a poem that is at once prophetic and journalistic, spoken by one who sees all time spread out before him, and also by a poet responding month by month to a political landscape that was changing as he wrote, and changing with worrying unpredictability.

Religious Musings is at once a poem spoken by a prophet, from a commanding height, and a poem made up of a series of bulletins scribbled down by someone caught up in the press of events, and the difficulty of defining whom the poem is spoken by is matched by the difficulty of deciding whom it is spoken to. There is the problem of whether it is a poem spoken by a 'Sage' to his peers among the 'Elect' or by one of the 'eloquent men' who transmit the Sages' teaching to a wider audience, but there is also the problem of how narrowly membership of the Elect is defined. The status of Milton, Newton, Hartley, Priestley and Franklin is explicitly acknowledged. Apart from Hartley, who is an eccentric addition, this is a fairly standard pantheon amongst the radical dissenters of the 1790s, who commonly sought to equate 'science' and 'freedom', and it suggests that Coleridge is addressing himself to the shared concerns of the wide radical community. His emphatic opposition to the war against republican France, and his insistence that the war that really needs fighting is against social evils, particularly poverty and lack of education, are positions that he could expect to command general agreement. But in other of its aspects the poem seems much more exclusive. Its insistent religiosity, for example, pointedly excludes two influential groups within the radical community; the sceptical rationalists associated wth Godwin, and those who sympathized with the deism promulgated by Tom Paine.[19] But *Religious Musings* is also precise and dogmatic in its Unitarianism. Christ is divine only by virue of the fact that

> The Great Invisible (by symbols only seen)
> With peculiar and concentred light
> When all of Self regardless the scourg'd Saint
> Mourns for th'oppressor.
> (10–13, 1796 version)

This excludes the great majority even of dissenters, confining the poem to one sect, very small in numbers, however distinguished some of its members.[20] But there would be few Unitarians, who included in their number a disproportionately large number of wealthy traders and manufacturers, who would happily have followed Coleridge in his rejection of the notion of private property. If Coleridge's poem sets out to address the radical community, it must be concluded that it does so ineptly, alienating in its course all but a tiny minority of the radical constituency.

Religious Musings is, as Coleridge acknowledges, a 'desultory poem', but it is precisely because of its desultory character that it serves so well to introduce the first section of this book, which is concerned with the political poetry of the 1790s. Its hesitations summarize those of a decade in which poets tried to locate some commanding position from which they could survey the political turmoil through which they were living, only to find that the prophetic voice, the voice removed from time, was unavailable to them, and a decade in which they tried to locate a voice that could harmonize, like Coleridge's 'glad stream', the diverse and contradictory currents that together constituted the English radical tradition only to find that no such voice was available.

1
Erasmus Darwin: from the Bastille to Birmingham

Erasmus Darwin was the most popular poet of the 1790s, and his *The Botanic Garden* (1791), in which *The Economy of Vegetation* formed the first part, and *The Loves of the Plants* (1789) the second, was the decade's most popular poem. In 1796 Coleridge was in a rather small minority in his distaste – 'I absolutely nauseate Darwin's poem' – and even Coleridge remained of the opinion that Darwin was 'the first *literary* character in Europe, and the most original-minded man'.[1] But if it was not at the time representative, Coleridge's repugnance was at least prescient. Darwin's posthumous poem, *The Temple of Nature* (1803), is in many ways his best, but it made little stir. The enthusiasm for Darwin's verse had waned.

In the 1790s Darwin's popularity did not rest simply on a new enthusiasm for botany. The four cantos of *The Economy of Vegetation*, on Fire, Earth, Water and Air, offer a grandly comprehensive panorama of the workings of the world as they were explained by contemporary science, and *The Loves of the Plants* does more than wittily and decoratively summarize Linnaeus's sexual system of botanical classification. The poem celebrates Darwin's Lucretian creed that found in sexuality or 'love' the governing impulse of all creation. The beautifully and expensively produced edition of *The Botanic Garden* published by Joseph Johnson in 1791, with its elegant typefaces, and its engravings from Fuseli and others, in itself proclaims a confidence in the book's unusual importance. Joseph Johnson was the leading radical publisher of his day. His associates included Priestley, Fuseli, Mrs Barbauld, Mary Wollstonecraft, William Godwin, Joel Barlow and Tom Paine, as well as the scarcely known William Blake. His edition of Darwin's poem registers his recognition of the book's commercial prospects but also his recognition that the poem gave vivid expression to a set of beliefs shared by Johnson's stable of authors, and his confidence that in 1791 such beliefs could be expressed triumphally, by the publication of a volume as costly and elegant as one of Wedgwood's copies of the Portland Vase, itself reproduced by Blake in the book's most elaborate engraving.

Darwin's 'general design', as he explains in his preface, 'is to inlist Imagination under the banner of Science; and to lead her votaries from the looser analogies, which dress out the imagery of poetry, to the stricter, ones which form the ratiocination of philosophy'.[2] This is a typically enlightenment project, its ambition to incorporate art and science into a single encyclopedic structure of knowledge. The book includes more than 4000 lines of poetry, more than twice as much prose, and some 18 illustrations. The illustrations themselves are startlingly various. There is a sentimental Boucheresque frontispiece by Emma Crewe, elaborate double-page engravings of the sections of the Portland Vase, scientific diagrams illustrating, for example, the structure of the earth's crust, flower engravings, some of them of rare beauty, and several engravings from Fuseli, most remarkably Blake's of the 'Fertilization of Egypt'. The prose is just as diverse. There are speculations on the significance of mythological episodes, journalistic anecdotes, as for example the account of the unfortunate death of an inventor asphyxiated while demonstrating his diving-bell, descriptions of Renaissance medals, tributes to admired friends and contemporaries, beautifully lucid summaries of scientific discoveries, such as Newton's of the structure of light and the operation of the tides, work in progress such as the lengthy essay recording observations of the wind and suggesting how a theory might be developed to account for them, descriptions of manufacturing processes, moral and political observations, and the essays on aesthetic theory that appear as 'Interludes' between the four cantos of *The Loves of the Plants*. The verse is formally less various. Darwin writes in end-stopped couplets, only twice interrupted by attempts at a lyric measure, but the formal consistency is offset by an extraordinary diversity of subject matter signalled in *The Economy of Vegetation* by the 'Argument' that precedes each Canto. This is a section of the argument of Canto II:

> Production of Clays; manufacture of Porcelain in China; in Italy; in England. Mr Wedgewood's works at Etruria in Staffordshire. Cameo of a Slave in Chains; of Hope. Figures on the Portland or Barberini vase explained. Coal; Pyrite; Naphtha; Jet; Amber. Dr Franklin's discovery of disarming the Tempest of it's lightning. Liberty of

America; of Ireland; of France. Antient central; subterraneous fires. Production of Tin, Copper, Zink, Lead, Mercury, Platina, Gold and Silver. Destruction of Mexico. Slavery of Africa. Destruction of the Armies of Cambyses. Gnomes like stars of an Orrery.

It looks like a farrago, but it is by admitting into his poem such apparently disparate materials that Darwin is able to document so completely the system of belief that he held in common with his publisher and most of his publisher's authors.[3]

Darwin's whole project depends from a single premise, the notion that physics and metaphysics are not two disciplines but one. Hence his habit, as the *Edinburgh Review* complained in 1803, of 'constantly blending and confounding together the two distinct sciences of matter and of mind'. The most obvious consequence of this was to reunite poetry, an expression of human experience, with physics, the study of the material properties of the world. But there were many others. Emotion and energy are conflated. The universe is created:

> When LOVE DIVINE, with brooding wings unfurl'd,
> Call'd from the rude abyss the living world.
> *(The Economy of Vegetation*, subsequently *EV*, 1, 101–2)

Divine love, in this scheme of things, is an energy immanent in matter rather than a transcendent, supernatural agent. It follows, too, that there is no radical distinction between natural and technological processes, between 'mills' and the 'green and pleasant land' in which they are built. In Darwin's Rosicrucian machinery the geosphere is the province of the gnomes:

> Gnomes! you then bade dissolving SHELLS distil
> From the loose summits of each shatter'd hill,
> To each fine pore and dark interstice flow,
> And fill with liquid chalk the mass below.
> *(EV*, 2, 93–6)

Limestone landscape is itself the product of a subterranean factory. To move to Matthew Boulton's Birmingham mint is just to travel from one industrial plant to another:

> With iron lips his rapid rollers seize
> The lengthening bars, in thin expansion squeeze;

> Descending screws with ponderous fly-wheels wound
> The tawny plates, the new medallions round...
>
>> (*EV*, 1, 281–4)

Darwin, as this quotation makes clear, takes a professional interest in new technology, but his response is also moral – machines like Boulton's diminish the hard physical labour of production – and aesthetic. There is no difference in kind in Darwin's appreciation of such a machine and his appreciation of the Portland Vase. Nature, art and industry are all, for Darwin, processes, and processes that are radically similar.

Take, for example, the tribute to James Brindley, canal-builder to the Duke of Bridgewater (*EV*, 3, 321–44). Brindley is 'the unletter'd child' smiled on in his cradle by the water nymphs. Darwin's diction echoes Gray's 'Elegy', but only to reverse its import. Brindley's humble origins did not debar him from great achievement. In fact, he achieved precisely what Gray's villagers are denied. He became one of those whose glory it was:

> To scatter plenty o'er a smiling land,
> And read their history in a nation's eyes...
>
>> (63–4)

Darwin urges that trophies be raised over his tomb, and an 'animated bust' be placed as a memorial of his achievement in Lichfield Cathedral. He praises the canal system that Brindley helped to build for its contribution to national prosperity – 'Plenty, Arts, and Commerce freight the waves' – but also because of the human powers displayed in its construction, as Brindley 'Mines the firm rock, or loads the deep morass', and also, and not least, because the canals are a beautiful addition to the landscape, winding through the English countryside like a

> bright serpent, now in flowers conceal'd;
> Far shine the scales, that gild his sinuous back,
> And lucid undulations mark his track...
>
>> (3, 326–8)

The benign serpent marks this as an Edenic landscape, a land of plenty, where artificial social distinctions no longer obtain, but it is the reverse of a nostalgic Eden: it can be celebrated by poets only because it has been realized by engineers.

For Darwin, Josiah Wedgwood is an exemplary figure not just because he was a friend, and a fellow member of the Birmingham Lunar Society, but because in his pottery art and industry were fully unified, and put to the service of Wedgwood's Whiggish philanthropic impulses, not just in the conditions of employment that Wedgwood offered but in some of the products of his factory. Darwin includes an illustration of the Wedgwood cameo depicting

> the poor fetter'd SLAVE on bended knee
> From Britain's sons imploring to be free...
> (315–16)

The slave's appeal, 'Am I not a man and a brother', superscribed on the cameo, makes clear the union here of factory production, art and philanthropy, as did Wedgwood's distribution of 'many hundreds' of these cameos 'to excite the humane to attend to and to assist in the abolition of the detestable traffic in human creatures' (note to line 315). Like Brindley, Wedgwood is both an artist and an industrialist, and one effect of this conjunction is to democratize art. The Duke of Portland may have paid the Barberini family a thousand guineas for his ten-inch high vase, but its beauty was available to many more in Wedgwood's reproductions. The same effect is produced by Darwin's consistent refusal to organize his aesthetic enthusiasms within an artistic hierarchy. He admires the high academic art of his friend Fuseli:

> Whose daring tints, with SHAKESPEAR'S happiest grace,
> Gave to the airy phantom form and place.
> (*The Loves of the Plants*, subsequently *LP*, 3, 56–7)

But he is just as appreciative of the paper flower gardens, the 'mimic bowers', produced by Mrs Delaney in her seventies (*LP*, 2, 153 and note).

Wedgwood best exemplifies Darwin's democratic moral sympathies in their philanthropic aspect. In their more narrowly political manifestations the exemplary figure is Benjamin Franklin, also a member for a time of the Birmingham Lunar Society. Franklin's experiments with lightning, for Darwin as for so many of his contemporaries, were fraught with political resonance. To discover the electrical energy contained in clouds was to produce the metaphor that enabled Franklin to enthuse his countrymen in their struggle for independence:

> The patriot-flame with quick contagion ran,
> Hill lighted hill, and man electrised man...
> (*EV*, 2, 367–8)

And just as lightning has the power to pass from cloud to cloud, Liberty passes from land to land; from America to 'fair HIBERNIA'S vales' (2, 372), and from Ireland to 'GALLIA'S plains' where the 'Giant form' of Liberty was imprisoned in the 'stern Bastile'.[4]

In 1790 such sentiments united Whigs and Reformers. The French Revolution is celebrated as the overthrow of tyranny, and an event that has brought to an end a period of almost a century in which Britain and France had been engaged intermittently in dynastic wars. The first canto of *The Economy of Vegetation* ends with a firework display of the kind which was held on the ruins of the Bastille to mark the first anniversary of its fall:

> So from fierce wars when lawless Monarchs cease,
> Or Liberty returns with laurel'd Peace;
> Bright fly the sparks, the colour'd lustres burn,
> Flash follows flash, and flame-wing'd circles turn...
> (*EV*, 1, 589–92)

Even in 1791 it was apparent of course that it was mob violence that had destroyed the power of a militaristic tyranny, and Darwin does not disguise this. He celebrates the invention of gunpowder, which makes 'Tyrants tremble on their blood-stain'd thrones' (*EV*, 1, 252), and adds a note reproving as aristocratic Cervantes's invective against an invention that 'levels the strong with the weak, the knight cased in steel with the naked shepherd, those who have been trained to the sword, with those who are totally unskilful in the use of it; and throws down all the splendid distinctions of mankind' (note to *EV*, 1, 242). But if the sympathies here are democratic, it remains a qualified and urbane variety of democracy. Darwin's detestation of tyrants, for example, does not extend itself to kings. At the end of *The Economy of Vegetation* he celebrates British constitutional monarchy in a charming cameo that is not merely dutiful. George and his Queen are represented walking around Kew Gardens:

> Sometimes retiring, from the public weal
> One tranquil hour the ROYAL PARTNERS steal;
> Through glades exotic pass with step sublime,
> Or mark the growths of Britain's happier clime;
> With beauty blossom'd and with virtue blaz'd,
> Mark the fair Scions that themselves have rais'd;
> Sweet blooms the Rose, the towering Oak expands,
> The Grace and Guard of Britain's golden lands.
> (*EV*, 4, 579–86)

The oak may guard Britain by furnishing the wood for its navy, but that navy is represented as purely defensive, its role simply to guard from invasion a garden kingdom. Darwin bestows on his King a 'wreath', but the trophy has a new appropriateness because it is won by agricultural not military achievement: the coronet of leaves is properly worn by a King who has planted trees. Louis XVI has not, suggests Darwin, been deposed, but rather freed to enjoy the calm, pastoral happiness of his neighbour monarch.

It is the third of Darwin's admired friends, Joseph Priestley, who directs his religious thought. Priestley is admired as a chemist who showed, for example, how the nymphs of the air 'wed the enamour'd OXYGENE to LIGHT' (*EV*, 4, 34 and note), but his authority is more general. For Darwin he is simply 'the Sage' (*EV*, 4, 168, and 195). In particular, it is Priestley who lends authority to Darwin's insistence on a purely natural religion, and his revulsion from religion of the kind that sanctioned the Spanish conquests in South America:

> Spain's deathless shame! the crimes of modern days!
> When Avarice, shrouded in Religion's robe,
> Sail'd to the West, and slaughter'd half the globe;
> While Superstition, stalking by his side,
> Mock'd the loud groans, and lap'd the bloody tide...
> (*EV*, 2, 414–18)

Mythology, both Christian and pagan, is offered as an allegorical description of natural process. Anubis, shown fertilizing Egypt in the extraordinary design by Fuseli that Blake engraved, is dog-headed to mark the

Egyptian astronomers' observation that the annual flood of the Nile coincided with the rising of Sirius, the dog-star (*EV*, 3, note on 129, citing Volney and the Abbé Le Pluche as authorities). This was already a conventional enough interpretative strategy amongst mythographers, but Darwin more unsettlingly extends the technique to biblical narrative. Elijah dowses the flames of the altar to Baal in a simile illustrating how the cycle of evaporation and condensation is preserved by electrical exchanges, a theory that allows every experimenter to become a rain-maker, by giving 'reason to conclude that very numerous metallic rods with fine points erected high in the air might induce it at any time to part with some of its water' (*EV*, note to 1, 551). When the assembled tribes witness Elijah's miracle they are immediately converted: 'shouting nations own THE LIVING GOD' (1, 584), but the conversion that interests Darwin is of one form of electrical energy to another. The miracle worked by the prophet functions only as a colourful illustration of the natural wonder.

It is Darwin's treatment of gender and of sexuality that is most distinctive in his verse. His enthusiasm for breast-feeding is predictable enough, as is his hostility to mothers who are 'bless'd in vain with tumid bosoms, and respond to the 'tender wailings' of their infants with 'unfeeling ear' (*EV*, 3, 353–76). Rousseau and Beaumarchais had made breast-feeding a popular issue amongst reformers, but there is an unusual tenderness in Darwin's gaze as he pictures the infant at the breast, as he 'Spreads his inquiring hands, and smiles, and sips' (3, 360). More remarkable, though, is Darwin's happy acknowledgement that the mother who breast-feeds both gives and receives pleasure in an exchange of gratification that marks this as an 'excellent contrivance' (note to *EV*, 1, 278). Darwin's is a male world, its heroes scientists and engineers, almost exclusively, then, a world of men, and yet one senses that, wherever possible, he writes in praise of women: Mrs French, who was proficient in 'botany and natural history' (note to *EV*, 3, 308), Miss Jones, a young Irishwoman remarkable for her charities (*EV*, 3, 455–62 and note), and a rather large group of women artists, not only Mrs Delany and Mrs North with their paper gardens of flowers (*LP*, 2, 154–62 and note), but also the painters Mrs Cosway (*EV*, 1, 413 note), Emma Crewe (*LP*, 2, 291–300 and note), and Angelica Kauffman (*LP*, 'Interlude' between Cantos 1 and 2), and the sculptor Mrs Damer (*EV*, 2, 111–14, and note). This admiration for women seems not so much principled as an amiable ebullition of a rather highly developed erotic susceptibility. Even a simple galvanic experiment furnishes Darwin with an excuse for a suggestive interlude. A 'fearless Beauty' stands on wax and touches 'with graceful hand' 'the sparkling rod':

> Through her fine limbs the mimic lightnings dart,
> And flames innocuous eddy round her heart;
> O'er her fair brow the kindling lustres glare,
> Blue rays diverging from the bristling hair;
> While some fond youth the kiss ethereal sips,
> And soft fires issue from their meeting lips.
> (*EV*, 1, 351–6)

But it is in *The Loves of the Plants* that Darwin gives fullest expression to his amative instincts. Linnaeus's sexual system for the classification of plants from the arrangement of their stamens and pistils stimulated Darwin to compose a poem that, because of it botanical subject matter could be addressed explicitly to young women, and yet remain a poem distinguished by its sustained and polymorphous eroticism. It is a light, witty, sometimes satirical eroticism, but it is continuous throughout the poem's four cantos. In just eight lines of Canto 1, for example, Darwin chronicles the alcea or double hollyhock, in which the female petals are so luxuriant as utterly to exclude any male stamen; the Iris, in which three stamens are matched with a single pistil; the cypress, in which the pistil and stamen occupy different flowers on the same plant; and the osyris, in which the pistil and stamen occupy different plants altogether:

> With vain desires the pensive ALCEA burns,
> And, like sad ELOISA, loves and mourns.
> The freckled IRIS owns a fiercer flame,
> And *three* unjealous husbands wed the dame.
> Cupressus dark disdains his dusky bride,
> *One* dome contains them, but *two* beds divide.
> The proud OSYRIS flies his angry fair,
> *Two* houses hold the fashionable pair.
> (*LP*, 1, 69–76)

The cumulative effect of such passages is to construct a rhetoric in which sexual foibles of all conceivable kinds are surveyed with an affectionate equanimity, which from time to time effervesces into a headier delight, as when the springtime wind robustly assaults an anemone:

> When Zephyr wafts her deep calash aside;
> Tears with rude kiss her bosoms gauzy veil,
> And flings the fluttering kerchief to the gale.
> (*LP*, 1, 286–8)

The Botanic Garden is remarkably consistent in its articulation of a set of principles that are predicated on Darwin's refusal to accept a distinction between mind and matter. It follows that the only tenable kind of religious belief would be a variety of deism, in which no distinction is admitted between God and Nature. It also follows that there is no distinction in kind between the works of nature and the works of man. Human activity appropriately figures natural process not only or primarily because Darwin's is an anthropomorphic imagination, but because human activity is itself a product of natural evolution, and therefore matter and mind share a common origin. As he put it in *Zoonomia*: '*the whole is one family of one parent*. On this similitude is founded all rational analogy' (p. 1, Preface). Darwin's refusal to accept any radical distinction between the divine, the natural and the human provides both the model and the justification for his refusal of other distinctions. His philanthropy, for example, is founded on the notion succinctly expressed on Wedgwood's cameo of the supplicating slave: 'Am I not a man and a brother?'. The brotherhood of man remains a moral imperative, but one securely founded on a scientific fact. Darwin's lack of interest in merely social distinctions, his suggestion that it is the canal-builder Brindley who should be commemorated by the nation, rather than the Duke of Bridgewater who financed him, has a similar basis. So, too, do Darwin's reformist politics, his hatred of 'tyranny', and his celebration of the democratic potential of gunpowder. His refusal to accept a difference in kind between poetry and science or between art and technology, and his willingness to allow women the possibility of successful entry into the public sphere of achievement follow from the same premise. Most obviously Darwin's refusal to distinguish between mind and body makes possible his frank and unconstrained celebration of a sexuality that is shared equally by men and women.

In *The Botanic Garden* there is an intellectual foundation of remarkable consistency supporting Darwin's encyclopaedic ambitions, but the structure of both poems remains precarious. Both incorporate a pre-existing organizing principle, the four elements in *The Economy of Vegetation*, and the Linnaean system in *The Loves of the Plants*, and trust that this will be sufficient to hold together the disparate subject matter of the poems. But the poems remain monstrous; that is, their different parts seem arbitrarily or wittily rather than naturally connected, and Darwin is aware of this. In the dialogue at the end of the first canto of *The Loves of the Plants*, the Poet contrasts 'the gardens of a

Sicilian nobleman' which contain 'six hundred statues of imaginary monsters; which so disgust the spectators, that the state had once a serious design of destroying them', with 'the very improbable monsters in Ovid's Metamorphoses' which 'have entertained the world for many centuries'. He leaves it to the 'candid reader' to determine in which class his own monsters should be placed, but their monstrousness is not at issue. Darwin's account of hybrid plants in Canto IV of *The Loves of the Plants* provokes an unusually intense simile:

> So, when the Nightingale in eastern bowers
> On quivering pinion woos the Queen of flowers;
> Inhales her fragrance, as he hangs in air,
> And melts with melody the blushing fair;
> Half-rose, half-bird, a beauteous Monster springs,
> Waves his thin leaves, or clasps his glossy wings;
> Long horrent thorns his mossy legs surround,
> And tendril-talons root him to the ground;
> Green films of rind his wrinkled neck o'erspread,
> And crimson petals crest his curled head;
> Soft warbling beaks in each bright blossom move,
> And vocal Rosebuds thrill the enchanted grove!
> (4, 211–22)

This is Darwin writing in the manner that prompted Coleridge to compare him to Cowley and Marino as a purveyor of corruptingly witty verse, in which disparate beauties are so mingled that they contrive to provoke, like Darwin's rose-nightingale, a shudder.[5] For Coleridge, of course, this was evidence that Darwin's verse was fanciful rather than imaginative, but it is at least worth considering whether it is not just Darwin's style that is fanciful but the system of thought that the style expresses.

Darwin's explicit claim for his volume is that it is designed to 'inlist Imagination under the banner of Science', a project that promises to dismantle, but in fact reinforces the distinction between the two spheres. The imaginative is not unified with the scientific, but press-ganged into its service, in a structure of knowledge that, as Darwin's metaphor reveals, has its true counterpart in the hierarchical, militaristic regimes ruled by those that Darwin berated as tyrants rather than in the reformed constitutions that he celebrated. The volume is designed to tempt its readers away from 'the looser analogies, which dress out the imagery of poetry, to the stricter, ones which form the ratiocination of philosophy'. In other words, Darwin's verse serves only as an enticement to a reader who, it is hoped, will be educated by the volume into a proper appreciation of the superior value of scientific prose. The eye of the reader of *The Botanic Garden*, as it travels down the page to read a footnote, or flicks through the volume to find the essays collected at the end of the poems, mimics the educative progress that Darwin's whole volume is designed to accomplish. Poetry functions, like sugar, to make robust tastes acceptable to the young: the mature palate is one that has outgrown the need for sweetening. Even the denial of the distinction between mind and matter, the premise on which all of Darwin's thought rests, emerges on inspection as a position sustained not by a reconciliation of the two terms, but by collapsing one into the other. Mind, for Darwin, is simply one form of matter, like all other forms of matter a product of natural evolution, and like all other forms, too, subject to the laws of motion. Coleridge was surely right to recognize Darwin's science of life as simply a variety of materialism.

Darwin's more narrowly political feints towards egalitarianism are similarly partial or deceptive. Maureen McNeil, for example, has pointed out that Darwin's celebration of the technologies that powered the industrial revolution characteristically elides the role of labour.[6] Brindley, the unlettered engineer, is honoured, but when Darwin writes his eulogy, the army of navvies whose physical labour produced Britain's canal system somehow disappears:

> So with strong arm immortal Brindley leads
> His long canals, and parts the velvet meads;
> Winding in lucid lines, the watery mass
> Mines the firm rock, or loads the deep morass...
>   (3, 329–32)

All the muscular strength of that labouring army seeps into Brindley's strong arm where it becomes the attribute of an individual rather than the common possession of a class. Even when, as in the description of Wedgwood's pottery, the industrial workforce is allowed an independent existence, its human identity is removed:

> Gnomes! as you now dissect with hammers fine,
> The granite-rock, the nodul'd flint calcine;
> Grind with strong arm, the circling chertz betwixt,

Your pure Ka-o-lins and Pe-tun-tses mixt;
O'er each red saggars burning cave preside,
The keen-eyed Fire-Nymphs blazing by your side;
And pleased on WEDGWOOD ray your partial smile,
A new Etruria decks Britannia's isle.

(2, 297–304)

This is not Wellsian allegory, in which the gnomes and the fire-nymphs take the place of the Morlocks, but rather an industrial romance, a Disney film before its time, in which the factory owner presides as a benevolent sorcerer over a troop of busy but smiling elves. McNeil accurately identifies the ideological implications of poetic figures such as these by quoting Marx's dictum that capitalism, when fully developed, institutes a mode of production in which 'the entire production process appears as not subsumed under the direct skilfulness of the worker, but rather as the technological application of science'.[7] In *The Botanic Garden*, the glorification of the scientist, the engineer, and the factory owner is achieved by rendering invisible the activity of the industrial workers, or by redesignating their labour so that it becomes an attribute of the engineer or the inventor or his machine. It was Wedgwood's ultimate ambition to 'make such machines of *Men* as cannot err'.[8] He may not have achieved this in the management of his own factories, but his friend, Erasmus Darwin, manipulating a more ductile material, poetic rhetoric, fully expressed in his poems a vision of the industrial future to which Wedgwood aspired.

Darwin's eroticism is clearly an expression of his own hearty sexual appetite. Darwin was enlightened in his treatment of his own illegitimate children and of their mother, but without ever relinquishing the distinction between his legitimate and illegitimate offspring, or between his mistress, whom he seems to have chosen from among his domestic servants, and his wives.[9] This would just be a matter of anecdotal interest were it not that the attitudes that he revealed in his own sexual history also inform many of his erotic descriptions. In *The Loves of the Plants*, for example, Zephyr's delighted relish of Anemone's beauty, as he tears off 'her bosoms gauzy veil', expresses itself in behaviour uncomfortably close to that of a lusty young gentleman towards a pretty domestic servant or a hotel chambermaid. *The Loves of the Plants*, in particular, was often attacked for its licentiousness. There is almost always a comically prudish element in these attacks that is scarcely avoidable when the outrage is provoked by the shenanigans of plants.

42   *The Revolutionary Years*

In 1794, in the first of these attacks, T. J. Mathias wondered whether the poem's rhetoric was not improper:

> In filmy, gawzy, gossamery lines,
> With *lucid* language, and most dark designs,
> In sweet *tetrandryan, monogynian* strains,
> Pant for a *pystill* in botanick pains;
> On the luxurious lap of Flora thrown,
> On beds of yielding, vegetable down,
> Raise lust in pinks; and with unhallow'd fire
> Bid the soft virgin violet expire?[10]

This is superior parody, but the misgivings made explicit in a note are intended to be taken seriously: 'I would just hint that it is a matter of some curiosity to conceive, how young ladies are instructed in the terms of botany, which are *very significant.*' In 1798, Richard Polwhele defended Darwin against Mathias's attack in his *The Unsex'd Females* (note to line 5),[11] but immediately afterwards he proceeds to implicate Darwin in the degenerate female fashions of the age adopted by women who:

> Scarce by a gossamery film carest,
> Sport, in full view, the meretricious breast...
>   (23–4)

Darwin has helped popularize such fashionable excesses by divulging to an audience of women a system of botanical classification that cannot 'accord with female modesty', and hence by educating a generation of young women, who:

> More eager for illicit knowledge pant,
> With lustful boys anatomise a plant;
> The virtues of its dust prolific speak,
> Or point its pistil with unblushing cheek.
>   (note to line 29)

In the same note Polwhele compares Darwin's offence with Mary Wollstonecraft's when she claims that 'it would be right to speak of our organs of generation as freely as we mention our eyes or our hands', but the comparison works only to point the difference between Wollstonecraft's demand that sexual language be purged of innuendo, and a poetic language that relies almost entirely on such innuendoes for its vitality. Mathias and Polwhele deploy against Darwin a priggish conservatism, but his poem remains vulnerable to their attacks, because the smile with which Darwin beams his approval of all sexuality is never securely disentangled from a smirk. In Darwin liberated joy merges with a sleazier libertine pleasure, and it does so because very often his eroticism gathers its intensity by transgressing conventional proprieties, and hence remains dependent on the proprieties that it flouts. Darwin is enamoured, as Mathias and Polwhele noticed, by gauzes and gossamers – by fabrics, that is, that excite by mimicking without performing the function of clothing, by covering but not concealing. He is not excited by women's bodies in a state of Edenic nudity, but by those bodies draped in materials that leave them vulnerable to a prying male gaze, and this is a symptom of a sexuality that, like Darwin's utopian visions of industry, remains committed to the conventional hierarchies that it pretends to overthrow.

For Darwin, the Revolution of 1789 liberated a giant who had until then been bound by the weak hands of a tyrant king, and blindfolded by the similarly weak machinations of the Catholic priesthood:

> Round his large limbs were wound a thousand strings
> By the weak hands of Confessors and Kings;
> Oer his closed eyes a triple veil was bound,
> And steely rivets lock'd him to the ground;
> While stern Bastile with iron cage inthralls
> His folded limbs, and hems in marble walls.
> Touch'd by the patriot-flame, he rent amazed
> The flimsy bonds, and round and round him gazed;
> Starts up from earth, above the admiring throng
> Lifts his Colossal form, and towers along;
> High o'er his foes his hundred arms He rears,
> Plowshares his swords, and pruning hooks his spears;
> Calls to the Good and Brave with voice, that rolls
> Like Heaven's own thunder round the echoing poles;
> Gives to the winds his banners broad unfurl'd,
> And gathers in its shade the living world!
> (*EV*, 2, 372–94)

There are two, contradictory metaphorical sequences here. One represents a 'Giant-form' shackled by 'steely rivets', caged in iron, and imprisoned within marble. Such a figure, like Blake's Orc, could win its freedom only through a frightening display of muscular energy. But the other sequence identifies the giant as Gulliver in Lilliput, not locked to the ground by 'steely rivets' but bound only by threads. Such a creature need only awake, sit up and yawn for the flimsy strings that bind him to snap. In the moment of Revolution, Orc is decisively rejected in favour of Gulliver:

> Touch'd by the patriot-flame, he rent amazed
> The flimsy bonds, and round and round him gazed...
> (2, 385–6)

Freeing himself so easily, there is no need for him to be other than a gentle giant, content to use his strength to convert military weaponry into agricultural equipment. Like Briareus, he has a hundred arms, a feature which seems to establish him as an embodiment of the people of France, but as soon as he has freed himself he issues a proclamation addressed to 'the Good and Brave', and then strikes his standard which 'gathers in its shade the living world!' (2, 394). In just a few lines he is converted from a personification of the popular will to a benevolent despot who governs by virtue of his appeal to a virtuous elite of 'the Good and Brave'. The 'Tyrant-power' of Louis XVI is overthrown, and its place is taken not by a mob, nor a Revolutionary leader, nor even by a Parliament, but by a figure who more strikingly resembles a Midlands factory-owner, his hundred hands being the work force that he employs, a figure rather like Darwin's industrialist friends, Josiah Wedgwood, Matthew Boulton and James Watt.

On the second anniversary of the fall of the Bastille, in 1791, the year in which *The Botanic Garden* was first published, a dinner was held in Birmingham to celebrate the occasion. The dinner, attended by wealthy reformers, provoked three nights of riots during which Priestley's library and laboratory were destroyed. The mob who inflicted the damage did so in the name of 'Church and King'. Priestley was a target because of his Unitarianism, because of his politics (like Franklin and Paine, Priestley was made an honorary French citizen and elected a Deputy to the National Convention), and because he was rich. In 1783 Darwin himself had left the Birmingham area, moving from Lichfield to Derby, but those of his Lunar Society friends who had stayed in Birmingham seem to have been singled out for attack. Priestley himself accused 'the friends of the court, if not the prime ministers themselves' of having fomented the riots, but R. B. Rose, the historian of the affair, has found no persuasive evidence to substantiate his claim.[12] It may well have been that three local magistrates played a somewhat sinister role, but even that possibility remains conjectural. It seems likely that their guilt extended no further than responding so passively to an outbreak of popular violence as to raise suspicions that they condoned it. The revealing evidence is in the trades followed by those implicated in the riots, almost all of whom were described as 'labourers', and who included a toy-maker, a harness-maker, a gardener, an errand-boy, a dealer in bones, two carpenters, two glaziers, a huxter, a cordwainer, a button-maker and a bricklayer. These were townspeople who had not shared in Birmingham's rise to prosperity, who remained almost certainly among the five-eighths of the town's population who, in 1781, were still too poor to be assessed for poor rates. Priestley, an active campaigner for universal suffrage, wanted to enfranchise these men, and their destruction of his house must have seemed an example of black, mindless ingratitude. But Darwin's poem, though it cannot serve to justify such actions, at least allows us to explain them, for these are the men that Darwin's poem renders invisible.

The cry of 'Church and King' may strike us as almost as empty of meaning as the other slogan, 'No Popery', that was shouted by some rioters during their attacks on Dissenting Chapels. Impoverished labourers seem not to have had much reason for gratitude to either institution. But this would be a naive response. The cry summed up for the rioters the threat to their own identity to which they were responding. Their national church and their monarch represented for them the assurance that they were not simply ill-paid exponents of trades that were becoming peripheral as Birmingham developed into a centre of heavy industry. They were, in addition, Englishmen whose pride in themselves was secured by the power and the status of their nation. The wealthy industrialists, many of them Dissenters, who gathered on 14 July to attend a dinner celebrating the anniversary of the fall of the Bastille must have seemed to be flaunting an economic power that had freed them from those patriotic ties on which the rioters depended for their sense of their own dignity, and they responded with brutal, destructive fury.

Darwin's *Botanic Garden* is the most complete expression of the ethic that they found so infuriating. In its calmly superior indifference to 'superstition' it denied their religion. In its domestication of the royal family, and its reduction of the King to a horticulturalist, it emasculated the most potent symbol of their nationhood. It allows from time to time a dutiful rehearsal of patriotic commonplaces, but these are rigorously subordinated to the scientific universalism that controls the structure of the volume. Darwin appears to enfranchise the powerless, but does so by depriving those he would empower of all identity. Just as he celebrates women, while reducing them to a tempting fleshiness veiled in gossamer, he celebrates labour in a rhetoric that wholly elides the person of the labourer. His work became simply a reflex of the inventor's cunning, of the entrepreneur's organizational skills, or of the machine's power. Darwin would certainly have admired his friend, Wedgwood's, lofty ambition 'to make *Artists*' rather than 'mere *men*', an ambition that seems utopian in its goal of recognizing each individual in Wedgwood's employment as an autonomous subject, but Wedgwood, it should be remembered, employed his painters and modellers within a disciplined factory system of his own devising, and it was the object of that system to make 'such *Machines* of the *Men* as cannot err'.[13]

The attack on the reformers' dinner on 14 July, and the rioting that followed, were the revenge of the 'bunting, beggarly, brass-making, brazen-faced, brazen-hearted, blackguard, bustling, booby Birmingham mob'[14] on a radical elite who threatened to deprive them of the boisterous individuality allowed them even by that array of cheerfully disapproving epithets. But to the more thoughtful members of that elite the riots revealed a more disturbing paradox. James Watt's radical son recognized that 'the town is divided into two parties who hate one another mortally, that the professed aristocrats are democrats in practice, that is, encouragers of the Mob; and that the democrats are those who have always contended for a police and good government in the town, therefore are in fact aristocratic, at least would have no objections to an aristocracy of which they themselves were members'.[15] The Bastille fell because in 1789 the radical elite in Paris made common cause with the mob. In 1791 the destruction of Priestley's house provided dramatic evidence that no such common cause existed in Birmingham, and in this, as in its new industrial technologies, Birmingham pointed the way for the nation. The mutual antipathy between the Mob and the wealthy radicals who sought to represent the Mob's interests secured England from any serious threat of revolutionary disturbances for a quarter of a century.

It is conventional to date the eclipse of Darwin's reputation as a poet to the Spring of 1798, when 'The Loves of the Triangles', a wickedly accurate parody of Darwin, was carried in three issues of *The Anti-Jacobin*.[16] Canning and Frere's poem ends apocalyptically, with a successful French invasion of Britain, the erection of the guillotine, and the execution of Pitt:

> Ye SYLPHS of DEATH, on demon pinions flit
> Where the tall *Guillotine* is raised for PITT.
> To the pois'd plank tie fast the monster's back,
> Close the nice slider, ope the' expectant sack;
> Then twitch, with fairy hands, the frolic pin –
> Down falls the' impatient axe with deafening din;
> The liberated head rolls off below,
> And simpering FREEDOM hails the happy blow![17]

It can remain an entirely comic apocalypse because the style of the lines is so happily discordant with their content. The scene is surveyed by a rapt engineer more entranced by the neatness of the mechanism than attentive to its purpose. Murderous revolutionary theatre is presented by a dramatist whose real enthusiasm is for stage machinery, so that the audience, as essential an element in such revolutionary spectacle as the victim, can be deprived of any bodily presence in the scene, its place usurped by the decorous abstraction, Freedom. The parody attacks Darwin's politics, but at the same time it celebrates the utter disconnection between those politics and the popular energies which alone could carry them into practice. It exposes the politics of Darwin's poem as, like Darwin's own 'rose-nightingale', a distasteful but unthreatening hybrid, and it gives the clue as to how it is that *The Botanic Garden* can be at once so comprehensive an expression of the ideology shared by the most advanced group of radical thinkers in Britain, and centred in Birmingham, its most advanced town, and yet remain so insubstantial. It was not Erasmus Darwin who developed a poetry that could speak to, and out of, the popular radicalism of the 1790s, but the most inventive of his illustrators, William Blake.[18]

2
William Blake and Revolutionary Prophecy

The central difficulty of *The Marriage of Heaven and Hell* is the problem of who it was written for. In his 'An Audience for *The Marriage of Heaven and Hell*', John Howard offers one solution. Blake wrote a satire on Swedenborgianism designed 'to amuse the Johnson circle', that is, the group of writers including Erasmus Darwin, Joseph Priestley, Mary Wollstonecraft and Tom Paine who gathered around the London publisher Joseph Johnson, attended his Tuesday dinners, and wrote, many of them, for his *The Analytical Review*.[1] In the years from 1789 to 1792 *The Analytical* repeatedly attacked the New Jerusalem Church of the Swedenborgians, and Priestley himself was engaged in a public controversy with its leader, Robert Hindmarsh. In the same period Blake did more engraving work for Johnson than any other publisher and it was Johnson who printed his *The French Revolution*.

Blake's title parodies Swedenborg's *Heaven and Hell and their Wonders as heard and seen by the Author*, and Blake's five 'memorable fancies' just as clearly parody Swedenborg's 'Memorable Relations'. Swedenborg is introduced by name immediately after the 'Argument', when we are told that thirty-three years after the new heaven which, according to Swedenborg, had been instituted in 1757, 'the Eternal Hell revives'. This seems to present *The Marriage* as a satirical supplement to Swedenborg's writings, a diabolic scripture that exposes the tameness of merely angelic vision. On plate 21 Swedenborg is accused of having perpetuated 'all the old falshoods':

> And now hear the reason. He conversed with Angels who are all religious, & conversed not with Devils who all hate religion, for he was incapable thro' his own conceited notions.

The Marriage of Heaven and Hell institutes the dialogue that Swedenborg refused, and one of its objects was surely to laugh him out of his conceit.

It is just possible that Blake's references to 'conceited notions' and to Swedenborgian 'vanity' (plate 21) involve a submerged play on the name of one prominent Swedenborgian leader, Joseph Proud. In 1797 Proud became the priest of the London Temple, but in 1791 he was in Birmingham, where he saved the Swedenborgian Temple from the mob who destroyed Priestley's Unitarian chapel, his library and laboratory by persuading them that the Swedenborgians had no interest in politics.[2] Their concern was with men's souls, and souls had no relation to the body politic. It was no doubt this that persuaded Priestley publicly to attack the Swedenborgians and their Church, and there is good reason to suppose that by 1791 Blake would have been in sympathy with him. In April, 1789, Blake and his wife had attended the General Conference of the Swedenborgians, but since then the Swedenborgians had formed their own church with its own priesthood, and, as Priestley and Blake agreed, it is the function of such priesthhoods to construct systems designed to take advantage of and enslave the vulgar (plate 11). It was, after all, just such a system that had prompted a mob of impoverished Birmingham labourers to burn down Priestley's chapel in order to register their devotion to 'Church and King'.

The strongest objection to the notion that Blake's primary object in *The Marriage of Heaven and Hell* was to poke fun at Swedenborg and his followers comes from the apparent disproportion between the target and the attack, between a minor and eccentric religious sect and Blake's monumental satire. But the objection disappears if we concede that for Blake the story of the Swedenborgians was emblematic, recapitulating in Blake's own time the process by which an enraptured recognition that everything that lives is holy decays into a religion, or a movement of the spirit in the course of time 'took the forms of books & were arranged in libraries' (plate 15). In 1789, when Blake and his wife attended the first General Conference, they passed under a portal on which was written, 'NUNC LICET', now it is allowed,[3] but in a year or two the Conference had constituted itself as a church like any other, 'Thou shalt not. writ over the door'. When Proud successfully protested to the Birmingham mob his innocence of any sympathy for the French revolutionaries he demonstrated that his church had very rapidly become, like all other churches, a defender of the political status quo, upholding as Robert Hindmarsh, the Swedenborgian leader and the historian of the movement, insisted, 'the Constitution and Government of their country', and staunchly opposed to all 'principles of infidelity and democracy'.[4] Even earlier, the Swedenborgians had nervously retreated from their teacher's enthusiastic recognition of 'the inborn *amor sexus*', the human sexual instinct that must itself be divine because 'there is no other idea of a God than that of a Man'. The first translator of Swedenborg's *Chaste Delights of Conjugal Love* was expelled from the society because he understood it to sanction fornication. By 1791 the Swedenborgians were preaching a repudiation of the body in favour of the soul, and representing a concern for the body politic as a sinful distraction from a proper concern for God. *The Marriage of Heaven and Hell* is written in defiance of both these positions, for both reinstitute the opposition between the divine and the human. It insists that 'the notion that man has a body distinct from his soul, is to be expunged', that the world is to be re-created, that this 'will come to pass by an improvement of sensual enjoyment' (plate 14), and that the new world will be characterized by the absence of priests, tyrants, war, indeed any system of government: 'Empire is no more! and now the lion & wolf shall cease' (plate 27).

Since 1789, when he attended their general conference, Blake had developed a lively contempt for Swedenborgians that he shared with the group of radical intellectuals gathered together by Joseph Johnson. But for Howard this is much more than an accidental agreement. For him, as for Erdman, *The Marriage of Heaven and Hell* decisively signals Blake's progression from 'humanitarian Christianity' to 'political radicalism',[5] a development made possible by his abandonment of Swedenborg in favour of Priestley, Paine, and the Enlightenment tradition within which they worked. Priestley, like Johnson himself, was a Unitarian. In plate 23 the Devil responds to the Angel's aggressive statement of the orthodox paradox – 'is not God One? & is not he visible in Jesus Christ?' – much as Priestley did, by insisting that Jesus is no more than 'the greatest man'. Priestley, despite being a materialist, retained a literal belief in scripture. Blake at times seems closer to other, more sceptical members of the circle. Like Paine, Darwin, and their French counterparts such as Volney, he locates the origin of religious belief in the tendency of primitive peoples to animate 'all sensible objects with Gods or Geniuses, calling them by the names and adorning them with the properties of woods, rivers, mountains, lakes, cities, nations, and whatever their enlarged and numerous senses could perceive' (plate 11). Blake can offer aggressively inverted readings of the Bible of a kind favoured by polemical opponents of Christianity from Paine to Shelley. In *The Age of Reason* Paine remarks that the Bible sometimes seems rather 'the work of a demon than the work of God'.

Blake makes the same point still more roundly, 'the Jehovah of the Bible being no other than he, who dwells in flaming fire' (plate 5). Like Volney, Paine and many others Blake can demystify scripture by reading it acerbically as allegory. Isaiah explains that although 'only the vulgar came to think that all nations would at last be subject to the jews', this 'like all firm perswasions is come to pass', because all nations now worship money, that is, they 'believe the jews code and worship the jews god, and what greater subjection can be' (plate 13). In the description of his own printing method Blake even registers an aesthetic relish of new technological processes that comes close to Erasmus Darwin.

Nevertheless, it seems odd, as Michael Scrivener has pointed out, to represent Blake at this or any stage of his career as a religious sceptic, as a rationalist Christian, as a materialist, or as an enthusiastic publicist for new technology.[6] Scrivener quotes from the *Morning Chronicle* an account of the behaviour of an eccentric enthusiast identified, though, given his political opinions, almost certainly wrongly identified as 'the head of the Swedenborgians':

> Where will things end? There is a person now in this city, at the head of the Swedenborgians, who, besides possessing *their common faculty* of seeing Angels, has the privilege of conversing with the Jewish Prophets and Apostles, whom he frequently meets in the streets of this metropolis; but very seldom if he is not in company with a third person. In this case, where the other cannot see any person near them, he frequently makes a full stop; and with an air of astonishment, either falls upon one knee, or makes the handsomest bow he can! To the natural expression of surprise at this unaccountable conduct, he always retorts by asking the other party if he did not see anything? 'That,' says he, 'is Isaiah – this Apostle Paul!' He had a few days ago a very favourable vision of St. Paul, in St. Paul's Church-yard! and on that account detained two friends who were with him a considerable time. The Apostle, according to his account, was then listening to a song in favour of the French Revolution! He further says, that he can any time have a sight of Moses, and the other Jewish Prophets at a boxing match, or about Rag Fair!

As Scrivener notes, the *Chronicle*'s measured scorn anxiously distinguishes its own principled support for the Revolution from the pathetic dumb-shows staged by the Swedenborgian with the design of impressing his credulous associates, and, as Scrivener also points out, it is more difficult to associate Blake with the attitudes implicit in such a report than it is with the ostentatious enthusiasm of the person it mocks. 'The Prophets Isaiah and Ezekiel dined with me', writes Blake (plate 12). It is a comically outrageous claim, but it is a humour that it is easier to imagine the Swedenborgian appreciating than the reporter. A man who as a boy had seen angels on a tree in Peckham Rye, and 'the Prophet Ezekiel under a Tree in the Fields' could not comfortably have mocked someone who saw Moses 'about Rag Fair'. For Scrivener the conclusion is clear. The rational dissenters that made up the Johnson circle would have found *The Marriage of Heaven and Hell* as embarrassing as the *Chronicle*'s reporter found the antics of the Swedenborgian, because Blake's political radicalism, like the Swedenborgian's, remained inextricable from his visionary religious enthusiasm.

The task of reconciling the two positions has been undertaken by Jon Mee, who concludes that 'both Howard and Scrivener seem to have been partially right', because in the *Marriage* Blake sets limits to his enthusiasm, 'limits marked by the traces of a scepticism' akin to Volney's and Paine's, both of them authors published by Joseph Johnson.[7] Mee's metaphor, with its submerged quotation, hints that Blake's covert programme is to marry angelic scepticism with diabolic enthusiasm, but he does not pursue the suggestion. For him the imprints of the Johnson circle on the *Marriage* are no more than 'traces'. Its real kinship is with the apocalyptic tracts produced in the 1790s by visionaries for whom the French Revolution heralded the destruction of the old sinful world and the creation of a new. He places it alongside Richard Brothers's *A Revealed Knowledge of the Prophecies and Times* (1794), Thomas Webster's pamphlet *God's Awful Warning to a Giddy Careless Sinful World* (1795) and John Wright's *A Revealed Knowledge of some Things that will Speedily be Fulfilled in the World* (1794).[8]

Mee finds intriguing parallels between these tracts and the *Marriage*. The difference for him is the 'pious strain', so evident in Wright, but which seems 'entirely absent from Blake's text'. But Blake's text is better distinguished, surely, not by an absence of piety, but by the presence of a kind of wild hilarity, a fiercely comic exuberance that could not have been admitted by Brothers or Webster or Wright because it is inconsistent with the solemnity required of the enthusiast who has been delegated to communicate his visions to the world. Blake may, like them, write as a prophet, but on the one hand he offers a rigorously demystified definition of prophecy as 'the voice of honest indignation', and on the other hand he re-creates the prophet as a surreal humourist:

> I then asked Ezekiel. why he eat dung, & lay so long on his right & left side? he answerd. the desire of raising other men into a perception of the infinite
>
> (plate 12)

The *Marriage* is a prophetic tract that has been dipped, like the plates that make up the volume, in 'corrosives', the acid bath of Blake's humour. Nor is the humour accidental to the text. It is what allows Blake to hold together the multiple perspectives, or, as Blake calls them, phantasies, that the *Marriage* comprehends, and it is what prevents a single 'phantasy' from imposing itself on the others.

Plate 4 is headed 'THE VOICE OF THE DEVIL'. Critics have differed as to how much of what follows falls under this heading, but they have been perhaps too ready to accept that the devil speaks in one voice. Blake's Hell is a foreign country, and he is the besotted traveller, returning like Gulliver from the land of the houyhnhnms, to communicate the wisdom he has learned there. That wisdom is tabulated in the central plates of the *Marriage*, 7–11, in the form of a collection of proverbs, for, 'as the sayings used in a nation, mark its character, so the Proverbs of Hell, shew the nature of Infernal wisdom better than any description of buildings or garments'.[9] The proverbs establish Blake's devils as a folk, and like all folk wisdom theirs is not at all philosophically rigorous but compendious and flexible, as alert to the dangers of too many cooks as appreciative of the advantages of many hands. The proverbs do not define a code of knowledge, but work rather to describe a community of speakers.

There are proverbs that seem to be spoken by an amiably moralistic village elder, 'The busy bee has no time for sorrow'. Others seem to voice a rough common sense: 'Always be ready to speak your mind, and a base man will avoid you'. There are proverbs that record an acute understanding of human behaviour, 'Excess of sorrow laughs. Excess of joy weeps'. Some betray the characteristic conservatism of traditional wisdom, anxious that time-honoured differences be maintained, 'Let man wear the fell of the lion, woman the fleece of the sheep.' Some proverbs might be distributed as uplifting texts at any Sunday school, 'The most sublime act is to set another before you', 'To create a little flower is the labour of ages'. Others seem quite unsuitable for this purpose: 'The lust of the goat is the bounty of God'. Some proverbs seem to be the invention of a dottily eccentric allegorist, 'The eyes of fire, the nostrils of air, the mouth of water, the beard of earth'. One proverb optimistically asserts, 'Truth can never be told so as to be understood, and not be believ'd', a Godwinian proposition that could only have been found uncongenial in its sedate rationalism by the devotees of another proverb, 'Everything possible to be believ'd is an image of truth'.

The group of proverbs that has attracted most attention has in common a transgressive antinomian enthusiasm, but again it is an enthusiasm that seems on inspection to fragment into a babble of different voices. Some proverbs of this kind seem to give voice to a prelapsarian innocence, 'The soul of sweet delight, can never be defil'd'. Others read like anarchist slogans, 'Prisons are built with stones of Law, Brothels with bricks of Religion'. Some proverbs seem to insist that the revolution can only be secured by a steely fixity of purpose that refuses any sentimental concern for its victims. Saint-Just might have claimed, 'The cut worm forgives the plow'. Elsewhere revolutionary rigour is superseded by an altogether wilder tone, 'Sooner murder an infant in its cradle than nurse unacted desires'. This is the antinomian as psychopath.

The Marriage of Heaven and Hell is a party manifesto, and like most such manifestos it is marked not by ideological consistency but by a desire to embrace as wide as possible a spectrum of opinion.[10] It is a party that must somehow accept the membership of Richard Brothers, self-styled Prince of the Hebrews, who recognized the French revolutionaries as God's instruments in the destruction of the old, corrupt world that must precede the building of the new Jerusalem: 'Now is the dominion of Edom, & the return of Adam into Paradise; see Isaiah XXXIs and XXXV Chap' (plate 3). But it must accept too the membership of Tom Paine, for whom the respect accorded to prophecy is simply the consequence of a misunderstanding of the word. Prophets, properly understood, are simply poets and musicians, and hence the Bible never describes Abraham, Isaac and Jacob as prophets, because 'it does not appear from any accounts we have that they could either sing, play music, or make poetry'.[11] The fierce comedy of the *Marriage* is the solvent that Blake employs in his attempt to hold together in a single suspension these apparently irreconcilable alternatives.

Many critics have noted that the 'marriage' prophesied in the title of the piece never takes place. It is true that in plate 24 Blake records that one angel has become his 'particular friend', but only after his conversion to the devil's party. Plates 16 and 17 seem to accept that angels and devils are alike 'necessary to Human existence': 'the Prolific would cease to be Prolific unless the Devourer as a sea recieved the excess of his delights'. But the metaphor here must be understood as that of a proud Englishman, an islander, for whom the sea is the necessary limit that guarantees his own diabolical identity. The 'two classes of men' may always coexist on earth, but they must coexist as 'enemies': 'whoever tries to reconcile them seeks to destroy existence'. Clearly, if the two groups must remain enemies, theirs is not the opposition of 'true friendship', and the relationship between them could be described as a marriage only in a flamboyant gesture that might accord with the cynicism of Byron, but not of Blake even in his most Quid-like mood. Blake does not imagine any reconciliation between angels and devils, and the reason is clear enough: all the energies of the piece are occupied, and in the end defeated, by the attempt to reconcile one devil with another.

To that end Blake develops a rhetoric that celebrates difference. One substantial group amongst the proverbs of Hell is devoted to affirmations of the joy of difference: between seed time and harvest, the fool and the wise man, the rat and the elephant, the fox and the lion, tygers and horses, or the apple tree and the beech. It is a stance emphatically reassertd in Blake's conclusion: 'One Law for the Lion & Ox is Oppression'. Blake's more angelic readers have again been anxious to convert this celebration of difference into an even-handedly liberal acceptance at once of diabolic and of angelic wisdom, but this is surely a misreading. Angelic wisdom is marked by an attempt to repress all those differences that move those 'of the devil's party' to laughter. So, in plate 20 when Blake shows an angel a vision of the universe as conceived by the angelic, a void Newtonian space inhabited by cannibalistic Yahoo-like creatures, the angel complains that he has been the victim of a conjuring trick: 'thy phantasy has imposed upon me, & thou oughtest to be ashamed.' But the diabolic Blake, unlike the angel, knows that there is no escape from 'phantasy', and that the angels are angelic only by virtue of self-deception, only by permitting themselves to forget that 'All deities', both the deities of Newtonian science and those of religion, 'reside in the human breast'. Hence he is not reduced to parroting the angel's accusation, to representing himself as the angel's victim when he was shown a vision of Hell opening up at his feet. He can reply to the angel smilingly: 'we impose on one another'.

The celebration of difference in the *Marriage* is as evident in the text's form as in its content. It is not just that the text contains both verse and prose, combining both with pictorial images, but that the verse, prose and images are themselves so various. Some pages, the title page and the 'argument', for example, are designed in a manner that closely resembles a page from *Songs of Innocence and Experience*, but the falling, ruined figures in plate 5 seem like a detail from some lost Last Judgement. In plate 16 the five enclosed figures who seem to represent the Giant progenitors of our five senses huddle together in an exaggeratedly Gothic design, whereas the Blake-like figure of plate 21 seems to be equipped with a body out of Michelangelo topped by a head from a contemporary political cartoon.[12] The 'argument' is in free verse, the beautiful couplet on the 'Bird that cuts the airy way' in fourteeners, and the 'Song of Liberty' is written in a form that is verse only by analogy with English translations of the Psalms. The prose incorporates proverbs, allegoric visions, biblical prophecy, scatological satire, travel writing, and philosophy, the different modes linked only by the glee with which each is parodied. For Jon Mee the product of this formal diversity is 'bricolage', a text that repudiates the possibility of generic classification.[13] This seems sensible, and is certainly to be preferred to the commoner description of Blake's text as ironic. Irony works almost always by establishing a hierarchy of meaning, whereas it is precisely the purpose of the *bricoleur* to refuse such hierarchies.

This is presumably what underpins Mee's tentative and unargued claim that its defiance of generic categories is an aspect of the text's political radicalism. But if so, it is an aspect that other radical texts of the period – Paine's *Rights of Man*, Godwin's *Political Justice*, Blake's own *The French Revolution*, or Wordsworth's *Descriptive Sketches* – seem perfectly happy to forgo. It seems truer to say that Blake is forced into his role as *bricoleur* by the multiplicity of the points of view that he feels the need to accommodate. In this *The Marriage of Heaven and Hell* has something in common with a text which is its ideological opposite, Swift's *A Tale of a Tub*. Particularly in the digressions Swift develops an ironic manner designed to undermine equally contrary points of view. Blake works similarly but to opposite effect, to produce a text in which contrary points of view are both of them accepted, a world in which 'Attraction and Repulsion, Reason and Energy, Love and Hate, are necessary to Human existence' (plate 3). The sentence has a beguiling vigour, an enlightened antithetical firmness that works hard to distract the reader from considering whether the Newtonian view, the view of fellow radicals such as Erasmus Darwin, Priestley, and Tom Paine, that existence is sustained by 'attraction and repulsion' is compatible with the notion that existence is a spiritual state sustained by the contraries of love and hate.[14]

Most obviously, the *Marriage* works hard to hold together various incompatible theologies; the atheism of fellow radicals such as Holbach, and, perhaps, Erasmus Darwin; the deism of Tom Paine, the unitarianism of Joseph Johnson and Priestley; those who accept the Bible as a literal revelation of God's purposes, and those who prefer to understand it as a collection of poetic allegories. But the *Marriage* also attempts to wed incompatible philosophical traditions. Terence Hoagwood has pointed out that the *Marriage* includes a near translation from Holbach's *Système de la Nature*: 'The more man reflects, the more he will be convinced that the soul, very far from being distinguished from the body, is only the body itself, considered relatively to some of its functions.'[15] In Blake's version this becomes: 'Man has no Body distinct from his Soul; for that call'd Body is a portion of Soul discern'd by the five senses, the chief inlets of Soul in this age' (plate 4). As Hoagwood rightly indicates, Holbach denies that the soul should be distinguished from the body, whereas Blake denies that the body should be distinguished from the soul, but the effect is surely not to effect a sharp distinction between Holbach's materialism and Blake's visionary spiritualism, but to devise a rhetoric that allows one to glide, as it were, without noticing it from one position to the other.[16] The *Marriage* includes a sequence of proverbs that ringingly endorse the value of sensuality. 'The nakedness of woman is the work of God' we are told, 'the genitals' represent 'Beauty'. In the short span of 200 years Eden will be regained, and 'This will come to pass by an improvement of sensual enjoyment' (plate 14). Sentences such as these perform their own work of reconciliation, marrying the kind of hearty endorsement of sexuality that one finds in Erasmus Darwin with the rapt celebration of human sexuality as divine characteristic of a large number of visionary Christian sects, including a group amongst the Swedenborgians. When Blake describes 'the five Senses' as 'the chief inlets of Soul in this age' he comes close to endorsing, even if he makes the position historically relative, the empiricism shared by almost the entire group of radical intellectuals, but the *Marriage* finds room too to embrace a quite different tradition within which the five senses are represented not as conduits for the spirit, but as barriers obstructing its apprehension:

> How do you know but ev'ry Bird that cuts the airy way,
> Is an immense world of delight, clos'd by your senses five?
>
> (plate 7)

I have no doubt exaggerated the self-contradictoriness of Blake's discourse in *The Marriage of Heaven and Hell*, and also its eccentricity. The case of Joseph Priestley, the most celebrated of all those radical intellectuals who made up the Johnson circle, is a useful corrective. Priestley was a scientist, and as consistent an exponent of philosophical materialism as Holbach, but he was also a Unitarian minister, a teacher of the Christian gospel for all that he did not accept the divinity of Christ, he was a proponent of universal suffrage, and, together with his friend Richard Price, one of those who had led the English campaign to rally support for the French revolutionaries, and he was also a man who read the Bible as prophesying the future course of political history, as in his *Institutes of Natural and Revealed Religion* of 1772:

> The present kingdoms of Europe are unquestionably represented by the feet and toes of the great image which Nebuchadnezzar saw in his prophetical dream... From Daniel's interpretation of this vision it may be clearly inferred, that the forms of government, ecclesiastical and civil, which now subsist in Europe, must be dissolved; but that something very different from them, and greatly superior to them, more favourable to the virtue and happiness of mankind, will take place in their stead.[17]

But two points need to be made. First, Priestley, in comparison with Blake, decorously maintains distinctions between his various kinds of writing. His scientific publications, the *Observations of different kinds of air*, for example, are quite distinct from his political and theological writings. He would not have thought, like Blake, to publicize his discovery of a new method of engraving, 'printing in the infernal method', by offering it as Blake does in plate 14 as an allegory of how in the course of time 'the whole creation will be consumed and appear infinite and holy'. Priestley's politics and his religion interpenetrate one another much more completely, but still he separated his apocalyptic readings of the Bible from his more conventional expositions of Unitarian theology, and separated both from his pamphlets on the proper relation between Church and State. Blake retains none of these distinctions. Second, and more crucially, Priestley, even in his apocalyptic writings, anxiously maintains his distinction from all those he regarded as vulgar and ignorant religious enthusiasts, from the Swedenborgian who saw 'Moses, and the other Jewish Prophets at a boxing match, or about Rag Fair', and from the writers of the pamphlets that Jon Mee has studied, from Richard Brothers, Thomas Webster and John Wright. Priestley looks to the Apocalypse to secure 'forms of government... more favourable to the virtue and happiness of mankind': he is the apocalyptic prophet in the incongruous guise of liberal reformer. He maintains between himself and Richard Brothers the same pitying compassionate distance that he maintained between himself and the Birmingham mob, whose rights he had championed, and who had responded by destroying his library and his laboratory. Blake makes no such concessions. *The Marriage of Heaven and Hell* is written by a man who recognizes his kinship equally with Priestley and with Thomas Webster, and is prompted by this recognition to the fierce hilarity that distinguishes his tract from the productions of either. The points of view that the *Marriage* accommodates are so diverse that they cannot be reconciled by argument, only by laughter.

Jon Mee is right to claim that the *Marriage* participates 'both in the ethos of [the Johnson] circle and the culture of radical enthusiasm', but Blake attempts to go further than this, and to reveal that the 'opposition' between the two is in fact 'true friendship'. He invites these very different voices to recognize that they are brothers, both 'sons of joy', who may join together to swell the harmony of the final chorus, the 'Song of Liberty'.

In Britain, as it happened, 'the stony law' was never stamped to dust. It was preserved by the inability of the radical intelligentsia to make common cause with the enthusiasm of popular radicalism. That this is not a perception available only to hindsight is amply demonstrated by the case of Tom Paine. Throughout the period treated in this book successive governments made a more sustained and vigorous attempt to prevent the publication of Paine's writings than those of any other radical propagandist, and the reason is obvious enough. They correctly detected in Tom Paine's prose the achievement of the alliance between intellectual and popular radicalism that they most feared. Their campaign was strikingly unsuccessful. They were unable to prevent Paine's works becoming more widely available through cheap reprints than the works of any other contemporary writer, and yet the consequence they feared never came to pass. There are no doubt many reasons for this, but one of them, surely, is that by publishing *The Age of Reason* Paine isolated himself from one of the dominant characteristics of popular radicalism, its distinctively Christian religious enthusiasm. Blake came to understand this very well, though perhaps not until some years after he had written *The Marriage of Heaven and Hell*, and yet even then, in the early 1790s, Blake is evidently intent on arranging a wedding between the radical intellectuals and the radical enthusiasts, between, as it were, Tom Paine and Richard Brothers. For this reason *The Marriage of Heaven and Hell* remains a central text in the political history of the early revolutionary years.

But it would be idle to deny that it remains for all that an entirely eccentric text.

Up to a point Blake's printing methods in themselves account for this. *The Marriage of Heaven and Hell* exists in nine complete and two incomplete copies, and it seems improbable that very many more copies were ever produced. The contrast with the thousands of copies circulating of Paine's *Rights of Man* needs no underlining. But it would be idle to pretend that the *Marriage*, even if Blake had devised a way of printing that made possible a wide circulation, would ever have achieved wide popularity, and this not because Blake was eccentric, though he may have been, but because his project was. The *Marriage* collects together 'the sayings used in a nation', radical England, but the sayings used in that nation contradicted one another too often to be resolved except by being plunged into the acid bath of Blake's humour. The fierceness of that humour, its hysterical wildness, is not so much an expression of Blake's personality as it is a response to a political situation, a crisis of English radicalism. The *Marriage* may be Blake's attempt to persuade his political allies that they are all citizens of one nation, all 'sons of joy', but it is haunted by the recognition that even in making such an attempt Blake is likely to succeed only in writing the manifesto of a party of which he is the only member. The *Marriage* ends with a communal chorus, 'A Song of Liberty', but the 'Argument' with which it begins may be a truer prophecy. There, 'the just man' finds no colleagues to share with him the task of making a just society, and is reduced to raging 'in the wilds / Where lions roam'.

3
The English Jacobins

At the end of *The Marriage of Heaven and Hell* Blake makes a characteristically flamboyant promise: 'I have also: The Bible of Hell: which the world shall have whether they will or no' (plate 24). It was a promise that he kept, publishing in 1794 the *Book of Urizen*, and in 1795 the *Book of Ahania* and the *Book of Los*. Then Blake fell silent. For more than a decade he pursued his trade as an engraver, but kept his own writings private. He explained himself in a note written on the title page of the Bishop of Llandaff's *An Apology for The Bible in a Series of Letters addressed to Thomas Paine*: 'To defend the Bible in this year 1798 would cost a man his life', and he added, in words that seem deliberately to recall and to retract the jauntily defiant conclusion of *The Marriage of Heaven and Hell*, 'I have been commanded from Hell not to print this, as it is what our Enemies wish'.[1]

1798 was the year of *The Anti-Jacobin*. In its first incarnation, as a weekly review, it survived for only 37 issues, but by 9 July 1798, when the last of these appeared, its work was done. It was a journal that could reasonably be categorized by the *Courier*, the *Post*, and the *Chronicle*, its principal targets, as a ministerial mouthpiece.[2] *The Anti-Jacobin* supported Pitt and assailed his enemies. It defended, that is, a Prime Minister who seemed, for all practical purposes, to have little need for defenders. At the end of the Parliamentary session in 1797 Fox recognized his impotence by announcing his secession from the Commons, an absence that served only to underwrite Pitt's Parliamentary supremacy. Pitt was able to pass his Gagging Acts, after the failure of Lord Malmesbury's peace negotiations to pursue his war policy, to finance it by an unprecedented increase in taxation, and to crush vigorously a rebellion in Ireland, without effective Parliamentary opposition. It was the achievement of *The Anti-Jacobin* to harness in the defence of established power the kind of fierce rhetorical energy that in normal circumstances is a resource available only to those in opposition. In this achievement the most significant precursors of Gifford, the journal's editor, and Canning, George Ellis and John Hookham Frere, his chief assistants, were, paradoxically, the Jacobins themselves.

It would be foolish, of course, to suggest an analogy between the sharp satirical thrusts of *The Anti-Jacobin*, and the blade of the guillotine with which the French Jacobins defended their own ideological purity. Gifford was personal and vindictive in his attacks – no one could claim of him what Shelley claimed for Peacock's satire, that it inflicted 'a wound so wide the knife was lost in it' – but there remains a wide difference between ridicule and state execution. Gifford openly displayed his chagrin that Horne Tooke, Thelwall, and the other members of the London Corresponding Society remained 'acquitted felons', he registered grim satisfaction at the death of Lord Edward Fitzgerald, and triumphed in the execution of the Irish rebel, 'O'Quigley' (properly O'Coigley), but, by and large, he exercised a surveillance over the country's political and cultural life in which the agent of discipline was contempt rather than revolutionary terror. Nevertheless, he repeated the distinctive Jacobin strategy, that is, he cultivated paranoia. No state power was secure, for there were a multitude of ideological enemies busily attempting to undermine it. The stability of the nation, the survival of its institutions, values, and traditions could be secured only by an unremitting vigilance.

The Anti-Jacobin presented itself as the spokesman of sentiments held in common by an overwhelming majority of the nation. It spoke for 'the people of England', but the manner in which it did so relied on it simultaneously representing itself as the mouthpiece of an embattled minority, of that tiny section of the cultural elite that had remained true to the nation and its people. The journal's heroes were few. Among statesmen it championed Pitt, among poets T. J. Mathias, the anonymous author of *The Pursuits of Literature*, and, most enthusiastically of all, it assumed the mantle of Burke, the 'mighty Sea-Mark of these troubled days'. Its enemies were legion. They are graphically assembled in the caricature Gillray published to accompany *The New Morality*, the poem with which Canning and Frere marked the final issue of the journal.[3] The Duke of Bedford, Burke's 'Noble Lord', is a podgy Leviathan. Fox and the Whig Parliamentary leaders ride on him, with Thelwall serving as their mahout. Behind them are a confused throng of Whigs, Irishmen and pamphleteers, among them Erskine, Whitbread, and O'Connor. Borne in front of Bedford is a huge 'cornucopia of ignorance' constructed from the monthly reviews, the *Analytical*, the *Monthly*, and the *Critical*, from which a welter of literature is spewing. The procession is moving towards the Priest Lepaux, the atheist cleric of France, who is instructing four baboons, the *Courier*, the *Chronicle*, and the *Morning Post*, and, still more grotesque in appearance, the Irish revolutionary newspaper, the *Star*. Also crowded into the picture are pamphlets by or portraits of almost the whole end-of-century world of letters: Southey, Coleridge and Godwin as donkeys, Paine as a crocodile, Horne Tooke, Mary Wollstonecraft, Priestley, Erasmus Darwin as a basket of liberty cap flowers, even the Charleses, Lamb and Lloyd, as a pair of frogs. It is a magnificently undiscriminating print, joining together the most unlikely associates, and insisting by the ubiquitous liberty caps that all belong to a single party, all are Jacobins. Gifford's tactic, in other words, was to define the term Jacobin as widely as the Jacobins themselves had defined the term enemy of the revolution. For the years during which France was threatened by an alliance of European monarchies, it was a tactic that had been effective enough to secure Jacobin power in France. It worked for *The Anti-Jacobin* for precisely the same reason, because the appearance of the journal coincided with the months in which the Army of England, under the command of Napoleon, was assembling across the Channel.

In Gillray's cartoon, as in Canning and Frere's poem, Lepaux is the high priest of a trinity of goddesses. Egalité, a wild-haired hag, her shrivelled breasts exposed, a dagger in each hand, is re-named 'Justice'; Liberté, a stout, truculent woman compressing the globe in a fierce embrace and trampling on 'Ties of Nature' and 'Amor Patriae', is named 'Philanthropy', and Fraternité becomes 'Sensibility', a sulky woman who weeps over a dead bird held in one hand, holds a copy of Rousseau in the other, and casually rests her right foot on the severed head of Louis XVI. The point of both poem and cartoon is to expose the anodyne disguises under which the British fellow-travellers pursue their propaganda work for Jacobin principles. Jacobin 'Justice', for example, is 'The avenging Angel of regenerate France', not anything to be found in 'British courts'. 'Sensibility' is the 'child of sickly Fancy' nurtured by Rousseau, the possession of those who weep over 'a dead Jack-ass',[4] but will contemplate unflinchingly even the foulest crimes when they are 'sicklied o'er with Freedom's name', and

'Philanthropy' is that 'general love of all mankind' proclaimed by those whose infatuation with France has made them traitors to their own country:

> Each pert adept disowns a Briton's part,
> And plucks the name of England from his heart.
> (99–100)

Jacobins are identified by their lack of patriotism, by their lack of piety, construed fairly narrowly as a devotion to the Church of England, and by their libertinism; by their assumption, that is, as Canning pithily expresses it in *The New Morality*, that a man might 'act from *taste in morals* all his own'. In the Prospectus to *The Anti-Jacobin*, the Jacobin mentality was more extensively defined as 'that wild and unshackled freedom of thought, which rejects all habits, all wisdom of former times, all restraints of ancient usage, and of local attachment: and which judges upon each subject, whether of politics or morals, as it arises, by lights entirely its own, without reference to recognised principle, or established practice'.[5] Jacobinism, then, was not an exclusively political phenomenon: it contaminated social life, particularly the relationships between the sexes, and it permeated the national culture, particularly its literature. Jacobinism, as Canning put it, propounded a comprehensive 'new morality', the necessary result of which was anarchy.

The vigorous heroic couplets in which Canning and Frere denounce the exponents of the 'new morality' function in themselves as a defence of the established order against anarchic metrical experiment, such monstrosities as 'Coleridge's Dactylics' and 'Southey's Saphics' [*sic*], which in Gillray's print are being declaimed by a pair of donkeys. Gillray's print is more subversive than the poem in its evident fascination with the anarchic tumult of the procession, but even he distances himself from it. His Jacobins are contained within a formal composition that imitates a conventional Triumph. In the centre background the three massive classical pillars grouped in parody of the three Jacobin goddesses, whose statues are clumsily huddled together on the altar table, function as a memento of the established aesthetic order that these celebrants would overthrow. The goddesses, in their unwomanly savagery and the immodesty of their dress, have rejected the feminine decorum which maintains the necessary distinction between the sexes, but Gillray preserves it anyway. His procession includes men, and men transformed into animals, but women take part only as a name in a dedication, 'Lady Oxford', and as the title of a book, 'Wrongs of Women'. Gillray resists the Jacobin tendency to extend their war against all distinctions to the difference between genders, a tendency which produces such unnatural creatures as 'STAEL the Epicene', denounced by Canning and Frere, or the *'unsexed* female writers' who alarmed Mathias by presuming to 'instruct, or confuse, us and themselves in the labyrinth of politicks, or turn us wild with Gallick frenzy'.[6]

For Canning, Frere and Mathias the struggle to preserve the political traditions of Britain against the Jacobin threat had as its necessary corollary an anxiety to maintain literary traditions, particularly the tradition of the heroic couplet, and traditional gender roles.[7] Poetry and women were deeply implicated in the struggle against France. Mathias wrote his *Pursuits of Literature* as his own contribution to the national effort to defeat those who would introduce the 'horrid system' of revolutionary government to England. Believing that 'Government and Literature are now more than ever intimately connected', it seemed clear to him that literary experimentation was inseparable from the rage for political experimentation that united the French revolutionaries and their English sympathizers. Hannah More's *Strictures on the Modern System of Female Education*, like *The Pursuits of Literature* a remarkable publishing success, calls on women 'to come forward, and contribute their full and fair proportion towards the saving of their country', but to do so 'without departing from the refinement of their character'. It quickly emerges that the retention of their femininity is, in fact, not the condition of the service they owe the nation, but itself constitutes that service. It empowers women to go about their true task, 'to raise the depressed tone of public morals, and to awaken the drowsy spirit of religious principle' (1, p. 4).[8] Their 'refinement' is as much needed in the struggle against Jacobin principles as is the courage with which British men must engage the French on the battlefield.

Mathias presents himself as an embattled voice. He assumes the state of affairs lamented in the first issue of *The Anti-Jacobin*: 'whether it be that good Morals, and what we should call good Politics, are inconsistent with the spirit of true Poetry... we have not been able to find one good and true Poet, of sound principles and of sober practice, upon whom we could rely for furnishing us with a handsome quantity of good and approved verse.' The editors have no option, they complain, but 'to go to the only market where it is to be had good and ready made – that of the *Jacobins*', and they offer a poem by Southey followed by their own parody of it. Their choice is not casual. Southey is, for the editors of *The Anti-Jacobin*, the representative Jacobin poet, and *Joan of Arc*, published in its second edition in 1798, the exemplary Jacobin poem.

In *Joan of Arc* Southey had established all the parameters of the Jacobin poem that are identified in *The Anti-Jacobin*.[9] He 'improves' the contempt of riches and grandeur shared by 'poets of all ages' into 'a hatred of the rich and great'. The action of Southey's poem takes place in 'the king-curst realm of France' (4, 163),[10] a land in which the 'low cottager' has 'little cause to love the mighty ones' (5, 92–3). Conrade, the poem's warrior hero, condenses these sentiments, which recur throughout the poem, into a comprehensive biblical curse:

> Come that hour,
> When in the Sun the Angel of the Lord
> Shall stand and cry to all the fowls of Heaven,
> 'Gather ye to the supper of your God,
> That ye may eat the flesh of mighty men,
> Of captains, and of kings!' Then shall be peace.
>
> (5, 476–81)

Unlike the poet of former times, who had been 'an enthusiast in the love of his native soil', the Jacobin poet's 'love is enlarged and expanded to comprehend all human kind'. Southey's Joan proclaims herself 'To England friendly as to all the world' (8, 628), and, as he makes clear in the poem's original preface, she is speaking for Southey:

> It has been established as a necessary rule for the epic that the subject should be national. To this rule I have acted in direct opposition, and chosen for the subject of my poem the defeat of the English. If there be any readers who can wish success to an unjust cause, because their country was engaged in it, I desire not their approbation.

Southey's theme may be an Anglo-French war, but he develops a special use of the epic simile to extend the poem's sympathies to all religions and nations, indeed 'all human kind'. In its similes the poem ranges from the Aztecs of Mexico (6, 97–111), to Arabia where the young Ali becomes the Prophet's Vizier (6, 127–38), to a Rajah tiger-hunting outside Delhi (8, 348–58), an African swimmer threatened by a shark (10, 504–8), a Persian worshipping Mithra (10, 209–13), and to the land of the Norsemen where winds blow when Hraesvelger flaps his eagle wings (10, 289–94). Lastly, whereas the poet of former times was 'a Warrior, at least in imagination', for the Jacobin poet thoughts of war bring to mind 'nothing but contusions and amputations, plundered peasants and deserted looms'. An exception is made only for the military prowess of Britain's enemies. Bonaparte's victories, for example, are apt to be represented by 'phalanxes of Republicans shouting victory, satellites of Despotism biting the ground, and geniusses of Liberty planting standards on mountain-tops'. Southey follows both these principles. His poem is thickly populated with characters like Wordsworth's Margaret, their husbands snatched from them by war:

> All the long summer did she live in hope
> Of tidings from the war; and as at eve
> She with her mother by the cottage door
> Sat in the sunshine, if a traveller
> Appear'd at distance coming o'er the brow,
> Her eye was on him, and it might be seen
> By the flushed cheek what thoughts were in her heart,
> And by the deadly paleness which ensued,
> How her heart died within her.
>
> (1, 282–90)

He develops a technique for the description of battles in which the deaths of individual soldiers are punctuated by descriptions of the domestic tranquillity from which they have been removed, and the grieving families who survive them. And yet Southey's detestation of war somehow coincides with an apparently wholehearted admiration of warrior prowess, such as Conrade's, that is directed against the English armies.

This is a Jacobin rhetoric, of course, because it is designed to express support for revolutionary France in its war against Britain. *Joan of Arc* does not bother to hide its intentions. In the section of the poem removed from its second edition, but only to be separately published, Henry V is exposed as a flimsy mask for Pitt:

> Seeing the realms of France by faction torn,
> I thought in pride of heart that it would fall
> An easy prey. I persecuted those
> Who taught new doctrines, though they taught the truth:
> And when I heard of thousands by the sword
> Cut off, or blasted by the pestilence,
> I calmly counted up my proper gains,
> And sent new herds to slaughter.
>
> (*The Vision of the Maid of Orleans*, 2, 353–60)

The Jacobin nature of the poem is apparent, too, in its generic character, for *Joan of Arc* is, Southey insists, an 'epic' poem, but a poem that insists just as strongly that the epic is subordinate to the pastoral. Joan is impelled into epic heroism by the corruption of the French court and the vicious belligerence of the British, cruelly snatched from her pastoral life in Arc, and from the life of quiet domestic contentment, married to Theodore, which ought to have been her lot. Throughout the poem the epic is represented as a vicious interruption of that pastoral happiness which it is the highest human ambition to achieve. Finally, *Joan of Arc* is Jacobin in its dismantling of gender differences. The poem's heroine is flagrantly 'unsexed', she wears armour, and wreaks havoc among the English: 'fast they fell / Pierced by her forceful spear' (10, 331–2). Her warrior virtues are not, of course, proper to her, but forced on her by circumstance. Nevertheless, she is a woman who dedicates herself to 'active duties' (9, 167), rejecting alike a life of cloistered contemplation, and a life of married love. It is Theodore, not Joan, who is sent back to Arc to 'sojourn safe at home' devoting himself to the care of his aged mother, and it is he who is reduced to the stratagem proper to the heroine of romance: he assumes a disguise and follows Joan to the wars.

It is significant that Southey republished *Joan of Arc* in 1798, and it is equally significant that he removed from the poem its most inflammatory section.[11] In this he showed himself more resolute than most of his fellow Jacobins, yet responsive, like them, to the kinds of pressure to which *The Anti-Jacobin* gave the most forceful expression. To borrow the title under which Coleridge first published his 'France: an Ode', it was a year of 'recantation'. In *Joan of Arc* Southey had constructed the monumental version of the plot that united the English Jacobins, a plot that represented Britain as having enthusiastically joined in the 'dire array' of European monarchs engaged in an aggressive war against revolutionary France. It was a story that Coleridge maintained even in his 'Recantation', but it was a story that, as Coleridge recognized, had been overtaken by events; by the invasion of Switzerland, and by the preparations to invade Britain itself. The French, it seems, were as much infatuated with 'the low lust of sway' as any 'kings'. 'Fears in Solitude' and 'France: an Ode' are uncomfortable poems, at once recantations and reaffirmations. They are candid poems, but poems written at a time when candour itself, the determination to maintain the full complexity of moral judgement, had come under attack. For Canning and Frere it is the 'driveling Virtue of this moral Age' (211), the recourse of those too feeble to attain 'the bold uncompromising mind' (223).

The Anti-Jacobin succeeded by being more Jacobinical than its enemies, by being itself so uncompromising that it successfully forced compromise on its opponents. The Jacobin was established as a compound beast, made up of impiety, lack of patriotism, profligacy, sentimentality, inhuman rationality, murderous violence, a character so Protean, adept at assuming so many disguises, that it seemed monstrous even to the 'Jacobins' themselves. The typical 'Jacobin' text of 1797 and 1798 is concerned less to enunciate principles, than to repudiate a distorted reflection of the self. Wordsworth's and Coleridge's tragedies of 1797 both choose historical settings that allegorize their own place and time. In the Spain of *Osorio*, the Moors have been defeated, even to wear Moorish costume is to make oneself vulnerable to the Christian victors, who use the Inquisition rather than Pitt's Gagging Acts to enforce conformity to their own ideology. The play's hero, Albert, is a Christian, but dresses in Moorish costume 'as if he courted death' (2, 143). But it is Osorio, the villain of the piece, Albert's younger brother, who has ousted him from his inheritance, and plotted his murder, who gives the play all its energy. He is a character recurrent in the fiction of the time, who recognizes no religion, no law, and no human ties. He feels himself to be a creature of 'some other planet' (4, 86), condemned all his life to mimic the 'occupations and the semblances/Of ordinary men' (4, 117–18). He represses within himself all the emotions that define humanity, notably the emotion of remorse, by denying his responsibility for his own actions:

> What have I done but that which nature destin'd
> Or the blind elements stirred up within me?
> (1, 114–15)

The Borderers takes place in the marches between England and Scotland, in a period when noble and active young men like Marmaduke have been driven into outlawry, but the play's energies are focused on Oswald, Wordsworth's version of Osorio, who recognises only one law, 'the immediate law,/From the clear light of circumstance, flashed/Upon an independent Intellect' (1494–6). Only in this recognition is freedom to be found, even if it is a freedom that condemns one to 'walk in solitude' amongst one's fellow men. All who refuse such freedom submit to:

> a tyranny
> That lives but in the torpid acquiescence

> Of our emasculated souls, the tyranny
> Of the world's masters, with the musty rules
> By which they uphold their craft from age to age...
> (1488–92)

The persecuted Moors and the young men driven into outlawry may express something of Wordsworth's and Coleridge's sense of themselves as the victims of Pitt's repression, but the characterization of Osorio and Oswald seems complicit in the conservative attempt to demonize the kind of revolutionary rationalism that was embodied most powerfully in England in the person of William Godwin.

The plot of both plays hinges on betrayal, but in holding up, however indirectly, to hatred and contempt a once-admired fellow radical they might also be seen as treacherous plays. In this, they are characteristic of a kind of Jacobin fiction that is best represented by Charles Lloyd's 1798 novel, *Edmund Oliver*. Coleridge felt betrayed by the novel because Lloyd borrowed episodes from Coleridge's life, notably his attempt to escape from his university debts by enlisting as a dragoon, in constructing the biography of his central character. But the novel constitutes a much more extensive act of betrayal than this. It is at once a radical novel and a rather broad satire on radicalism. It maintains a fairly full set of Jacobin principles. When Oliver enlists in the army, he comes to recognize the ignominy of employment as a hired murderer for the state. Notions of patriotism are tartly repudiated: 'When the word country...expresses a track of land inhabited by human beings, I am anxious for its welfare; but not particularly because I place the pronoun *my* before it' (2, 115). We are urged to throw aside the whole 'panoply of artificial and personal distinction (1, 103), and maintain 'the principle of equality, whereby we deem it robbery to hold useless property in defiance of a poor and suffering neighbour' (2, 150). The ideal community is pantisocratic, a community whose members 'have banished the words *mine* and *thine*'. We are invited to maintain the notion of perfectibility by fixing our minds on 'the grand spectacle of universal final happiness to the whole creation' (1, 72). All these are Godwinian positions, lightly flavoured with Coleridge. Lloyd leans on Godwin, too, in his attack on politically active radicalism, represented in the novel by Edward D'Oyley, a member of the London Corresponding Society who is apt to indulge in 'some very sanguinary wishes with regard to the present ministers and governors of this country' (1, 178). D'Oyley is counselled to 'desist from meddling with political bodies', and conform to 'a system of complete passiveness' directed by 'a principle of political non-resistance' (1, 184–5). But Godwin remains, as Lloyd clearly suggests in his preface, the novel's principal target. The novel consistently assails radical scepticism, the representation of the pious as 'dupes' to 'superstitions' (1, 39), and of religion as a tool of government, 'convenient as a political restraint on the minds of the vulgar' (1, 85). More pointedly the novel repudiates Godwin's denial that promises can be binding by placing his argument in the mouth of Gertrude, Oliver's first love, who uses it to excuse herself for jilting him. Once, the attack on Godwin is explicit: 'A modern writer recommends a person, who should see a house on fire, in which a philosopher and his own mother are contained, it being impossible to rescue both, to effect the escape of the former rather than of the latter, as a being most likely to be of benefit to the human race.' To subordinate the domestic affections, 'the attachment of a sister to a brother, of a father to a son, or of one friend to another', to 'the conduct of general existence' is, we are advised, not an advance in philosophy, but the wanton rejection of a tendency without which 'we should not be human' (1, 127–9). Finally, Godwin's argument against marriage is rebutted when Gertrude finds that it has enabled Edward D'Oyley to persuade her to become his mistress only to abandon her when she is pregnant in favour of a rich heiress.

Gertrude's fate is particularly revealing. She and Edmund had early formed an attachment to each other founded on a shared idealism. Both were determined to become 'benefactors of mankind' (1, 38). They are separated when Edmund goes to university, where he is tempted into dissipation, frequents brothels, falls into debt, and is forced into flight. His moral reformation is accomplished by Charles Maurice, his friend and benefactor. After some years, during which he has not written to her, he meets Gertrude by chance in London, and renews his suit. She has formed a new attachment to Edward D'Oyley, and rejects him, a decision which is unaccountably represented as vicious. D'Oyley abandons her when pregnant. Maurice rescues her. She gives birth, but remains sunk in a wild despair which brings her, at last, to suicide. Edmund is more fortunate. He may have 'plunged in all the depths of sensuality', and 'rioted in all the wildness of youthful passion and imagination', but these have been 'trials' for which he is now grateful: 'less severe discipline would never have tamed my impetuous nature'. He eventually finds happiness in marriage to Edith Alwynne, who has led a 'solitary life, and a life which has cherished meek and quiet sensibilities'. Edmund flies to her bosom 'as a shelter from the vexations and ruffling business of a wearying world'. Gertrude's story would have struck all its readers as a pointed allusion to the career of Mary Wollstonecraft, who was also abandoned by a lover when pregnant. *Edmund Oliver* and the vituperative reception in 1798 of Godwin's *Memoirs* of his late wife both mark a violent reaction against the possibility that women might engage blamelessly in active, public roles. Joan of Arc as an ideal of womanhood withers to an Edith Alwynne, or to a Maria or an Idonea, the unimpeachably passive heroines of Coleridge's and Wordsworth's plays.

In 1798 the Jacobin poets surrendered to their opponents 'the bold, uncompromising mind', and sought an alternative virtue in 'candour'. But it would be wrong to represent this development as a response simply to external pressure, to the propaganda of journals such as *The Anti-Jacobin* or the more direct pressure embodied in Pitt's repressive legislation and in the agents through which he maintained his surveillance over suspected radicals. The Jacobin poets seem to have been more susceptible to internalized pressures, in particular guilt. The most powerful image of the year is of a man condemned to an utter solitude, adrift at sea, surrounded by the dead bodies of comrades who have died in punishment for a senseless and blasphemous act of violence that he knows himself to have committed, but no longer knows why. It is an image that has complex origins, no doubt, but one of them surely lies in Coleridge's newly awakened sense that he might wilfully have deafened himself to 'blasphemy's loud scream', and blunted a properly sympathetic response to Revolutionary terror by dehumanizing its victims, casting them as reptilian monsters in some allegorical mummery, 'Domestic treason' writhing 'like a wounded dragon in his gore'.

There was both guilt and fear, and it produced various responses; an impulse to confession of the kind evident in 'France, an Ode', and in 'Fears in Solitude' – 'Oh, shrieve me, shrieve me, holy man!' – but also, and more emphatically, an impulse to retreat into an isolated rural society and into domesticity, an impulse that the Jacobin poets pursued both in their lives and in their fictions. At the end of *Edmund Oliver*, Edmund and his friends Charles and Basil establish with their wives an emotionally self-sufficient community in the Lake District, in the hope that nature, like their womenfolk, will offer them 'a shelter from the vexations and ruffling business of the world'. Canning and Frere had sought to rouse the 'bashful Genius', as:

> far aloof retiring from the strife
> Of busy talents and of active life,

> As, from the loop-hole of retreat, he views
> Our stage, Verse, Pamphlets, Politics and News...
> (63–6)

They seem to have succeeded so well that the writers of the 'Verse' and 'Pamphlets' – Wordsworth, Coleridge, Southey, Thelwall – were persuaded to occupy the loop-holes of retreat that had been vacated.

But it was never simply a defensive retreat. It was also restorative: Coleridge describes the 'dell' within which he writes 'Fears in Solitude' as 'a spirit-healing nook'. From within such nooks a new aesthetic could be constructed. Instead of a heady commitment to the universal, and a dismissal of the notion that one should be more interested in the welfare of a particular 'track of land' because 'the pronoun *my*' is placed before it, there is a new emphasis on 'local attachments', and love of a locality broadens into a newly proclaimed patriotism:

> Oh native Britain! Oh my mother isle!
> How shouldst thou prove aught else but dear and holy
> To me, who from thy lakes and mountain hills,
> Thy clouds, thy quiet dales, thy rocks, and seas,
> Have drunk in all my intellectual life...
> (179–83)

Philanthropy is no longer allowed to trample either 'Amor Patriae' or 'Ties of Nature': instead the most intimate of such ties are celebrated. The poet proclaims himself 'a son, a brother, and a friend,/A husband and a father' (175–6), and finds in domestic intimacies the proper model for all social relations. There is a new distrust of the printed word, a revulsion from that great welter of pamphlets pouring from the cornucopia of the monthly reviews in Gillray's 'New Morality': 'Books! 'tis a dull and endless strife' ('The Tables Turned'). There is a continuing reverence for the 'spirit of divinest liberty', but liberty is no longer a quality that inheres in political institutions, but in 'an impulse from a vernal wood', felt, as Coleridge has it:

> on the sea-cliff's verge,
> Whose pines, scarce travelled by the breeze above,
> Had made one murmur with the distant surge!
> ('France: an Ode' 99–101)

One understands the puzzlement of a reviewer: 'What does Mr. Coleridge mean by liberty in this passage? or what connexion has it with the subject of civil freedom?'[12] This poetry may be Romantic, but it is emphatically not Jacobin.

Only two substantial Jacobin poems were published in 1798. One of them was Southey's second edition of *Joan of Arc*, the other a poem of which Southey was the first and greatest admirer, Landor's *Gebir*. Landor found the story of his poem in a translation from the French by Clara Reeves, 'The History of Charoba, Queen of Egypt', appended to her *The Progress of Romance*, a lengthy dialogue in which a pair of learned ladies defend, to the astonished admiration of their male adversary, the claim that prose fiction, the romance, should be granted a status equal to that of epic poetry. Landor, he tells us, came across the book 'on the shelf of a circulating library', and he affects a loftily dismissive response towards it: 'the work itself had little remarkable in it, except indeed we reckon remarkable the pertness and petulance of female criticism'. But there is reason for suspecting that he was more receptive to Reeves's argument than he finds it politic to admit. In his own first substantial poem, *Birth of Poesy*, published in 1795 when Landor was only twenty, he attempts an even more extreme revision of conventional hierarchies. The poem traces in three cantos the history of poetry, from its beginnings in a mysterious prehistoric past to the death of Anacreon at the end of the fifth century BC. In this, it simply shares an interest in the origins of poetry common in the later eighteenth century. It is in its structure that the poem reveals its originality. The first canto ends with the death of Orpheus, the second with the death of Sappho, and the third with the death of Anacreon. These three comprise Landor's great trinity of early poets, a trinity remarkable for the poet that it excludes, Homer. He is there, in the second canto, but Landor happily turns from the *Iliad* to the higher art of Sappho, from a poetry of war to a poetry of love. His point becomes explicit at the end of the third canto in the praise of Anacreon:

> All cruel wars the Teian bard resign'd
> That tend to slaughter and enslave mankind.
> (3, 248–9)

Anacreon sang of love and of wine, and this is a nobler poetry than any epic celebration of conquerors like Alexander, Caesar or Augustus. Landor points the contemporary relevance of his argument when he interrupts his history of Greek poetry with an address to his own countrymen:

> Britons! at last will come the fated hour
> With ample vengeance for abuse of pow'r.
> (3, 262–3)

He elevates lyric poetry over epic because he convicts epic poetry of gratifying the kinds of ambition, for imperial aggrandizement and for martial glory, that led George III and Pitt to pursue their war against revolutionary France:

> O lust of empire! brutal thirst of war!
> Which fiends delight in, Gods and Men abhor.
> (3, 252–3)

It is the same topic that lies behind *Gebir*.

'I sing the fates of Gebir' (1, 12), Landor begins, announcing his epic ambitions, but only after a preludium which makes a very different claim:

> When old Silenus call'd the Satyrs home,
> Satyrs then tender-hoof't and ruddy-horn'd,
> With Bacchus and the Nymphs, he sometimes rose
> Amidst the tale or pastoral, and shews
> The light of purest wisdom; and the God
> Scatter'd with wholesome fruit the pleasant plains.
> (1, 1–6)

Even before the epic claim is made, the poem has affiliated itself with the pastoral. Gebir is about to summon with his battle-horn 'whole nations', 'ten thousand, mightiest men', to accomplish with him the conquest of Egypt, but the poem has already given priority over epic glory to a quite different ideal, the bucolic abundance of those fruit-filled plains. In the poem's plot it is an opposition embodied in the contrast between Gebir, the warrior king of the island, Gibraltar, to which he gave his name, and his brother Tamar, the shepherd prince. Gebir's desire is to regain the throne of Egypt once held by his ancestors. Tamar is content to tend the 'royal flocks, entrusted to his care' (1, 89), unburdened by dynastic ambitions.[13] Each brother has his own love story.

Charoba, Queen of Egypt, is helpless to oppose the army that has landed on her shores. Encouraged by her nurse, Dalica, she travels to Gebir's camp and throws herself on his mercy. She appears before him:

> Faint, hanging on her handmaids, and her knees
> Tott'ring, as from the motions of the car...
> (1, 73–4)

Gebir is disturbed by the intensity of his response to the young Queen. He salutes her formally and retires:

> lest Pity go beyond,
> And crost Ambition lose her lofty aim...
> (1, 79–80)

He wilfully dams up within himself the capacity for emotional spontaneity, for trust, on which all human intimacy depends. It is a quality that even his dogs display when they are frightened by the cries of animals that are unfamiliar to them. They:

> raise their flaccid ears,
> And push their heads within their master's hand.
> (1, 66–7)

By trying to be more than simply human, Gebir makes himself less even than them.

Charoba is no different. She is unable to admit the love she feels for Gebir, persuading her nurse, admittedly an imperceptive woman, that Egypt is not to be saved by a marriage between Charoba and Gebir, and that she must pursue another policy and plot Gebir's murder:

> I have asked
> If she loved Gebir: 'love him!' she exclaim'd,
> With such a start of terror, such a flush
> Of anger, 'I love Gebir? I in love?'
> Then, looked so piteous, so impatient looked –
> Then saw I, plainly saw I, 'twas not love.
> For, such her natural temper, what she likes
> She speaks it out, or rather, she commands.
> (5, 180–7)

Charoba is inhibited from speaking her love by feminine modesty, by maidenly fear of Gebir's masculine power, his 'gigantic force, gigantic arms' (1, 24), and also by her recognition that to confess her love would be to lose that queenly self-possession that she was bred to, a self-possession that was hers even as a child, when, for the very first time, she saw the sea:

> 'Is this the mighty ocean? is this all!'
> (5, 130)

Gebir and Charoba are both of them trapped within their genders, he within his masculine code in which private affection must be subordinated to public duty – 'My people, not my passion fills my heart' (2, 90), as he tells his brother – and she within her feminine code of modesty and fear.

Gebir's invasion of Egypt is evidently designed to suggest Britain's war against Revolutionary France, but the allegory is not simple. The Egyptian resentment that Gebir's men build 'fairer cities than our own', with 'wider streets in purer air than ours' (4, 88–94), obviously recalls the chagrin of Londoners contemplating the new civic grandeur of Paris. The contemporary allusions cluster most thickly in Book 3, in which Gebir descends to the Underworld. There, in an utterly sterile region, all 'glowing with one sullen sunless heat' (3, 87) Gebir's ancestors expiate their crimes:

> their's was loud acclaim
> When living: but their pleasure was in war.
> (3, 36–7)

One representative of his line strikes Gebir as particularly repulsive:

> what wretch
> Is that, with eyebrows white and slanting brow?
> (3, 184–5)

As De Quincey saw immediately, these are features that identify George III. He 'was no warrior', but stands convicted of a 'thousand lives/Squander'd, as stones to exercise a sling!' (3, 196–7). Another is distinguished by a 'pale visage', and a horrifying 'space' between his 'purple' and his 'crown' (3, 222). This 'wretch accurst/Who sold his people to a rival king' is clearly Charles I, but he can also be identified with the executed Louis. Finally, Gebir meets his own father, who is suffering there in punishment for the vow he had inflicted on the infant Gebir, binding him to make war on Egypt. It is Pitt's meeting with the shade of his own dead father.

Two nations are in conflict whose shared culture would have made them friends had they not been plunged by a succession of warrior monarchs into a sequence of wars that stretch back through the centuries. The monarchic thirst for glory has repeatedly forged an alliance with the 'vulgar' hatred of the 'foreign face' to overpower the voices of 'the wiser few' who 'dare to cry' even in Charoba's Egypt:

> 'People! these men are not your enemies:
> Enquire their errand; and resist when wrong'd.'
> (3, 81–2)

The two nations are driven to war by a failure of frankness, by an ability to converse across national divisions, and the same failure blights the relationship between Gebir and Charoba. He cannot voice the emotions that she has aroused in him, and she is in the same plight. The result is that their story ends not in marriage but in murder. Dalica believes Charoba when she affects repugnance at the suggestion that she might neutralize the threat posed by Gebir's army by marrying him, and so Dalica pursues another plan. She impregnates a costly gown with poison, and presents it to Gebir. He dies in agony, realizing only as he dies that he has dedicated his life to the pursuit of illusory, worthless ambitions:

> Ah! what is grandeur – glory – they are past!
> (7, 265)

Charoba, too, ends calling on the Gods to obliterate her sovereignty, to 'hurl / From this accursed land, this faithless throne' (7, 199–200). Both learn the truth that Gebir announces as he dies, that the only possession worth acquiring is the love of a fellow human being:

> When nothing else, nor life itself, remains,
> Still the fond mourner may be call'd our own.
> (7, 266–7)

But it is a lesson that both learn too late. In the tears Charoba sheds she at last confesses her love, and Gebir at last reciprocates, but only in the moment before he dies.

It is not the King but his shepherd brother, who is content to feed his flocks and does not 'pant for sway', who has the power to usher in the future that his bride foretells:

> The Hour, in vain held back by War, arrives
> When Justice shall unite the Iberian hinds,
> And equal Egypt bid her shepherds reign.
> (6, 225–7)

Tamar is from the first a pastoral figure, free from the epic ambitions that deform Gebir, and unencumbered by the occupation of a throne that renders both Gebir and Charoba 'wretched up to royalty' (4, 48). He engages in a trial of strength with his nymph, like Gebir with Charoba, but it remains a pastoral contest in which Tamar stakes a sheep, and the nymph a collection of seashells. Gebir and Charoba are imprisoned within roles conferred on them by their gender, but Tamar and his nymph inhabit their roles much more freely. Unlike his brother, Tamar does not allow any code of warrior sternness to stifle the pangs of love. Instead, 'the tear stole silent down his cheek', as he tells Gebir how he first met his nymph. She came to Tamar, swimming through the waves as he sat by the shore playing his pipe. She is dressed in sailor fashion, and challenges him to a wrestling match, which he accepts, not because he has failed to penetrate her male disguise, but because he is already smitten. He had expected to win the contest easily, and was intent only on lingering it out, on contriving 'By pressing not too strongly, still to press' (1, 161). But as soon as he grapples with the woman all his strength evaporates. As he surrenders the sheep to her, he is filled with 'confusion', not because he has been overcome by a woman, but because he knows that, now the contest is over, she will leave:

> then ran I to the highest ground
> To watch her; she was gone; gone down the tide;
> And the long moon-beam on the hard wet sand
> Lay like a jaspar column half uprear'd.
> (1, 225–8)

It is a simile that accommodates the masculinity of Tamar's desire but dissolves all its unyielding rigidity into a beam of moonlight. The episode establishes Tamar as not by any means a 'fierce frightful man' like his brother, and the nymph as quite free of Charoba's maidenly affections. Their equal union makes them the proper progenitors of a new race, which, at the end of Book 6, the nymph predicts will colonize the whole world, until

> They shall o'er Europe, shall o'er Earth extend
> Empire that seas alone and skies confine,
> And glory that shall strike the crystal stars.
> (6, 306–8)

It is a Jacobin vision, and it concludes the last Jacobin poem to be published in England until Shelley was to reinvent a modified version of the kind some fifteen years later. *Gebir* is Jacobin in its internationalism, in a geographical sweep that takes the poem from the Iberian peninsula to Egypt, and then to the new western world, presumably America, colonized by Tamar and his nymph. It is Jacobin, too, in employing this internationalist rhetoric to articulate a condemnation of Britain in its war against France. It is Jacobin in its contempt of royalty, in its fierce anti-militarism, and in maintaining the myth of an original, natural state of peaceful plenty, the birthright of all, until mankind was cheated of it by the machinations of warmongering kings. It is Jacobin in its distrust of the recalcitrant prejudices of the 'vulgar', and in its desire to redraw the boundaries both of gender and of genre. But by 1798 it was already a Jacobin poem written out of its time, and it carries the marks of its belatedness.

In part the poem suffers simply from the accident of its timing. It was unlucky to publish a poem that figured the English war against France by an Iberian invasion of Egypt at a time when Napoleon was about to sail for Egypt at the head of his army of occupation.[14] It was also unlucky, though it was not entirely a matter of luck, that Landor should rehearse the myth of original pastoral abundance just as Malthus assailed that myth with an argument that its proponents were powerless to refute. But it is Landor himself who has Tamar and his nymph pause on their western journey as they pass the island of Corsica:

> *there* shall one arise,
> From Tamar shall arise, 'tis Fate's decree,
> A mortal man above all mortal praise.
> (191–3)[15]

But Napoleon, after all, was a general, the 'victor of Lodi', his fame founded on his Italian conquests, and hence already, even for those who saw him as Italy's liberator, marked as a descendant not of Tamar but of Gebir.[16] Landor innocently convicts himself of an inconsistency that the editors of *The Anti-Jacobin* found characteristic of the Jacobin poet. His detestation of war somehow fails to embrace the feats of his country's enemies:

> The prowess of BUONAPARTE indeed he might chaunt in his loftiest strain of exultation. *There* we should find nothing but trophies, and triumphs, and branches of laurel and olive. Phalanxes of Republicans shouting victory, satellites of Despotism biting the ground, and geniusses of Liberty planting standards on mountain-tops.

It is not an inconsistency confined to a digression. It marks both the poem's structure and its plot. Tamar's fruitful union with the nymph may be opposed to the sterile relationship between Gebir and Charoba in token that the epic is subordinate to the pastoral, war a perversion of peace, and the warrior inferior to the shepherd, but it is Gebir who gives his name to the poem. The utopian vision of innocence regained ends Book 6, but the seventh and final book ends with the death of the epic hero:

> Cold sweat and shivering ran o'er every limb,
> His eyes grew stiff; he struggled and expired.
> (7, 275–6)

Just as much as Southey Landor is half in love with the epic conventions that he seeks to overthrow, and implicated, too, in the warrior ethic that supports them. It is, after all, Gebir who wins for Tamar his bride. Tamar has arranged a return match with the nymph at the next full moon, and Gebir takes his place. The ruse seems at first designed to allow Tamar the opportunity to overcome the pang of jealousy with which he responds when Gebir first volunteers to impersonate him. Masculine possessiveness, it seems, is as incompatible with love as the masculine desire for mastery that Tamar has already forgone. But Tamar rises above his jealous suspicions only as a prelude to Gebir's violent encounter with the nymph:

> Nearer he drew her, and still nearer, clasp'd
> Above the knees midway; and now one arm
> Fell; and the other, lapsing o'er the neck
> Of Gebir, swung against his back incurved,
> The swoln veins glowing deep; and with a groan
> On his broad shoulder fell her face reclined.
> (2, 127–32)

She is forced to submit to Gebir, to surrender to him the secret that will safeguard his regal authority, and to receive from his hands the shepherd that she loves. It is a victory achieved by a pitiless exercise of male power:

> And thus, in prowess like a god, the chief
> Subdued her strength, nor soften'd at her charms...
> (2, 149–50)

The brave ambition of English Jacobin poetry is to escape from history, like the French revolutionaries to rewrite the calendar so that time might begin again, all the distinctions that deformed the old world obliterated, distinctions between ranks, between sexes, between nations, between genres. It is the vision that ends Book 6 of Landor's poem, when Time 'throws off his motley garb / Figur'd with monstrous men and monstrous gods' and assumes a 'pure vesture', pristinely blank, but in 1798, the year of the first publication of *Gebir*, it was the vision rather than history that came to an end, the victim of government repression, of anti-Jacobin propaganda, and of the potent allure of the traditional for a nation at war and under threat of invasion. But it was more than that. The nymph assures Tamar that the just society will inevitably and soon be established:

> The Hour, in vain held back by War, arrives
> When Justice shall unite the Iberian hinds,
> And equal Egypt bid her shepherds reign.
> (6, 225–7)

But she does so within a poem that is itself contaminated by the 'lust for sway' that it seeks to repudiate, a poem the proper hero of which is not Tamar but Gebir, who is 'generous, just, humane', but finds that not enough to free him from his history, from that long line of ancestors from which he has 'inhaled/Rank venom' (6, 219–20).

The Anti-Jacobin put an end to Jacobin poetry not because Gifford was savage and Canning and Frere were witty, but because Jacobin poems were from the first divided against themselves. Just as the French Jacobins led a campaign of opposition to monarchical government that culminated, not by accident but inevitably, in a nation that found strength and unity only in its fealty to a single warrior-leader, an emperor, so the Jacobin poets reproduced the generic hierarchy that they were bent on destroying. Their epic parodies served only to perpetuate the epic values that they were attempting to disclaim. In 1798 Southey and Landor continued to write a Jacobin poetry that their peers, including Wordsworth and Coleridge, had chosen to abandon, but by 1798 their project was eccentric. In comparison with *Lyrical Ballads*, *Joan of Arc* and *Gebir* staunchly maintain the tradition of radical political poetry, but these poems – and again the appropriate comparison is with *Lyrical Ballads* – remain, despite themselves, formally conservative. They represent not a new beginning, but a belated attempt to maintain the tradition of classical epic in 1798, in the very year in which Wordsworth, distanced in Germany alike from Home Office spies and radical friends in whose company he was no longer comfortable, began to write the verse that he was to collect into his own long poem, the *Prelude*, his epic of the self that would break decisively with Homeric and Virgilian epic models, and would institute a quite new poetic tradition. The ideology of the classical epic remained potent, and was to re-emerge within a few years in the poetry of Walter Scott, in which the epic re-enters English poetry disguised as romance. But in Scott's version it serves political ends quite foreign to Southey's and Landor's.

Part Two
The War against Napoleon

Introduction
The Poet's Pilgrimage to Waterloo

Howard Weinbrot has traced through the eighteenth century the slow creation of the idea of Britain, the idea, that is, of a nation that is empowered rather than threatened by its diversity.[1] His is a benevolent account of a nationalism that has its origin in liberal tolerance, but it must be supplemented by Linda Colley's story of a nationalism produced by xenophobia, a Britain that came into existence through the course of a century-long struggle against France, for it was in the first decade of the nineteenth century that the idea of Britain achieved an unprecedented potency.[2] Throughout that decade Britain's status in the world was under threat, and for much of it so, too, was its continued existence. The last, and perhaps the most powerful of the architects of the idea of Britain was Napoleon. In the following two chapters I will trace the vitality of the British idea in the poems of Scott and of Wordsworth, before turning, in the succeeding chapter, to the poems of Byron. Writing during another great war, Arthur Bryant wrote the history of these years as a great national epic: long years of endurance rewarded, at last, by the years of victory. My story will be quite different. It begins with the proud patriotism of Scott's Minstrel:

> Breathes there the man, with soul so dead,
> Who never to himself hath said,
> This is my own, my native land!

But it ends with Byron's Childe Harold bidding adieu to his own native land in a gesture that establishes not the deadness of his soul but its vitality, its demand for unfettered freedom. The story must change, of course, because Bryant's earnest patriotism has become embarrassing. It could not survive the feeble attempts to re-create it at the time of the

Falklands or the Gulf. All historical perspectives obscure some things and illuminate others. What ours enables us to see is that final victory, Waterloo, even in the poets who celebrated it, inspired oddly troubled thanksgivings.

Philip Shaw has found in Wordsworth's Waterloo poems not a ringing proclamation of 'the idealised symbiosis of individual and national genius', but a nostalgia for the time when such a thing might be, for a time when, as Josiah Conder tartly put it in his review of these poems, 'wars left us no legacy of taxes', and victory might preserve its epically simple symbolic significance.[3] Wordsworth, as Shaw points out, found himself in 1815 in the difficult position of the poet who claims to speak for a nation that persisted in regarding his poems with contempt. But the embarrassment is more general. Scott undermines his patriotic sentiments by seeking to excuse the 'imperfections' of his 'The Field of Waterloo' on the ground that the poem was composed at a time when 'the Author's labours were liable to frequent interruption'. Its best excuse is that its profits will be donated to the Waterloo Subscription. The poem's proud assertions of British courage and British justice are awkwardly introduced by a preface that begs for the poem the indulgence expected of buyers at a charity sale. Hunt's mask, *The Descent of Liberty*, is similarly burdened by an awkward self-consciousness. His preface anxiously distinguishes his own mask from the king-centred masks of the seventeenth century, and the 'Genius of Britain' that his poem celebrates from the fat regent who presided over the London celebrations as if the downfall of Napoleon had been his own work. As soon, remarks Hunt, 'ascribe victory to the trumpeter's tassels'. This is confidently jaunty enough, but the need to make similar distinctions infiltrates the poem. The entrance of 'True Glory', figured as pastoral abundance and the cultivation of the arts, is preceded by the entry of 'False Glory', a figure suspiciously like Wellington himself, who is militaristic and mercantile, and holds a golden chain to which are bound characters such as 'Misery' and 'Widowhood'. Liberty recognizes that the Genius of Britain wears the laurel wreath of freedom, but points out that it has become rather tattered: 'some under leaves' are 'torn/Here and there'. The ceremony in which Liberty honours the Allied Powers is interrupted by the 'Sable Genius of the South' who complains of Britain's continuing involvement in the slave trade, a 'thoughtful interruption' that, as Liberty points out, compromises 'Our joy's completeness'.[4] In such episodes Hunt yields to the moral demand that he register too complex a political awareness to be comfortably accommodated by the mask genre. Hunt, of course, might be expected to respond to Waterloo with a troubled complexity, but, as Philip Shaw notes, it is a common characteristic of Waterloo poems, no matter the politics of the poet, to lay bare a 'disparity between historical actuality and artistic form'. For Shaw, the exception is Southey's *The Poet's Pilgrimage to Waterloo*, in which Southey speaks as the laureate, fully confident of his right to speak to and for the nation. But Southey's poem scarcely seems to bear this out.

Southey's poem is divided into two parts, 'The Journey' and 'The Vision', which share a stanza form but not much else. The poem begins at journey's end, with the poet's homecoming. The children quickly recover from their shyness with parents they have not seen for some weeks, and the presents are distributed, a wooden ark with all its animals, the 'tumbler, loose of limb, the wrestlers twain'. The whole Poem is infused with Southey's paternal affection for his 'dark-eyed Bertha', his 'gentle Kate', 'sweet Isabel', and most of all his son:

> Aloft on yonder bench, with arms dispread,
> My boy stood, shouting there his father's name,
> Waving his hat around his happy head.

The poem ends as it begins, in joy, in celebration of a victory that has secured peace:

> Rightly for this shall all good men rejoice,
> They most who most abhor all deeds of blood;
> Rightly for this with reverential voice
> Exalt to Heaven their hymns of gratitude;
> For ne'er till now did Heaven thy country bless
> With such transcendent cause for joy and thankfulness.

Southey's point, of course, is that the two kinds of joy are connected, that his own domestic happiness has been secured by the victory for which he gives thanks. All the same, it is impossible not to feel a discrepancy between the assured ease with which Southey renders the joy of his homecoming and the nervously insistent injunctions to rejoice with which the poem ends:

> If they in heart all tyranny abhor
> . . .
> Their joy should be complete, their prayers of praise sincere.

The most obvious reason is that Southey is too scrupulous an observer of the battlefield. He notes the stench of the hastily buried corpses, the humdrum debris left behind, the shoes, the belts, the tattered hats, the 'One streak of blood' on a cottage wall, the mindless desecration of a Catholic shrine by British soldiers, even, in a note, the honourable burial which an inn-keeper had accorded 'Lord Uxbridge's leg'. Southey observes the field too closely, and hence too variously for it to be accommodated easily within the complete joy that we are instructed to feel at the poem's conclusion. But it is not just that. Southey is rancorous even in victory, lending his joy an edge of vindictive glee. It is not enough for him that the enemy is defeated. Like Scott, he insistently denigrates Napoleon's courage – 'Foremost...In flight, though not the foremost in the strife' – and, unlike Scott, he begrudges the Allied decision to spare Napoleon's life:

> Why had we not, as highest law required
> With ignominy closed the culprit's life?

The war has been triumphantly concluded, but it has left in Southey a residue of bitterness, which he comes closest to explaining in the poem's second part, 'The Vision'. The instruction offered by an old man masquerading as 'Wisdom', an embodiment, Southey explains, of 'the gross material philosophy which has been the guiding principle of the French politicians, from Mirabeau to Buonaparte', is corrected by a Muse who delivers Heavenly wisdom, and, at last, rewards the poet for his attention with a vision of Britain's future greatness and prosperity. It is a Britain of noble cities, fertile farms and flourishing commerce, a land of power and pastoral plenty, in which well-rewarded seamen and soldiers are allowed honoured rest from their labours, and a Britain, too, that commands a vast empire populated by diverse peoples united in their gratitude for the benefits of British rule:

> One people with their teachers were they made,
> Their arts, their language, and their faith the same,
> And blest in all, for all they blessed the British name.

It is a vision of the future, but a vision that is constantly threatened by the present that it so pointedly excludes the bad harvests that made the first years of peace hungry years, the bitterness of the soldiers who came home to find the labour market glutted, the taxes on staple foodstuffs imposed to pay for a war from which a few had made fortunes. The vision ends in a celebration of a world in which 'Slavery was gone', and at this point Southey admits, like Leigh Hunt, a 'thoughtful interruption'. In a 'great town' three statues are raised to honour those who had abolished this, the 'foulest blot' on Britain's honour: one of Southey's friend, Clarkson, another of Wilberforce, and a third, an unnamed absence, signifying Southey's recognition that Clarkson's work remains incomplete.

The vision of the future fails at the very last to sustain the erasure of the present on which its complete joy depends, but it was from the first a paradoxical vision, a prophecy dependent on the restoration of those old certainties that the 'gross material philosophy' of the French revolutionaries had destroyed. Southey's Heavenly wisdom delivers a restatement of the Christian providential view of history that never quite convincingly occludes Southey's Wordsworthian recognition that nothing can bring back that hour. The Belgian peasantry have only one wish, that in peace they might recover once again their former way of life:

> One general wish prevail'd... If they might see
> The happy order of old times restored!
> Give them their former laws and liberty,
> This their desires and secret prayers implored;...
> Forgetful, as the stream of time flows on,
> That that which passes is for ever gone.

That is why the 'Wisdom' of the 'lying Spirit' can only be superseded, not refuted, by a Heavenly voice who speaks prophecy, but is herself the embodiment of a futile nostalgia. Leigh Hunt happily accepts that the defeat of Napoleon cannot restore the world as it existed before 1789. Southey's poem is contorted by his recognition that Hunt is right, and that the 'gross material philosophy' has been defeated in the person of Napoleon only after it has infected the victorious nation. The nation is threatened by 'the wild hands of bestial Anarchy', and it is a more powerful threat than that posed by Napoleonic France:

> Easier to crush the foreign foe, than quell
> The malice which misleads the multitude...

So it is that Southey speaks as the laureate in the hour of national triumph, as the voice of a united nation, and also as a citizen of a divided state. In one of his voices Southey leads a national hymn of thanksgiving, in his other he prophesies class war.

Southey's poem is predicated on the fact of his laureateship, on the idea that an individual can speak for the nation:

> Me most of all men it behoved to raise
> The strain of triumph for this foe subdued,

> To give a voice to joy, and in my lays
> Exalt a nation's hymn of gratitude,
> And blazon forth in song that day's renown, ...
> For I was graced with England's laurel crown.

But his poem reveals that laureateship has become a mythical notion, another of those things that pass away and are forever gone. The wars against Napoleon had given the idea of Britain a potency that it had never before achieved, but even before their end the idea was disintegrating. The British had already recognized as their chief poet not the laureate, but a poet whose special talent was to articulate the fractured responses of a nation that knew itself to be divided, Byron.

What most struck Waterloo tourists who visited the scene in the following year was how quickly the battlefields had resumed their pastoral appearance. In Scott it produces an awkward epic simile:

> No vulger crop was theirs to reap,
> No stunted harvest thin and cheap!
> Heroes before each fatal sweep
> Fell thick as ripen'd grain...

This seems unintentionally callous. Southey notes how the grain had reassumed the land in lines that convey his sad puzzlement. In the very spots where the fight had been fiercest, and the blood had flowed most freely, the farmer had been at work:

> There had his ploughshare turned the guilty ground,
> And the green corn was springing all around.

It is a thought that Byron compresses into a single line: 'How that red rain hath made the harvest grow!' It is a line at once sad and mordant, indignant and cynically detached. Byron's account of Waterloo in Canto 3 of *Childe Harold* gains its authority from its failure to arrive at any settled stance, by retaining throughout a spirit like Napoleon's, 'antithetically mixt'. War, in these stanzas, is glorious, unutterably sad, a blackly comic display of human absurdity, and an outrage visited by the world's rulers on those over whom they exert power. The political import of the battle is no clearer. It demonstrates the futility of Ambition, who now 'wears the links of the world's broken chain', an outcome too complexly ironic to be deciphered.

Byron's poem refuses Scott's simple patriotism, of course, in much the same way that Byron himself loftily withdrew from the victory celebrations in London. Communal emotion is disdained as incompatible with the maintenance of a proper aristocratic hauteur, as a bourgeois impingement on the aristocrat's freedom to express fully his own antithetical self. But by 1816 Byron's special variety of aristocratic individualism had created him, by an odd paradox, as the one truly national poet, the one poet who had constructed a voice that could seem to accommodate all the discordant voices of a fractured nation. This is the story that the following three chapters will tell.

4
Walter Scott and Anti-Gallican Minstrelsy

In Scott's continuation of the ballad, *Thomas the Rhymer*, the Rhymer tells the story of Tristram,[1] and his audience is moved:

> Then woe broke forth in murmurs weak:
> Nor ladies heaved alone the sigh;
> But, half ashamed, the rugged cheek
> Did many a gauntlet dry.
>
> (p. 291)

The gauntlet distinguishes the audience within the poem from Scott's contemporary readership – medieval knights, it seems, wore gauntlets at their evening entertainments rather than the kid gloves favoured by gentlemen at the beginning of the nineteenth century – but in their susceptibility to pathos the two audiences merge. Fashions may change, but feelings remain the same. Hence Scott's confidence that his collection of ancient ballads, *Minstrelsy of the Scottish Border*, will be appreciated by the modern reader, that the 'fragments of the lofty strain' that he has worked so hard to recover might 'Float down the tide of years' (p. 288), to awaken in his readers sympathetic emotions that would unite them with those who had listened to the ballads centuries ago. It is a precarious faith – though a faith, however sophisticated, on which all historical fiction ultimately depends[2] – and its precariousness reveals itself clearly enough in Scott's stanza. His knights shed tears of which they are only 'half ashamed', as if they already dimly glimpse a culture in which a man might wear his tears with pride, as a badge of his cultural attainment. Scott's knights inhabit at once a thirteenth century castle and an Edinburgh drawing room of the later eighteenth century: the 'tide of years' that separates them from their modern readers has shrunk to a stream so narrow that they can nonchalantly stand astride it.

Scott, it is agreed, made sentimental additions even to the authentic ballads in his collection, and rewrote lines to accommodate them to eighteenth-century taste. A couplet from 'The Dowie Dens of Yarrow' is adjusted to meet a modern demand for more finished pathos:

> A better rose will never spring
> Than him I've lost on Yarrow.
>
> A fairer rose did never bloom
> Than now lies cropp'd on Yarrow.[3]

But it is the presentation of the ballads rather than their emendation that works most powerfully to integrate the traditional material with the society that Scott was addressing. The ballads are prefaced by an introduction of more than a hundred pages, buttressed by five appendices, in which Scott applies to his traditional materials the methods of historical scholarship that had been developed only during the previous fifty years. He fixes in print poems many of which, until his publication of them, had survived only by oral transmission, and, in addition, he applies to them a scholarly method distinguished above all by its respect for the written document. So he adds to his introduction a letter from Surrey to Henry VIII, passages from the memoirs of Sir Robert Carey, and an indenture terminating a feud between the Scotts and the Kers. Individual ballads are furnished with an editorial apparatus that refers whenever possible to written documents. A typical example is 'Johnnie Armstrong', a ballad which is preceded in Scott's edition by a preface of eight pages offering an account of the career of the historical Armstrong, and followed by an appendix of two pages in which Scott transcribes a 'Bond of Manrent' given by Armstrong to the Warden of the Western Marches. The most extreme example is 'The Souters of Selkirk', a song of only twelve lines occupying a single page, but preceded by an introduction of thirteen pages, and followed by two pages of explanatory notes.

One effect of Scott's editorial labours is to bestow on the ballads a value quite independent of their literary merit. He presents the ballads in a manner designed to appeal not solely, nor even primarily, to a literary taste but to a taste for the antiquarian. The affectionately mocking and self-mocking representations of antiquarians so common in Scott's novels has secured our awareness of the fashion for antiquarianism in the later eighteenth and early nineteenth centuries, but the harmless eccentrics depicted by Scott, obsessive in their enthusiasm for the long ago, obscure one, obvious enough, aspect of the cult. The antiquarian object is distinguished not by any enhanced aesthetic value, but by an enhanced economic value. A better guide to this are the booksellers who continue to offer to the public 'second-hand and antiquarian books', a phrasing by which they distinguish their stock into two categories: books the value of which has been reduced by their having been previously owned, and books which, by virtue of the same fact, have acquired an enhanced value. Scott's *Minstrelsy* transforms ballads freely passed from speaker to speaker around cottage fires on the Scottish Borders into luxury items, items available only to book-buyers of some means – the original two volumes of the *Minstrelsy* sold for a guinea. James Ballantyne's printing of the volumes works in tandem with Scott's editorial work to secure this effect. Typefaces elegantly distinguish the ballads from the editorial matter, and the ballads themselves are displayed with an opulent disregard for economy, no more than eighteen lines to the page, so that the 134 lines of 'Johnnie Armstrong' occupy eight pages of the first volume.

In its sentimentalism, in its antiquarianism and in its scholarship, *Minstrelsy of the Scottish Border* is a characteristic product of the Edinburgh in which Scott was educated, and where, as a young man, he worked. It is fitting that the most important stimulus to antiquarian research in the later eighteenth century came from the improved road system that allowed scholars to extend the area of their investigations, because the growth of commerce, of which the activities of a man such as McAdam were both a cause and an effect, itself generated the surplus capital that made possible the cultivation of refined hobbies such as antiquarianism.[4] It was that same burgeoning of commerce that transformed the Scottish universities by creating a demand for professional men, not just ministers of the church, but doctors, and, most important of all, lawyers such as Scott himself. It was commerce, too, that supported the new respect for the written word, for in commerce the written contract supersedes the spoken agreement, a fact of which Scott, whose father's official designation was Writer to the Signet, and who, during his apprenticeship to his father, accustomed himself to covering in one sitting a hundred and twenty pages in his own swift, easy hand, could scarcely have been ignorant. Sentimentalism might seem important as offering an antidote to the economic motives prevailing in such a society. It seemed so to Burns, who denied that 'the man whose mind glows with sentiment' could ever 'descend to mind the paltry concerns about which the terrae-filial race fret, and fume, and vex themselves'.[5] But, in truth, sentimentalism, which locates ethical value not in principles of conduct, but in the play of the individual's emotional responses to the plight of his fellows is a moral system precisely adapted to a commercial society.[6] The sentimental man responds always as an individual, and if he responds in concert with others, like Scott's knights when all together they raise their gauntlets to wipe away a tear, then this can never be more than a happy coincidence. The sentimental can only ever form themselves into accidental communities. The sentimental pressure towards individualism is so strong that its representative hero becomes increasingly defined by his eccentricity, as a Parson Yorick or Uncle Toby. If the sentimental man's distinctive emotional state is to be tearful, his most distinctive action is to give money. He gives money because he has it to give, and he gives it in reponse to a sudden pressure of sympathetic emotion.[7] Hence, his charities, because they are performed in response to an emotional pang rather than in accordance with a rule of conduct, can never threaten the economic individualism on which a commercial society is founded.

In *Minstrelsy of the Scottish Border*, Scott, one might say, remakes ballads that had survived until that point by circulating freely amongst a community of speakers by converting them into items that could be sold. Scott's scrupulously kept annual accounts allowed Lockhart to determine that for the sale of the first edition of the *Minstrelsy*, Scott's half share of the profits yielded him £78.10s, and he was able to sell the copyright to subsequent editions to Longman for £500.[8] Such information serves to reveal the startling disparity between the society within which Scott's volumes were designed to circulate, and the society out of which the ballads themselves were produced, which was regulated by an economy that Scott himself liked to characterize in an anecdote concerning his grandfather's great-great-grandfather, Auld Watt of Harden, husband of the beautiful 'Flower of Yarrow'. When the last stolen English bullock had been consumed, the Flower of Yarrow would place on her husband's table a dish containing nothing but a clean pair of spurs, a signal to him that it was time he and his men rode out on a raid into England to replenish the castle's supplies.[9] In publishing *Minstrelsy of the Scottish Border*, Scott circulated within an economy powered by surplus capital and founded on trade, a collection of ballads which celebrated the exploits of those living within a subsistence economy founded on theft. It was a combination piquant enough to secure the success of the volumes, but Lockhart is surely wrong to point to it as the achievement on which the whole of Scott's subsequent career was founded.[10] The combination may be piquant, but it remains inert, for the two societies are related only by their difference.

The difference between Scotland's present and its past was obviously important to Scott. His biographers have done no more than recognize this when they fashion Scott's youth, as biographers will, into a sequence of emblematic moments – the childhood divided between his father's genteel and pious house in Edinburgh, and the border farm at Sandy-knowe where his grandmother enthralled him with tales of Watt of Harden, Wight Willie of Aikwood, and Jamie Telfer of the fair Dodhead; or the days spent in his father's office refreshing himself amidst 'the barren wilderness of forms and conveyances' by devouring 'like a tiger... every collection of old songs or romances that chance threw in [his] way'.[11] It was Scott's sense of this difference, after all, that enabled him to maintain at once a staunch Hanoverian patriotism that expressed itself most comfortably in a cultivation of the civic virtues, and a sentimental Jacobite nostalgia, rival impulses that powered his first novel, and led him towards the principle of organization on which his achievement in fiction is founded. But difference, by itself, could never have served this purpose. Had Scott been content with a simple relish of the difference between the past and the present he would have remained like one of his own antiquaries, a charming, harmless eccentric. It is at the moment that he found a vital connection between the two that he became a historian, and a writer of historical fiction, and he found that connection first in his poems. It was in *The Lay of the Last Minstrel* that Scott first succeeded in expressing his awareness that the interest of historical fiction lies not in the past, but in the past's relation to the present, and it was in that poem, too, that he first discovered the device through which this awareness manifests itself in fiction, the device that Lukacs has named, in a phrase borrowed from Hegel, 'the necessary anachronism'.[12]

Scott recalls his discovery in his characteristic manner, modestly and casually. The *Lay* was all but finished when a friend suggested to him that 'some sort of prologue might be necessary to place the mind of the hearers in the situation to understand and enjoy the poem', and, in response, Scott 'introduced the Old Minstrel, as an appropriate prolocutor, by whom the lay might be sung, or spoken'.[13] The old minstrel tells his tale to the Duchess of Buccleuch. She has mourned the death of Montrose, and survived to see the Stuarts restored to the throne and banished once again. The minstrel entertains her with a tale of her ancestor, the widow of Sir Walter Scott of Buccleuch, of how she was reconciled to the marriage of her daughter to Lord Cranstoun, who belonged to a family with whom the Scotts were at feud. The minstrel is himself the representative within the poem of the young Walter Scott, who wrote his poem at the suggestion of his noble kinswoman, who was herself to become Duchess of Buccleuch, and dedicated it to her husband. As Lockhart notes, a system of 'arch allusions' runs through all the framing passages of the lay, which allows Scott to register his gratitude for the hospitality and the patronage he has received from the house of Buccleuch.[14] But the allusions work, too, to interweave within the poem three generations of the Buccleuch family stretching from the middle of the sixteenth century to the end of the seventeenth and up to the present. The poem does not simply tell the story of a sixteenth-century border conflict: it includes the lapse of centuries that separates Scott from his material, and in doing so it decisively distinguishes *The Lay of the Last Minstrel* from the modern imitations of old ballads that Scott included in the third volume of his *Minstrelsy*. The invention of the old minstrel is an indication that Scott has found a new subject, his own belatedness.

Scott's minstrel is an anachronism, a product of sixteenth-century Scottish culture who has survived improbably into the time of the Hanoverian settlement. His role is as a mediator between Scott, writing at the beginning of the nineteenth century, and the writers of the sixteenth-century border ballads whose subject matter Scott appropriates. The minstrel tells his tale to the Duchess of Buccleuch and her ladies, and their role too is mediatory. He is a warrior poet, but he responds to his audience of women with a tale which celebrates martial exploits, and yet subordinates the theme of war to the theme of love. Warmed by the women's presence, and by their wine, he belies his own account of his abilities, and sings a hymn in praise of the power of love. The women arouse in him, too, a new tenderness, so that his pride in his son, who died bravely in battle, is complicated by a father's grief. The fierce sixteenth-century border widow, whose business in life it is to defend her castle and to uphold the pride of her clan, must be violently persuaded that pride must yield to love: she is a sorceress, an embodiment of unnatural and threatening female power who must be forced into the proper mould of womanhood. But in her seventeenth-century successor, also a widow and a patriot, pride has given way to pathos, the chivalric obligation to uphold the honour of the family name has been modified into the obligation of politeness.

Scott invented his minstrel as the source of a deliberately anachronistic language, a mediating language that has 'caught somewhat of the refinement of modern poetry, without losing the simplicity of the original models'.[15] The texture of the poem becomes a palimpsest, inviting its reader to reconstruct its history. It can include a celebrated passage of picturesque description, the ruins of Melrose Abbey seen by moonlight. But for Scott the description is completed only when he registers Deloraine's indifference to its beauty: 'Little reck'd he of the scene so fair.'[16] For the sixteenth-century moss-trooper's indifference inscribes in the text the centuries that separate Deloraine from the contemporary taste for the picturesque. Scott offers his reader a picture, which is to be enjoyed but also understood as itself an item of cultural history.

The largest difference between Scott and his minstrel is that the minstrel speaks or sings, whereas Scott writes his poem. Between them stretch the centuries that have changed Scotland's from an oral to a literary culture. The minstrel accompanies his poem with a harp, Scott prefers quite other accompaniments, the detailed historical notes with which he furnishes his poem. Again the difference is allowed to infiltrate the text, the first three cantos of which are dominated by a book, the book in which the wizard, Michael Scott, has recorded his spells. The book of spells achieves a mighty presence in the poem, a presence only underlined by its negligible role in the poem's plot. One of Deloraine's qualifications when he is given the mission to collect the book from the wizard's grave is that he would be quite unable to read it – 'Letter nor line know I never a one'. When the illiterate Deloraine rides back from Melrose to Branksome Hall with the book tucked close to his chest, he becomes a living emblem of the poem in which he appears, the true subject of which is the difference between the society Scott writes about, and the society that he writes within, between a society that trusts in 'gramarye', and a society that confines its trust to grammar.

Lukacs was right to claim *Waverley* as the first historical novel, but Scott was able to write it because he had already written the first historical poem, and he went on, in *Marmion*, to refine his invention. For Lukacs the enabling condition of Scott's invention was the revolutionary conflict throughout Europe which had been inaugurated by the French Revolution. Lukacs's thesis gains its strength from his insistence on the need to identify the political and economic circumstances that produced Scott's achievement, but in his choice of which circumstances to adduce he leaves himself vulnerable. He is forced to present Scott as a man who wrote in ignorance of the import of his own novels. His Scott is a reactionary legitimist who somehow managed to achieve a truly realistic mastery of his materals despite the fact that this realism was 'in conflict' with his 'personal views and prejudices'. It is notorious that Lukacs writes on the assumption that Scotland is a district of England, and the correction of that error has resulted in the most persuasive modification of Lukacs's argument. David Brown contends that Scott's historical understanding has its foundation not in the condition of Europe, but in the specific condition of Scotland, a nation that had lost its independence in 1707 and had failed to reassert it in two rebellions. The rapid development of historical studies in Scottish universities, according to Brown, was a direct consequence of this. The need to recover a sense of national identity impelled Scots in the later eighteenth century to develop a new understanding of the nature of historical process.[17] Brown's argument has obvious advantages over Lukacs's. It can be shown that Scott was exposed to this newly developed historical understanding while a student at Edinburgh, and that he was deeply influenced by it. By contrast, his contact with revolutionary ideas seems to have been negligible. But Lukacs's argument has one striking advantage over Brown's. Scott – and in this it is only Byron of all his contemporaries who can be compared with him – was a peculiarly European figure, whose novels were very quickly translated into the major European languages, and became the most significant models in the development of the novel all over Europe, from Russia to France. It seems somehow inappropriate to locate the ground of this achievement in the conditions peculiar to one, small European nation. But it may be that Brown's and Lukacs's arguments are not so inconsistent as they seem.

Scott's earliest reference to the *Lay* is in a letter to Ellis, when he mentions that he is working on a long poem, 'a kind of romance of Border chivalry, in a light horseman sort of stanza'.[18] He was later to acknowledge that he had adopted his stanza after hearing Coleridge's *Christabel* recited,[19] but Scott's stanza has a galloping momentum that Coleridge's entirely lacks. Lockhart helpfully suggests that the stanza may have something to do with 'the circumstances under which the greater part of the original draft was composed'.[20] In the autumn of 1802, Scott was carrying out his duties as Quartermaster of the Edinburgh Light Horse, who were in camp at Musselburgh. This was a volunteer force, and Scott had himself been the prime mover in its formation in 1797, in response to the threat of French invasion. It was surely his service in the Light Horse that prompted Scott to describe the *Lay* as written in 'a light horseman sort of stanza'. It seems more than a coincidence that the years of Scott's significant poetic achievement, the years in which he compiled the *Minstrelsy* and wrote his first three narrative poems, coincided with those years in which there were recurrent invasion alarms. During this period Scott devoted himself to his duties as a cavalryman with just as much enthusiasm as he pursued literature and his legal profession. Scott may be self-mocking when he describes himself as 'a complete hussar',[21] but it is characteristic of Scott to mock himself when he is at his most serious. Scott's friend, Skene, suggests the connection between Scott's military enthusiasm and his love of border ballads. Unable to serve on foot because of his lameness, Scott, Skene remarks, 'had seen nothing for it but to raise the spirit of the moss-trooper', and set about the formation of the Edinburgh Light Horse.[22] From 1797 and for the greater part of the first decade of the nineteenth century, the professional and cultural life of Edinburgh went in tandem with a quite different kind of activity. Edgar Johnson vividly describes the summer of 1803: 'Drums and bugles sounded above the rumble of drays in the street; the evening quiet was broken by the pop of muskets and the thunder of the volley.'[23] It is out of this coincidence that Scott's narrative poetry was born. He was no longer an Edinburgh lawyer who delighted to recall in his daydreams a lost time of moss-troopers, border raids and clan feuds. The commercial ethos of Edinburgh and the warrior ethos of the Borders in the sixteenth century were no longer related only by their difference: there was a vital association between them that was visibly and dramatically evident in the everyday texture of Edinburgh life.

In *Marmion* the introductory epistles confess Scott's distance from the centres of power. Four letters are written from Ashestiel in the Ettrick Forest, only one from Edinburgh, and at Ashestiel Scott represents his life as pastoral, devoted to country sports, to his children, and to memories of his own childhood. He offers his readers 'an old romance', a tale sheltered from the urgencies of contemporary life, a tale that appeals less to men than to boys, and to the nostalgia that grown men feel for their boyish passions. His poem is characterized by its distance from 'heroic song', and the freedom it allows him from the discipline of the 'classic poet'. The letters offer a definition of romance which associates it with the country rather than the city, with the childish rather than the adult, and with play rather than work. In writing such a poem, Scott acts like his own King James, exchanging his business dress for a suit of Lincoln green and retreating from his professional duties into the greenwood. But the epistles fit oddly with the poem that they introduce and interrupt, for *Marmion* is 'A Tale of Flodden Field', and if the subtitle agrees with the epistles in modestly disclaiming that the poem is any more than a tale, it nevertheless identifies its subject as the greatest military disaster in the history of Scott's nation. There is an odd discrepancy between the confession of a playful refusal of seriousness and the choice of theme, a disparity that the very first epistle, addressed to William Stewart Rose, works into the fabric of the poem. With his usual modesty Scott represents Nature as teaching him his unworthiness for the 'high theme' that he had once aspired to:

> Meeter, she says, for me to stray
> And waste the solitary day,
> In plucking from yon fen the reed,
> And watch it floating down the Tweed...

This is the aimlessly pastoral activity that Scott aligns with his own modest poetic ambition, the telling of a 'legendary lay'. But at once he is prompted to a defence of such legends:

> They gleam through Spenser's elfin dream,
> And mix in Milton's heavenly theme;
> And Dryden in immortal strain
> Had raised the Table Round again,
> But that a ribald King and Court
> Bade him toil on to make them sport...

Spenser, Milton and Dryden were, Scott claims, dedicated to the romance tradition, but they also constitute, for Scott, the great line of England's national poets. The argument has turned so completely that Dryden's distraction from romance is described in exactly the same terms as Scott's devotion to it, as a retreat from serious labour to 'sport'.

The 'high theme' of which Scott protests his unworthiness was given him by the death of Britain's two great statesmen, Pitt and Fox, and his letter begins as a memorial to their greatness. But Scott finds himself inadequate to his mighty subject:

> It will not be – it may not last –
> The vision of enchantment's past:
> Like frostwork in the morning ray,
> The fancied fabric melts away;
> Each Gothic arch, memorial-stone,
> And long, dim, lofty aisle are gone;

And lingering last, deception dear,
The choir's high sounds die on my ear.

The great patriotic theme dissolves to make way for the romance, the 'tale' that Scott will tell, but as it dissolves it reveals that it was itself a romance, a Gothic church like his own Melrose Abbey, and subject, like all the visions of romance, to dissolve in the hard light of day. Scott's opening epistle begins by rigorously distinguishing the 'high theme' of patriotic poets from the idle predilection for romance, a stern attention to the momentous present from the whimsical devotion to things that have long since passed away, and having established the distinction the poem works to confuse it. So does the tale that follows.

Marmion, the poem's central character, takes the place of the last minstrel by himself embodying the 'necessary anachronism' on which Scott's historical fiction depends. Marmion is at once a rational man of the eighteenth century, a man who accepts that 'Nature's laws' have made redundant any appeal to 'superhuman cause', and he is also a man prompted by an inn-keeper's tale to arm himself in the middle of the night and ride off to do battle with an 'Elfin Foe'. Marmion is Ralph de Wilton's rival for the hand of Lady Clare de Clare, but Marmion woos her not for love but for her land. It is avarice that prompts him to rid himself of his mistress Constance, the runaway nun. His is dastardly behaviour, but behaviour that aligns him as nearly with the villain of the novel as with the dishonourable knight of romance, with Jane Austen's Henry Crawford as closely as with Mordred. He defeats Wilton in a trial by combat, but only after incriminating him by planting forged letters in his possession. Again the effect is to make him straddle the gap between chivalric notions of dishonour and contemporary notions of criminality.[24] Forgery, after all, was the most distinctive crime of the first decades of the nineteenth century, a crime ushered into prominence by Pitt's decision to finance the war against Napoleon by massively increasing the supply of paper money. Marmion dies bravely, fighting at Flodden Field, and a monument to him is erected in Lichfield Cathedral, a monument that stood, Scott tells us, until the cathedral was despoiled during the Civil War, but the tomb in Lichfield cathedral never contained Marmion's body, for after the battle his corpse was confused with another body, and Marmion was interred in the 'nameless grave' dug for an ordinary Scottish peasant. Even in death Marmion is allowed to glide between the centuries, between a war such as that fought at Flodden, and the new kind of war inaugurated by Napoleon, mass war, of which the characteristic memorial is not the tomb built to house the remains of a hero, but the grave of the unknown soldier. In death Marmion still plays out his role as the necessary anachronism, an anachronism that can make the connection between Flodden Field and Austerlitz.

Scott's time of poetic creativity, the years when he wrote his first three narrative poems, and secured his place as, for a decade, the supreme poet of Britain, the 'Monarch of Parnassus' to whom Byron declared himself a humble subject,[25] coincided with the Napoleonic wars, and this is unsurprising, for the war with France constituted the historical moment at which Scott's antiquarian love of old ballads coincided with the demands of the present.[26] It was a moment that Tennyson was to rediscover some fifty years later. Maud's 'passionate ballad', her 'martial song like a trumpet's call', provokes at first only a weak nostalgia, tears for the difference between a time when men marched merrily 'to the death for their native land' and a present 'so sordid and mean', but the outbreak of the Crimean War brings into connection the well-kept meadow in which Maud sings, and the long-ago battles she sings of, fuses them into the 'blood-red blossom of war'. It is a point that was once obvious enough: it prompted Lockhart to pay tribute to the significance of Scott's poetic achievement by hailing him as 'the "mighty minstrel" of the Antigallican war',[27] a description that has the added merit of offering an explanation of why, after Waterloo, Scott's fame was so quickly eclipsed by Byron's. *Childe Harold* won its astonishing popularity by offering the most complete expression of a new national mood: it is the first post-war poem.

Unlike his greater contemporaries, Scott did not waver in his political allegiances throughout the war years. He remained a Tory and a fiercely partisan one, who viewed the war against Napoleon with uncomplicated enthusiasm. But whereas his Toryism had once found occasion to express itself only in outbreaks of patriotic hooliganism, as when he went to the theatre in Edinburgh armed with a cudgel for the express purpose of leading an attack on a group of Irish radicals who were intent on drowning out any attempt to sing the national anthem,[28] the war allowed him to present his conservatism in its most dignified guise, as an expression of national purpose within which mere party political differences were subsumed. So, in the opening epistle of *Marmion*, Scott's eulogy on the dead Pitt is extended to embrace Fox, in life Pitt's great opponent, but in death his brother. Fox had at the last participated in the Whig ministry that continued Pitt's policy of war against France, and Scott seizes on that fact as evidence of Fox's redemption: it allows him to cast aside 'partial feeling' and 'Record that Fox a Briton died'.[29]

Pitt and Fox in life opposed each other, but Scott supplements their antagonism by allowing them each a generous sense of the other's honour and greatness. Pitt and Fox become the prototypes of all those noble enemies that people Scott's fiction, differing in their principles but alike in their greatness of spirit. In writing his memorial to them Scott found the rhetoric that was to serve him equally well when Vich Ian Vohr confronted Colonel Talbot or when the Lionheart spoke with Saladin, a rhetoric that confers on his historical novels their rare generosity of spirit. But it was a rhetoric that was born out of war, and out of Scott's recognition that in war allegiance to a party must be subsumed within allegiance to a nation, that his own identity as a Tory must be subsumed within his identity as a 'Briton'.

It is significant that Pitt and Fox are celebrated by Scott as Britons rather than as Englishmen. Between them, they represent something more than just England: they embody what Scott calls 'the British world'. Robert Crawford has argued that the invention of British literature, that is, of a literature that included but was not comprehended by Englishness, was a distinctively Scottish achievement. For Crawford, *Waverley*, with its central figure who travels from England, and discovers in his travels the quite different life of the neighbouring kingdom, is the crucial text. Scott may have been anticipated by Smollett in a novel such as *Humphrey Clinker*, and he may have been indebted, as Scott himself acknowledged, to Maria Edgeworth's Irish novels, but the publication of *Waverley* marks for Crawford the decisive moment when the idea of an English literature gave way to an idea of British literature.[30] But if Smollett's *Humphrey Clinker* is one of *Waverley*'s precursors, Scott's own *Marmion* is another, for already in *Marmion* Scott's concern is to discover for both the English and the Scots a common identity that both nations might acknowledge without any requirement that the one subordinate itself to the other. Scott's English and Scots readers are invited to recognize themselves as 'Britons' and citizens of 'the British world'.

It may seem that Scott chose an odd subject for a poem dedicated to the idea of Britain, England and Scotland not in harmony, but at war. But in Scott conflict becomes an occasion for mutual compliment. In *The Lay of the Last Minstrel*, the English Howard marches against the Lady of Branksome, but the two forces agree to resolve their differences by single combat rather than in battle, and as soon as the decision is taken the hostile armies mingle in gruff good fellowship:

> The hands the spear that lately grasp'd,
> Still in the mailed gauntlet clasp'd,
> Were interchang'd in greeting dear...

Scott claims that such sudden transitions were characteristic of Border society, and it may be so, but they serve a wider rhetorical purpose. They transform the long history of war between England and Scotland into a lover's quarrel, the fierceness of the conflicts proving only the earnestness of the mutual attachment. Marmion, when he looks down on the Scottish camp spread over the plain, is so struck with admiration that he quite forgets his peacekeeping mission:

> For, by St George, were that host mine,
> Not power infernal or divine
> Should once to peace my soul incline,
> Till I had dimm'd their armour's shine.
> In glorious battle-fray.

And when Marmion rides into the Scottish camp, his admiration is returned:

> Fast ran the Scottish warriors there,
> Upon the Southern band to stare,
> And envy with their wonder rose,
> To see such well-appointed foes...

Each nation's soldiers serve as the other's appreciative audience. Scott, as it were, reviews the wars between nations through the ethical system that governed his own Edinburgh schoolyard, where a bout of fisticuffs served only as the prelude to the frank handshake that instituted a lifelong friendship. It may be a naive, though benign, understanding of international relations, but it is crucial to Scott's wider purpose, for it establishes the centuries of intermittent warfare between Scotland and England as a history that, far from threatening the union of the two nations, secures it.

By the time that Scott began to write the economic integration of Scotland and England was well advanced. The publication history of *Marmion* itself serves to indicate this. Constable, the Edinburgh publisher, bought the copyright before he had seen a line of the poem, indeed, before much of it had been written, for the unprecedented sum of a thousand guineas. But he immediately decided to secure the cooperation of London publishers, which he achieved by selling a quarter share of the copyright to William Miller and another quarter to the young John Murray.[31] The publication of *Marmion* became a tripartite venture in which London and Edinburgh shared the risk equally, and in this it was just one of countless commercial transactions that linked the capitals of the two nations. Throughout Scott's career, Scott was to depend on the economic ties between Scotland and England to secure his phenomenal literary earnings. But Scott did not welcome so kindly other kinds of integration. In 1807, for example, he was engaged not just in the composition of *Marmion*: he was also busy organizing opposition to the Whig government's attempts to reform the Scottish legal system by bringing it into conformity with English practice. When Jeffrey, who, as a Whig, supported the reform, good-naturedly complimented Scott on a spirited speech he had made on the matter, he was shocked by the intensity of Scott's response. 'No, no,' he said to Jeffrey – 'it is no laughing matter, little by little, whatever your wishes may be, you will destroy and undermine, until nothing of what makes Scotland Scotland shall remain'. Scott turned his face away, and Jeffrey noticed, when the two walked on together, that Scott's face was streaming with tears.[32] Taken together, the two stories represent well enough the coincidence in Scott of a thoroughgoing acceptance of the Union, in particular of its economic benefits and of the political stability that the Union had secured, and a passionately sentimental desire to preserve all that was distinctive in the Scottish national identity.

Scott had arrived early at both of these positions, but as a young man the Scottish patriotism that expressed itself in the cultivation of Jacobite sentimentality could exist only in inert contradiction to the loyal Hanoverian practice of his everyday life. It required some external stimulus to force the two aspects of Scott's identity into creative combination, and make possible, for example, the most famous lines of Scott's old minstrel:

> Breathes there a man, with soul so dead,
> Who never to himself hath said,
> This is my own, my native land!

The minstrel's land is Scotland, 'Caledonia', and for him Scotland is defined in opposition to the 'Southern land' of England. England may be generous to minstrels, but he scorns it, preferring poverty in the Ettrick hills and the free winds of Scotland even though they 'chill [his] wither'd cheek'. But the English generosity that the minstrel spurns, Scott reciprocates, for he allows the minstrel's patriotic sentiment to blow south across the border, until it becomes an expression of the passionate nationalism that united all of Britain in its war against Napoleon.

After the defeat of the '45, the English government had passed in quick succession a series of measures designed to extirpate Scotland's nationhood. The Disarming Act of 1746, the third such act of the century, banned not only the carrying of arms but the wearing of all distinctive forms of Highland dress. English soldiers garrisoned in the Highlands had instructions to arrest anyone wearing the plaid. The Heritable Jurisdictions Act was designed to destroy the common law practices on which the clan system was founded. An attempt to impose the English legal system on Scotland in its entirety was averted, but only narrowly. The status of Scotland, an equal partner in the Union of 1707, was reduced to that of an occupied colony.[33]

As a colony, Scotland had, of course, flourished remarkably. The foundation of the *Edinburgh Review* in 1802 conveniently marks the point at which Scotland's cultural preeminence within Britain became indisputable even by the English. By then, Glasgow was already the second city of the empire. It was an achievement that Scott was particularly well placed to recognize, because he was, himself, one of its products. But his Scottish patriotism could not have allowed him to ignore the truth that whatever Scotland's achievements, they were the achievements of a nation that had been for half a century ruled by its neighbour. Hence the Jacobite attachment that Scott preserved from his childhood until long after he had become an active member of the Edinburgh legal profession, upholding in all his professional activities the settlement enforced on Scotland by the victors of Culloden.

This is the context in which Scott's enthusiasm for his military duties as Quartermaster General of the Edinburgh Light Horse needs to be understood. When his troops mustered, he was taking part in something that had not been seen in Scotland since the '45, Scots in arms, preparing for the defence of their own nation against invasion. The demands of the war effort meant that Scotland was left to its own defence. In the midst of one invasion scare Scott dashed off a letter in which he noted that nothing stood in the way of Napoleon, should he land in Scotland, but Scottish volunteers. The tone of his letter is not at all fearful, it is jubilant.[34] Scott's joy in his soldiering, an enthusiasm that struck some of his friends as ridiculous, marks his sense that he and his fellow volunteers were not just offering their services for the defence of Britain, but were seizing the opportunity to reassert Scottish nationhood.

In each of his first three narrative poems, Scott describes a gathering of the clans, and on each occasion his verse swells with the pressure of patriotic sentiment. When Marmion views the Scottish camp, he sees a 'martial kingdom's vast array':

> For from Hebudes, dark with rain,
> To eastern Lodon's fertile plain,

> And from the southern Redswire edge,
> To farthest Rosse's rocky ledge;
> From west to east, from south to north,
> Scotland sent all her warriors forth.

These moments are thrilling precisely because they escape mere nostalgia. They are occasions on which Scotland's past intersects with its present. In March 1804, the beacon fires were lit in Kelso, the message passed from hill to hill, and all through Scotland men seized their arms and made for their meeting-places. Again in 1806 the beacon-fires were lit. Scott was holidaying over the border, and he rode the 100 miles to Musselburgh in twenty-four hours.[35] On both occasions the invasion warnings proved false, but for Scott the gatherings they brought about had symbolic importance: a conquered, disarmed and garrisoned nation was proclaiming itself once again a 'martial kingdom', and it was as a reflex of that reborn national confidence that Scott found his own creative talent. He was freed in *Marmion* to tell the tale of Scotland's greatest military defeat, and in his first novel he could tell the story of its most recent military disaster, because he had discovered a way to be both a British and a Scottish poet. Napoleon, or so it seemed to him, had resolved the contradiction between the two terms.[36] The war against France had made possible for every Scotsman the proud sentiment that in *The Heart of Midlothian* he allows the Duke of Argyll to express to the Queen: 'My sword, madam, like that of my fathers, has always been at the command of my lawful king, and of my native country – I trust it is impossible to separate their real rights and interests.'

In 1825, at the very end of Scott's career, Hazlitt wrote of him as a writer who cultivated a nostalgia for the past as an escape from a present that he found distasteful. Hazlitt's judgement is inherently implausible. It is hard to fathom how a man might become, what Hazlitt acknowledges Scott to be, 'the most popular writer of the age' by virtue of his refusal to speak to that age of any of the things that concerned it. But Hazlitt's essay is in any case inconsistent. He admires Scott's novels and hates his politics, and, since the novels are rather obviously political, he can rescue himself from self-contradiction only by claiming that their politics is of the past, and has no connection with the present time. But this is a desperate stratagem, and Hazlitt is reduced at the last to arguing that Scott's novels may entertain when they are impotent to persuade: 'Is he infatuated enough, or does he so doat and drivel over his own slothful and self-willed prejudices, as to believe that he will make a single convert to the beauty of Legitimacy, that is, of lawless power and savage bigotry?' This is strident enough to suggest that Hazlitt has not quite lost sight of the fact that for almost twenty years Britain had been governed in obedience to principles that for him are no more than 'slothful and self-willed prejudices', that in 1825 they seemed as firmly embedded as ever, and that in Scott's poems and later his novels they are given their most powerful and beguiling expression.

It was the war against Napoleon that prompted Scott first to develop a rhetoric in which difference, the difference pre-eminently between the Scots and the English, could be celebrated as the ground of a higher unity, the condition of the strong union between all of its peoples that was demanded of the nation in its war against the French. But when peace came, that rhetoric did not become obsolete. Scott turned from poetry to the novel at the moment when the stability of Britain was no longer threatened by a foreign nation but by divisions within itself, and the rhetoric that Scott had devised in his poems, when transferred to the novel, proved versatile enough to accommodate the new threat. The novels survey bitter ideological conflicts – between Jacobite and Hanoverian, Christian and Saracen, Cavalier and Roundhead, peasant and aristocrat – with a calm and disinterested tolerance, but that tolerance is not, as Hazlitt would have us believe, in contradiction to Scott's political beliefs, but their most seductive expression. He writes within a nation that, in the post-war years, seemed ever more fiercely divided, and delivers the smiling wisdom that its divisions are the source of its strength, and the mark of its broad humanity. Other writers in the period attempted to develop a similar rhetoric. None of them did so with equal success, but failure can be just as revealing. I turn now to one of Scott's friends and admirers, Wordsworth.

5
Wordsworth at War

In *Poems, in Two Volumes*, 1807, Wordsworth speaks to a nation at war. Wordsworth presented his poems to their readers as a response to an urgent national crisis. The poems are divided into seven sections only one of which, the 'Sonnets Dedicated to Liberty', is exclusively concerned with the progress of the war, but this is the group of poems around which the whole collection revolves.[1] In the first section, a note attached to 'Character of the Happy Warrior' informs the reader that the poem had been written 'soon after tidings had been received of the Death of Lord Nelson'. The firmness of mind that the poet finds in the leech gatherer becomes, in the poem's title, 'Resolution and Independence', a summary of the qualities that Wordsworth demands of his nation in its struggle against the French. Rob Roy, in the poem that opens the second volume, is praised by contrasting him with Napoleon. Both trusted to the sword to impose their 'sovereign will', but, unlike Napoleon, Rob Roy loved the '*liberty* of Man'. In the final section two neighbouring sonnets contrast the activity of Napoleon, who enslaves nations under the pretext of liberating them, with that of Wordsworth's friend, Thomas Clarkson, whose life's work had come to fruition in March, 1807, with 'the final passing of the Bill for the Abolition of the Slave Trade'. Most of the poems are written from Grasmere, from a position of rural retreat, and they celebrate the happiness that Wordsworth had found there, but even the most pastoral of the poems is likely to be infiltrated by an incongruous memory of the war in Europe, so that in March the snow retreats to the summits of the hills 'Like an army defeated'. The title of the sonnet that ends the first volume, 'November, 1806', suggests that Wordsworth thought of the whole collection as a 'timely utterance'.

It was Wordsworth's first major publication since *Lyrical Ballads*. In the 'advertisement' of 1798 Wordsworth had presented his poems as written in 'the language of conversation in the lower and middle classes of society'.[2] He addresses a divided nation. In the prefaces of 1800 and 1802 he describes the language that he has adopted as that of 'low and rustic life' (*Prose*, 1, 124, 125), supplementing the division between classes by a division between the rural and the urban. But in 1807 both distinctions are refused. Alice Fell, consoled for the damage to her cloak by the gift of a new one 'of duffil grey', is encountered directly after a sonnet which begins by quoting from the most courtly of English poets, 'With how sad steps, O Moon, thou climbst the sky'. The sonnet, 'Composed upon Westminster Bridge', is framed by two sonnets which dwell on the experience of rural retirement. The collection addresses a people whose divisions have been healed, and the 'Sonnets Dedicated to Liberty' make it clear that the healing agent has been the war against Napoleon.

In 1801, presenting a copy of *Lyrical Ballads* to Fox, Wordsworth had represented himself as the spokesman for a particular 'class of men', the statesmen of his own Westmorland, the class of 'small independent *proprietors* of land',[3] but in 1807 he presents himself as a champion of the independence not simply of the statesmen but of the state. He addresses 'England', his thoughts are those 'of a Briton'. In the 1805 *Prelude*, Wordsworth recalls how, in 1793, the outbreak of the war against France had ruptured the bonds that tied him to the nation. In *Poems*, 1807, he speaks as a poet who has become once again 'a green leaf on the blessed tree / Of [his] beloved country'.

Dorothy Wordsworth wrote of Scott, 'His local attachments are more strong than those of any person I ever saw' (*Letters*, 1, 590), but Scott had himself shown in *The Lay of the Last Minstrel* how local attachment might become the ground of a national poetry,[4] and Wordsworth displays a similar confidence. In the Lucy poems included in *Lyrical Ballads*, Lucy functions as a spirit of locality, of a place defined by its seclusion, but in 'I travell'd among unknown men', the 'green field' that Lucy inhabits is identified with 'England'. Here, even more emphatically than in *Lyrical Ballads*, Wordsworth presents himself as the poet of the Lakes, of that 'perfect Republic of Shepherds and Agriculturists', that had maintained 'in the midst of a powerful empire' a constitution that was 'imposed and regulated by the mountains which protected it' (*Prose*, 2, 206). The whole collection proclaims Wordsworth's allegiance to this 'pure Commonwealth', but it suggests, too, that in the war against Napoleon, the 'almost visionary' republic hemmed in by its mountains has become the type of the island nation protected by its seas, its 'barrier flood'.[5]

The purity of the mountain republic is preserved by the 'consciousness' of its citizens that 'the land, which they walked over and tilled, had for more than five hundred years been possessed by men of their name and blood', and it is preserved, too, by the subsistence economy of the Lakes, where 'the plough of each man was confined to the maintenance of his own family', and where 'two or three cows furnished each family with milk and cheese' (*Prose*, 2, 206). The war, Wordsworth suggests, has worked to reawaken in the whole nation the 'consciousness' shared by the Westmorland statesmen that their land is a living covenant between them and their ancestors. The British have come once again to recognize themselves as 'a people which, by the help of the surrounding ocean and its own virtues, had preserved to itself through ages its liberty, pure and unviolated by a foreign invader' (*Prose*, 1, 228). Under threat of invasion the British have come together to form once more that 'solemn fraternity which a great nation composes – gathered together, in a stormy season, under the shade of ancestral feeling' (*Prose*, 1, 305). The embargo on trade with Europe that Napoleon had enforced so successfully was itself a blessing, for it taught the nation the virtue of 'self-support and self-sufficing endeavours', and it demonstrated the moral bankruptcy of a nation that could judge its well-being in terms simply of its material prosperity. The ambition to acquire 'a dwelling more commodious and better furnished' (*Prose*, 1, 326) may be well enough, but Napoleon had shown all Wordsworth's countrymen what the Westmorland statesmen already knew, that material progress is worthless if bought at the price of the loss of independence. The war has shown that a nation cannot be animated by calculations of profit and loss, but 'by joy', 'by love', and 'by pride', by those qualities that for Wordsworth are summarized in the word 'imagination'.

The poems repeatedly inveigh against the 'idolatry' of wealth that defines a society for which commerce has become the one active religion, and which holds that 'The wealthiest man among us is the best', a society dominated by 'money'd Worldlings'. The pursuit of economic advantage is identified with spiritual loss, 'Getting and spending we lay waste our powers'. Wordsworth offers as an antidote to the cruel and demoralizing processes of capitalism an imaginative economy, in which the signs of 'wealth' are not golden coins but golden daffodils, and the most profitable investments are not those made by 'money'd Worldlings', but those that occur in the exchange between the outward and the 'inward eye'. He recognizes a 'debt', but it is to the daisy. He offers a world in which commercial exchanges are replaced by the exchanges that take place between the imaginative mind and the natural world around it, a world in which the 'thrifty cottager' can look at a 'careless prodigal' with unselfinterested joy, because the prodigal is a small celandine. It is a world in which economic value is wholly subordinated to imaginative value, in which the most precious objects are a singing-bird in a cage, a glow-worm, or a cloak of 'duffil grey'. So much we might have expected of Wordsworth at any time in his career, but in 1807 his confidence in an imaginative economy to which the economy of financial calculation is wholly subordinate is sustained by his understanding of the historical moment. 'These times touch money'd Wordlings with dismay', but 'tens of thousands' of his countrymen remain 'cheerful as the rising Sun in May', and prove by this that all those faculties that are not exercised in 'getting and spending' remain vital in them.

The freedom enjoyed by the Lake District statesmen is not compromised by its narrowness. It is rather the case that the geographical and economic constriction of their life is a condition of their liberty. In *Poems*, 1807, much more emphatically than in *Lyrical Ballads*, Wordsworth represents freedom as the condition of those who willingly accept restraint.[6] In 'Elegiac Stanzas' he claims to have 'submitted to a new controul', echoing his prayer in 'Ode to Duty', 'I supplicate for thy controul'. The preference in 1807 for demanding lyric forms rather than the ballad stanzas and blank verse that had dominated *Lyrical Ballads* registers in itself a new insistence that freedom is won in the act by which it is surrendered. One crucial difference between *Tintern Abbey* and the Immortality Ode is secured by Wordsworth's refusal of the 'uncharter'd freedom' of blank verse for the intricate discipline of the Pindaric ode. Freedom, as it is now defined, is appropriately figured in the 'jubilant activity' of the water fowl that Wordsworth describes in his 'Introduction' to Wilkinson's *Select Views* in a passage taken from his own *Home at Grasmere* (*Prose*, 2, 183). Their joyous freedom expressed in the 'Hundreds of curves and circlets' that they describe in the air is not compromised but enabled by the mountains that hem the vale, and limit the area of their flight. Almost half of the poems are exercises in a single verse form, the sonnet, and the 'Prefatory Sonnet' asks that the form be understood as in itself embodying the paradox that freedom is won not by release from imprisonment, but by freely choosing to be imprisoned: 'In truth, the prison unto which we doom/ Ourselves, no prison is.' Like Toussaint l'Ouverture, the sonneteer finds that formal constraints release him into the 'air, earth, and skies', freeing him from the shackles truly worn by those who bear 'the weight of too much liberty'. It is an ideal that for Wordsworth has its origins in his admiration of men like Michael, whose days are given over to tending his flock and his evenings to the spinning wheel, and in his pained memories of the revolutionary excesses in France. But Napoleon, by confining his countrymen to their island, and by imposing on them the discipline of war, has allowed Wordsworth to present it as an ideal to which the whole nation owes service.

Poems addressed to a nation must be written in a national language. In the various prefaces to *Lyrical Ballads*, Wordsworth had remained defiantly consistent in appealing from the conventional language of poetry to the language of living speech; 'the language of conversation in the middle and lower classes of society' (*Prose*, 1, 116), 'a selection of the real language of men in a state of vivid sensation' (*Prose*, 1, 118), a 'purified' version of the language of 'low and rustic life', which, it is insisted, is 'a more permanent and a far more philosophical language than that which is frequently substituted for it by Poets' (*Prose*, 1, 124, 125). In all cases Wordsworth appeals from writing to speech. 'Literature' is held in suspicion as a practice that has been used to enforce and maintain social divisions by 'Poets, who think that they are conferring honour upon themselves and their art in proportion as they separate themselves from the sympathies of men' (*Prose*, 1, 124, 125). The most obvious difference between *Lyrical Ballads* and *Poems, 1807*, is that in 1807 the appeal to the authority of the language spoken in the 'pure Commonwealth' of the Lakes has been replaced by an appeal to the authority of another Commonwealth, which had preserved its language in writing:

> The later Sydney, Marvel, Harrington,
> Young Vane, and others who call'd Milton Friend.

The inferiority of the French is shown by their lack of such men, but equally by their lack of the 'Books' that they wrote. The commonwealth of letters that Wordsworth invokes in 1807 is distinctively republican and nationalistic, but not exclusively so. It can find room for Michelangelo, for the earlier Sidney as well as the later, and for Chaucer, Spenser and Shakespeare. Milton is its chief of men,[7] but he presides over a Commonwealth that has been released from the constraints of ideological purity. Wordsworth can celebrate now the exploits of the King of Sweden, 'that great King', as well as the heroic suffering of Toussaint l'Ouverture. Literature is offered as a *polis* in which the political differences that divide the subliterary world may be resolved. It is a tactic that Wordsworth maintains in the *Essays upon Epitaphs*, when, for example, he praises Montrose's lines on the death of Charles I by invoking the example of the poet who had defended Charles's execution: 'The whole is instinct with spirit, and every word has its separate life; like the Chariot of the Messiah, and the wheels of that Chariot, as they appeared to the imagination of Milton aided by that of the Prophet Ezekiel' (*Prose*, 2, 71). In the 'advertisement' to *Lyrical Ballads*, Wordsworth may appeal to the example of 'our elder writers', but he is defiantly aware that many of his reader will read through his volume looking for poetry and 'will be induced to enquire by what species of courtesy these attempts can be permitted to assume that title' (*Prose*, 1, 116). He writes for a readership that, he fears, has lost understanding of what is most vital in its own literary heritage. But *Poems*, 1807, is written to a people who have learned once again to experience the 'ancestral feeling' that unites them with the past of their nation, and, in consequence, with their nation's literary heritage. They have become once more a nation 'who speak the tongue/That Shakespeare spake'.

For Wordsworth, the question of language is crucial, for 'Language, if it do not uphold, and feed, and leave in quiet, like the power of gravitation or the air we breathe, is a counter-spirit, unremittingly and noiselessly at work to derange, to subvert, to lay waste, to vitiate, and to dissolve.' It is in its language that 'the taste, intellectual Power, and morals of a Country' can be shown to be 'inseparably linked in mutual dependence' (*Prose*, 2, 85). It follows that the crucial evidence that Britain had once again become a nation would be its possession of a language that served once more to unite rather than to divide its speakers. In *The Convention of Cintra*, Wordsworth insists that politics, as understood by him and the 'vast majority of the nation', as opposed to politics as understood by Mr Pitt and Mr Fox, is not a branch of 'Experimental Philosophy' (*Prose*, 1, 325) but has its true kinship with poetry. The war is represented as an epic poem, a restaging of *Paradise Lost*, in which France figures as Lucifer, 'the Fallen Spirit, triumphant in misdeeds, which was formerly a blessed Angel' (*Prose*, 1, 302). It is for their failure to recognize that they are engaged in the creation of a poem rather than the formulation of a policy that the political and military leadership is indicted. They do not recognize that the appropriate appeal is to the imagination and to the passions rather than to the calculating faculty, and the symptom of their blindness, in politics as it is in poetry, is an insensitivity to language.

Wordsworth contemptuously analyses the clauses of the Convention to reveal that it is written in a political diction that is equivalent to artificial poetic diction in its refusal to attach words to things. The generals who wrote it were under the same misapprehension as the French general who insisted that a troop of Spanish soldiers were merely a group of 'Galician peasants' because they wore no uniforms, and hence lacked the 'outward appearance' of 'regular troops' (*Prose*, 1, 233). Wordsworth repeatedly contrasts the vigorous, passionate language of the Spanish patriots with the frigid conventionalities of their British allies, but, even more strikingly, when he wishes to insist on the importance of what is at stake in the contest, it is language that he invokes. The British generals failed to understand that the war was not fought for possession of fortresses made of stone, but for 'strong-holds in the imagination', and that the cities and soil of the Peninsula 'were chiefly prized by us as a *language*' (*Prose*, 1, 261–2). Even the religious faith of the Spanish, tainted as it might be by bigotry and superstition, is to be valued, for in the flames of war it will inevitably be refined until it becomes 'a language and a ceremony of imagination' (*Prose*, 1, 293) Wordsworth's pamphlet is written throughout from the premise that his authority derives not from the depth of his political knowledge but from the power of his imagination, that respect for language is a truer test of political aptitude than experience of the intricacies of government, and that therefore it is the poet rather than the professional politician who may properly claim to speak for and to the nation.

Poems, 1807, is a collection extraordinary for its heterogeneousness. It is as likely to memorialize objects such as a household tub or a friend's spade as a chivalric item such as 'The Horn of Egremont Castle'. Its characters range from Charles James Fox to a queenly beggar woman to Coleridge's six-year-old son. The poems may address a daisy or Milton, an infant girl or 'England'. They may chronicle domestic doings or great international events, and they do so in verse forms that range from the humble ballad to the Pindaric ode,[8] and in a diction that can accommodate both the infant prattle of 'The Kitten and the Falling Leaves' and the Miltonic sonorities of the political sonnets. It is a collection addressed, to use a distinction that became important to Wordsworth at this time, not to the 'public' but to the 'people',[9] not to the nation as a hierarchically ordered entity, held together by a system of difference, but to the nation as a 'solemn fraternity' that will recognize the variousness of Wordsworth's volumes as a proper representation of the spaciousness of its own heart. The collection wills such a people into being, but it dares to do so because the war has given Wordsworth a 'firmer faith' that his countrymen's 'virtue and the faculties within' remain 'vital'.

It is the 'faculties within' that remain his primary concern. The 'Sonnets Dedicated to Liberty' are placed at the centre of the collection, but Wordsworth reaches out to the public from the private. The first group of poems, 'The Orchard Pathway', is, as its title indicates, firmly rooted in Wordsworth's domestic life at Grasmere,[10] and in the second volume he withdraws from the public events that had preoccupied him at the end of the first. The collection ends with three elegiac poems that seem to underline the 'ebb and flow' of the whole collection. In the first Wordsworth shares at Grasmere the sadness that 'many thousands' of his countrymen feel at the news that Fox is dying, but in the second, 'Elegiac Stanzas', the grief that the poem records is private and familial, and the third, the Immortality Ode, narrows the focus from 'many' to 'one', as it elegizes a loss that can be recognized only by a process of introspection. The collection that begins with an address to the humblest of wild flowers, 'To the Daisy', ends with the lines:

> To me the meanest flower that blows can give
> Thoughts that do often lie too deep for tears.

Thus, the poems, like all things, as Wordsworth claims in his *Essays upon Epitaphs*, 'revolve upon each other' (*Prose*, 2, 53).

The shape of the collection works in itself to subordinate the public to the private. Wordsworth is happy to characterize his poems by their distance from the matters that preoccupy 'worldlings': 'what have they to do with routs, dinners, morning calls, hurry from door to door, from street to street, on foot or in Carriage; with Mr Pitt, Mr Paul or Sir Francis Burdett, the Westminster Election or the Borough of Honiton?' (*Letters*, 2, 145–6). But contempt of worldliness does not imply a detachment from politics.[11] The poems already assume an argument that becomes explicit in *The Convention of Cintra*. Those whose 'education has been pre-defined from childhood for the express purpose of future political power' are, precisely because of the exclusively political nature of their interests, less likely to achieve sound political judgement than those who have 'studied in the walks of common life' (*Prose*, 1, 305–6). In a bold manoeuvre Wordsworth offers his lack of interest in Mr Pitt and Mr Fox as the ground of his political authority. Professional soldiers share in still greater measure the deficiencies of professional politicians. Wellesley, in associating himself with the Convention of Cintra, had betrayed 'a deadness to the moral interests of the cause in which he was engaged' and 'a want of sympathy with the just feelings of his injured Ally', and such defects are predictable in 'a mind narrowed by exclusive and overweening attention to the *military* character' (*Prose*, 1, 251). In *Poems*, 1807, it is Napoleon's mind rather than Wellington's that typifies the moral deformity of those who have been educated only 'in battles'. Such minds have no access to 'Wisdom', for:

> Wisdom doth live with children round her knees:
> Books, leisure, perfect freedom, and the talk
> Man holds with weekday man in the hourly walk
> Of the mind's business...

Wellesley and Napoleon are 'unhappy warriors', deprived of 'a Soul whose master-bias leans/To home-felt pleasures and to gentle scenes'. Many of the 1807 lyrics celebrate the domestic happiness that Wordsworth had found at Grasmere, and in several poems Wordsworth represents himself with 'children round his knees'. But these are not trivial distractions from the weighty affairs that preoccupy Wordsworth in his 'Sonnets Dedicated to Liberty', rather they justify the authority that the political sonnets claim. Patriotic sentiment, as Wordsworth insists in *The Convention of Cintra*, is an overflowing of private virtue that has its origins in 'the domestic loves and sanctities'.

Poems, 1807, is in an important sense a collection of war poems, but they are war poems that always accede to the premise that to celebrate war in and for itself is to render oneself monstrous, like Napoleon. The 'happy warrior', by contrast, has a staunchness that is grounded in his knowledge that the warrior virtues are subordinate to the domestic virtues that sustain them. In 1807, Wordsworth was happy to associate his warrior with Nelson, so that the 'Ode to Duty', which ended the section in which the poem appeared, might achieve an additional resonance supplied by memories of Nelson's last signal, but the ode still insists that the duty Nelson recommended, like all other military virtues, is only an inflection of, and subordinate to, the virtue as it is displayed in private life. Similarly, the 'resolution' that Wordsworth exhorted the nation to display in protection of its own 'independence' and the independence of others, is a virtue more perfectly embodied in the humble life of the leech gatherer than in the public exploits of a military man. Wordsworth maintained the association with Nelson only for so long as he could feel that Nelson's heroism was validated by his final thoughts which were of 'early pleasures' and of 'home' (*Letters*, 1, 664–5). When he learned that Nelson, by his execution of Carocciolo, had shown a capacity to subordinate private virtue to military policy, he immediately disavowed it (*Letters*, 2, 154 and note).

In 1807, the shape of the whole collection, which curves outward from the private and domestic to embrace the public and political only to turn back in the second volume towards the individual life, expresses Wordsworth's sense that the language of politics is only ever a symbolic language, the meaning of which is sustained by its reference to the language of private reflection. The 'Tree of Liberty' is properly defended only by one able to feel the value of an ordinary tree, 'of many one'; military glory is truly valued only by one able to see 'glory in the flower'.[12]

For Wordsworth in 1807 the state is a generalization of the family, the political is an extension of the domestic, and he writes in the confidence that he shares this premise with the 'people' of Britain. In *The Convention of Cintra*, much more confidently than in the 1805 *Prelude*, he is prepared to offer his own political biography as both consistent and representative. His passionate opposition to the war against France has been converted into a passionate support for it, but this apparent volte face is evidence, as Wordsworth puts it in 'Ode to Duty', of 'no disturbance of my soul,/Or strong compunction in me wrought', but the result of principles stoutly maintained amidst the flux of political circumstance. The war against France became 'just and necessary' 'after the subjugation of Switzerland', at precisely the time when the nation's governors were negotiating the Treaty of Amiens in the hope of bringing the war to an end, and its justice and necessity were 'by none more clearly perceived' than by those who had for many years sided with the French: 'Their conduct was herein consistent: they proved that they kept their eyes steadily fixed upon principles; for, though there was a shifting or transfer of hostility in their minds as far as regarded persons, they only combated the same enemy opposed to them under a different shape; and that enemy was the spirit of selfish tyranny and lawless ambition.' Before 1801, Wordsworth argues, that spirit was embodied in Pitt, after 1801 in Napoleon, and he speaks, he claims, not simply on his own behalf, but on that of 'an immense majority of the people of Great Britain' (*Prose*, 1, 226). *Poems*, 1807, is enabled by a similar confidence that the time has come when Wordsworth can speak to and for his nation.

It was a confidence that did not survive the reception of the volumes. By 1807, Wordsworth had achieved a solid and growing reputation as the author of *Lyrical Ballads*, by then in its fourth edition. *Poems*, 1807, reduced his status to that of a coterie poet, championed by eccentric enthusiasts such as Lady Beaumont and John Wilson. The reviews of

Poems, 1807, were much more vituperative, and also more consistent than reviews of *Lyrical Ballads* had been. The charges brought against the volumes may be briefly summarized. First, the volumes displayed all of the defects of *Lyrical Ballads* with none or almost none of the redeeming merits. Both volumes, it was assumed, were written according to the 'system' that Wordsworth had expounded in his *Preface* of 1800, but in the poems of 1807 the idiosyncrasies, most marked of which was 'the extreme simplicity of their language', were, as Jeffrey put it, 'much more strongly marked', and hence more reprehensible. Linked to the diction was the habit of introducing mean and contemptible objects into the poems. Jeffrey was particularly exercised by the 'Household Tub' in which *The Blind Highland Boy* set sail: 'nor is there anything... which may not be introduced in poetry if this is tolerated.' One effect of the introduction of such items was to establish an absurd incongruity between the loftiness of the poet's feelings and the triviality of the objects that had prompted them. Reviewers mourned the spectacle of a grown man reduced to 'drivelling... to a common pile-wort'. Such habits betrayed the 'affectation' and 'egoism' of a poet who had, on system, repudiated 'illustrious predecessors' such as 'Virgil and Milton' in favour of 'vulgar ballads' and nursery rhymes, and who had, by living in Westmorland, wilfully become 'a humble recluse' condemned to 'starve his mind in solitude', freed from the wholesome checks that the habit of mingling with a cultured metropolitan class would inevitably have placed upon his eccentricities.[13]

Wordsworth responded combatively. The four prose works that he published between 1809 and 1810, despite their miscellaneous subject matter, all share an unacknowledged concern with Wordsworth's status in the republic of letters.[14] They are an attempt to undertake the task that, as Wordsworth explained to Lady Beaumont, fell to 'every great and original writer, in proportion as he is great and original': such a writer 'must himself create the taste by which he is relished' (*Letters*, 2, 150). There was obvious comfort to be found in an aphorism that represented hostile criticism as an index of literary merit, but a stronger indication of Wordsworth's gut response to the reviews is the loss of nerve that led him to abandon his plans for the immediate publication of *The White Doe of Rylstone*. In the event, it was to be seven years before Wordsworth felt able to risk the publication of another volume. It was a reaction prompted not only by Wordsworth's thin-skinned sensitivity, but by a growing recognition that in some sense his hostile critics were right. In a collection designed to express a national mood, Wordsworth had succeeded only in representing the 'moods of [his] own mind': in a collection of poems intended to speak to the nation, he had succeeded in speaking only to himself.

It was Jeffrey whose reviews most exercised Wordsworth, and he was well aware of the point at issue between them. He wrote to Southey:

> That, to a great number of persons, many objects such as I have written upon will be either unknown, or uninteresting, or even contemptible there can be no doubt, but I suppose, generally speaking, that these people are, so far, in a state of degradation, at least that it would be better for them if they were otherwise. Mr Jeffrey takes for granted the contrary. Here we are at issue.
>
> (*Letters*, 2, 162)

In 1808, in his review of Crabbe's *Poems*, Jeffrey clarified his position.[15] A comparison between Crabbe and Wordsworth leads to the conclusion that, unlike Wordsworth's, Crabbe's poems accord with 'our general knowledge of human nature'. Similar phrases recur throughout the review. Crabbe appeals to the 'common sympathies of our nature', he admits no 'wide and wilful aberration from ordinary nature', the value of his poems is upheld by 'that eternal and universal standard of truth and nature, which everyone is knowing enough to recognize, and no-one great enough to depart from with impunity'. The comparison reveals Wordsworth's poems as marked by 'fantastic and affected peculiarities', and as restricted to the analysis of Wordsworth's own 'capricious feelings', with the result that they are often 'strained and affected'. Jeffrey's tactic seems clear. He is deploying against Wordsworth a rhetoric borrowed from Wordsworth's own 'Preface' to *Lyrical Ballads* in order to expose Wordsworth as a mutant specimen of precisely the kind of poet that Wordsworth had himself deplored: 'Poets, who think that they are conferring honour upon themselves and their art in proportion as they separate themselves from the sympathies of men, and indulge in arbitrary and capricious habits of expression in order to furnish food for fickle tastes and fickle appetites of their own creation' (*Prose*, 1, 124, 125). Jeffrey takes as his key example the village schoolteacher, a character that had been delineated by Goldsmith, by Shenstone, and by Crabbe, and is credited by all three with particular traits: 'pedantry', 'an innocent vanity of learning', a 'mixture of indulgence with the pride of power, and of poverty with the consciousness of acquirements'. The truth of the characterization is suggested by the coincidence between the three poets, and demonstrated by an appeal to 'our common apprehension'. By contrast, Wordsworth's Matthew is revealed as entirely fantastical.

Wordsworth replies to Jeffrey in the second of the *Essays upon Epitaphs* by distinguishing between 'a living creature' and 'a character'. The character is produced when a person's qualities are separately abstracted, and 'put together again' according to the rules of art, that is, 'petty alliterations...combined with opposition in thoughts when there is no necessary or natural opposition' (*Prose*, 2, 75). Hence the 'character' never has more than 'an intellectual Existence' (*Prose*, 2, 77). In the *Essay* Wordsworth chooses his examples from Pope and Lyttelton, but Crabbe's schoolmaster, as Jeffrey recognizes, is constructed on their model. The character accords, Jeffrey claims, with 'our common apprehension', but, even in Jeffrey's summary, its impression of truthfulness seems suspiciously dependent on the patterns of antithesis and alliteration that Wordsworth identifies: 'poverty', 'pride', 'power'. Wordsworth's 'Character of the Happy Warrior' had offered an example of how one might construct a portrait in couplets without surrendering to the 'sparkling and tuneful' manner of Pope, but it is clear from the *Essays* that he recognized himself and Jeffrey as differing over more than a taste for alliteration and antithesis.

Jeffrey insists that the village schoolmaster, as Crabbe represents him, conforms to 'our general knowledge of human nature', but the portrait he offers, in which the schoolmaster is assembled as an arrangement of piquantly antithetical qualities, assumes a perspective that is available only to a limited community of cultured, metropolitan readers who are invited to regard the schoolmaster's rusticity and the modesty of his acquirements with an amused and sympathetic condescension. It is in protest against such notions that Wordsworth offers as the proper type of all poems, the epitaph, for 'an epitaph is not a proud writing shut up for the studious; it is exposed to all, and for all: – in the churchyard it is open to the day; the sun looks down upon the stone, and the rains of heaven beat against it' (*Prose*, 2, 59). The community of the parish, lingering at the end of the service amongst the gravestones, becomes the type of an ideal readership. But, however beautifully the prose accommodates the vision, it remains ideal. The strength of Jeffrey's argument remains that the community to which he appeals corresponds, as the community that Wordsworth imagines does not, with the social group amongst which poetry found its readership.

In the *Essays* Wordsworth meets the problem by comparing epitaphs transcribed from tombstones with poems selected from Knox's *Elegant Extracts*, and by demonstrating through 'minute criticism' that poetry is as likely to be found on the stones as in the book (*Prose*, 2, 77).

In the *Reply to Mathetes* he shows full confidence in the method: 'Range against each other as Advocates, oppose as Combatants, two several Intellects, each strenuously asserting doctrines which he sincerely believes; but the one contending for the worth and beauty of that garment which the other has outgrown and cast away', and 'the riper mind' will inevitably triumph. It would follow that Wordsworth need only publish his *Essays* for Jeffrey to be exposed as a critic 'duped by shews, enslaved by words, corrupted by mistaken delicacy and false refinement' (*Prose*, 2, 21). But as Wordsworth wrote the *Essays* his Godwinian confidence evaporated. He seeks to demonstrate that the taste of the cultured, literary community is founded on false principles, and that it cannot sustain his own critical practice of 'bringing words rigorously to the test of things' (*Prose*, 2, 77). Mason says of his wife that, when she visited a spa in an attempt to recover her health, she 'bow'd to taste the wave', whereas, in fact, 'the waters of a mineral spring' are drunk 'out of a goblet' (*Prose*, 2, 83). Because it is untrue, such prettification is vicious. But, as Jeffrey had pointed out, the demand for literal truth would hardly sanction the claim that it was 'duty' that preserved the physical order of the cosmos.[16] True poetry speaks out of the 'primary sensations of the human heart', and, 'unless correspondent ones listen promptly and submissively in the inner cell of the mind to whom it is addressed, the voice cannot be heard: its highest powers are wasted' (*Prose*, 2, 70). Minute criticism cannot summon these primary sensations into existence, and it is ultimately only by an appeal to them that it can be known whether the words of a poem are false or true. It follows that 'the taste, intellectual Power, and morals of a Country are inseparably linked in mutual dependence', and Wordsworth agreed with Mathetes that 'the moral spirit and intellectual Powers of this Country are declining' (*Prose*, 2, 10).

In *Poems*, 1807, the representations of poor people have an edginess less evident in *Lyrical Ballads*. *The Sailor's Mother* has a dignity 'like a Roman matron's': the poet is proud to recognize in her the persistence of an 'ancient Spirit', but it is a spirit that she would not be able to recognize in herself. Similarly the beggar woman's beauty, like an Amazonian queen's, is a beauty that Wordsworth can share with his reader but not with his subject. The ideal readership that Wordsworth imagined tracing the epitaphs inscribed on the gravestones of a country churchyard did not exist, and its absence generates the most uncomfortable moments in the collection, as when the moon and stars look down on a band of 'Gypsies' silently reproving their idleness: 'Then issued Vesper from the fulgent West'. The evening star is above the gypsies' heads, and so is the vocabulary that describes it, with the result that the astronomical reproof is couched in accents redolent of a cultivated contempt.[17] All true poems ought to be written, like those country epitaphs, 'to the wise and the most ignorant', but in 1807 there was no language that the two groups had in common. Wordsworth may well have published his poems in the belief that the war had made it possible to address a united nation in a common language, but the reception of the poems made it impossible to sustain that belief. Wordsworth ends the last of the *Essays* with the passage from Book VII of *The Excursion* that relates the life and death of Thomas Holme, an agricultural labourer (*Prose*, 2, 94–6). Wordsworth's elegy for him is an elegy, too, for the unified community of which he was a remnant. Holme died in 1773, and even then, the passage suggests, the blameless dignity of his life was secured by the affliction that cut him off from the spoken language of his neighbours, and confined him to his books. Holme was deaf.

Thomas Holme who retreated in his deafness from the society of men to the society of books becomes an exemplary figure, and one with whom Wordsworth claims special kinship. In 'I am not one who much or oft delight', he represents himself as preferring, somewhat morosely, 'Long barren silence' to the 'personal talk' of the fireside, for it is a silence that allows Wordsworth entry into a world free from 'evil-speaking' and 'rancour', the 'substantial world' of books. The *Essays upon Epitaphs* repeat and refine many of the views that Wordsworth had expounded in his Prefaces to *Lyrical Ballads*, but there remains a crucial difference. Whereas Wordsworth had once insisted on appealing from written language to speech, in the *Essays*, as in *Poems*, 1807, as a whole, the appeal is consistently from one kind of writing to another. The 'ideal Commonwealth' of the Lakes may once have been united by its common possession of a spoken language, but by 1807 Wordsworth had accepted that neither the society nor its language survived. He had been left with no option but to make his appeal to an alternative Commonwealth, the Commonwealth of seventeenth-century England, for that Commonwealth had preserved its language in writing. The most striking difference between *Lyrical Ballads* and *Poems*, 1807, is that the later collection, with its startling variety of traditional verse forms, and its tributes, both explicit and implied, to admired predecessors, asserts a claim that the poems be recognized as taking their place within the long tradition of English poetry. The whole collection expresses the ambition that Wordsworth articulates in 'I am not one who much or oft delight', when he celebrates the 'Poets': 'Oh! might my name be numbered among theirs'. Jeffrey's reviews were so disturbing because they denied so emphatically that the retreat from speech to the 'substantial world of books' might be a means to recover a language that transcended social divisions. For Jeffrey literature is a category that is secured only by a recognition of the social divisions that enable it, and that it reproduces. In *Poems*, 1807, Wordsworth recognizes in 'Hesperus' the type of his own lofty poetic ambitions, and in the very next poem describes how 'The Blind Highland Boy' set sail in his 'Household Tub', a collocation evidently designed to affront conventional notions of literary hierarchy. But for Jeffrey it seemed self-evident that the elegantly latinate star could function only as an unwitting satire on the irredeemably prosaic domestic utensil.[18]

Wordsworth offers the republic of letters as a substitute for the 'almost visionary mountain republic' that no longer existed. In his 'Introduction' to Wilkinson's *Select Views*, Wordsworth offers his most moving celebration of that republic, and at the same time writes its elegy. The section in which he describes the lives of its citizens is controlled by a single phrase three times repeated, 'Till within the last sixty years' (*Prose*, 2, 200, 203, 206). The statesmen, the 'humble sons of the hills', who lived on the land that supported them, and had 'for more than five hundred years been possessed by men of their name and blood' (*Prose*, 2, 206), were a dying class. The cottage industries on which they relied could not survive 'the invention and universal application of machinery', and the result has been that the statesmen have sunk into debt, and their land has fallen into the hands of 'wealthy purchasers' (*Prose*, 2, 224). The principles are the same as those explained by Wordsworth in his letter to Fox, but there is a new acceptance that the forces that have destroyed the 'visionary mountain republic' are impossible to withstand. The final section of the 'Introduction' is addressed to the 'wealthy purchasers' in an attempt to correct their taste, so that their 'disfigurement' of the landscape might remain within measure.

Wordsworth's 'Introduction' begins, as it were, as a defiant counterblast to the reviewers who had characterized him as a 'humble recluse' who had chosen to live in wilful isolation from the cultural centre of the nation. The Lakes become the central place, a 'national property' (*Prose*, 2, 225), and the urgent business is to control the encroachments upon them threatened by the inhabitants of the metropolitan margins. But he ends by apologizing to his readers for having been forced, in order to spare them from prospects spoiled by discordant modern buildings, to lead them 'through unfrequented paths so much out of the common road' (*Prose*, 2, 286). His Lakes, he ends by confessing, have become marginal even to themselves.

In the four prose works with which Wordsworth occupied himself immediately after the publication of *Poems*, 1807, Wordsworth seems to change from a man who addresses a nation in full confidence that his views are shared by 'an immense majority' of its citizens to a man who would rather claim kinship with Thomas Holme, isolated by his deafness and finding companionship only in his books. But it would be wrong to claim this transformation as a result of the critical reception that the poems received, for both stances were already adopted in the poems themselves.

In *Poems*, 1807, Wordsworth offers the war against Napoleon as a public event that will force his nation to discover once again the private virtues on which its greatness was founded. In war, words, the words of the Convention of Cintra, for example, must be tested by their relation to things, and in wartime there was a need so urgent that it could not but be met, for a national language that could speak 'to all, and for all', a language that functioned to bind its speakers into a community rather than to divide them one from another. In wartime, in other words, it seemed as if, by a pressure that could not be withstood, the 'visionary mountain republic', the small community that had retained by virtue of its isolation those virtues that the country as a whole had abandoned, must be recognized at last as embodying the political ideal to which the whole nation must aspire. By closing the markets of Europe to British goods, Napoleon was forcing on the nation the virtue of self-dependence that had secured for centuries the 'ideal Commonwealth' of the Lakes, and by threatening invasion he had exposed the shallowness of those who recognized the value only of economic motives, and who concluded that therefore 'the wealthiest man among us is the best'.

Wordsworth inveighs repeatedly against the idolatry of wealth that represented for him the strongest evidence of the moral degradation of his nation, but the imaginative economy that he substitutes for it, in which 'wealth' comes not from appropriating money but memories, not from golden coins but from golden daffodils, is an economy that is only ever ushered into being by the poems that memorialize such objects. It is an economy that can regulate Wordsworth's volumes, but not, as his introduction to Wilkinson's *Select Views* acknowledges, his neighbourhood. So, even while Wordsworth registers a hope that the war will extend the virtues of the self-subsistent Westmorland statesmen to the whole nation, the poems betray the futility of such an ambition given the fact that the statesmen themselves have been unable to defend their way of life against the unimaginative economic forces that have destroyed it. In the last of the 'Miscellaneous Sonnets', Wordsworth thanks Raisley Calvert for permitting him to enjoy a 'liberty' that is not limited but confirmed by the 'frugal and severe' way of life that Calvert's legacy required of him. It has allowed him what their land and spinning wheels once allowed the statesmen, a subsistence that protected them from the 'getting and spending' that so damagingly preoccupied the world outside the mountains. It is bleakly revealing that the true heir and the last representative of the 'almost visionary Republic' should be the poet.[19]

Wordsworth's ambition to stand forward as a poet who speaks to and for a nation comes into conflict with a quite contrary recognition that the war has failed to transform in other than an entirely superficial way a country that has willingly abandoned its constitution in favour of an economy, and that remains on that account irremediably divided. It is Milton who presides over the volume, but he is a radically divided figure, at once the poet of an 'ideal Commonwealth', and the poet who lived to see how willingly his countrymen 'forfeited' the 'manners, virtue, freedom, power' that were their inheritance. It is the second figure that proves the more powerful. At the last, the poems represent Wordsworth as a citizen of a nation that is constituted only by the poems themselves.[20] Hence the appropriateness that its final poem should be the Immortality Ode, and that the collection should end with 'thoughts too deep for tears', thoughts so deep that they have no content at all except in relation to the poem that they conclude.

In *Poems in Two Volumes* Wordsworth tried to speak to the nation, and ended up speaking to himself. It was to be almost five years before Britain was to find a new poet that spoke to it and for it, and that poet, oddly enough, achieved his position by writing in open contempt of the nation and everything that it stood for.

6
Mapping
Childe Harold I and II

Carl Woodring has described the landscape of *Childe Harold* as 'a palimpsest of political maps'.[1] In the poem's first two cantos maps are invoked that would, if bound together, make up a moderately comprehensive historical atlas of Europe. As he rides over the Greek mainland, or sails through the Greek islands, Byron traces a map of the ancient world; from Troy to Marathon, from the Athens of Pericles to the site of the Battle of Actium. In Spain he understands the indignity of suffering occupation by a foreign power by recalling how Spain's own 'fell Pizarros' had three centuries before subjugated large tracts of South America. All over Europe he notes the sites that mark the slow decline of the Ottoman empire, from its first check with the expulsion of the Moors from Spain to the Battle of Lepanto and its present enfeebled state when a warlord such as Ali Pasha could exercise a rule all but independent of his Turkish overlords. But in the first two cantos one map dominates all others, the map of Napoleonic Europe. This was a volatile map, changing even as Byron wrote, but it controls all of the experience that the poem records.

Harold's pilgrimage closely follows Byron's own travels, and from one point of view the itineraries of both journeys seem haphazard, governed by chance and whim.[2] Byron after all had sailed to Lisbon only because he had arrived at Falmouth too late to catch the Malta packet. He travelled from Greece to Constantinople because naval officers happened to offer him passage, and from Constantinople he returned to Greece rather than continuing his journey to India, as he had once intended, because he had lost interest in the earlier project and because he was short of funds. The course of Harold's journey, even more emphatically than Byron's, seems governed by impulse rather than by plan. From the first Harold travels without a goal, impelled on his journey not by curiosity but by ennui. But looked at otherwise the journeys of both are controlled at every stage by the contours of the political map of the Europe through which they travel. Byron visited Seville and Cadiz, but had he arrived in Spain just six months later he would have visited neither, for by then Seville had fallen to the French and Cadiz was under siege. He could dally with Mrs Spencer Smith at Malta because Malta was a naval base so important that the British had chosen to risk the breakdown of the Peace of Amiens rather than to withdraw and risk losing the island to the French. From Malta he had planned to sail to Friuli, 'but, lo! the Peace spoilt everything by putting this in the possession of the French'.[3] Byron was flattered by his reception by Ali Pasha in Albania, but the warmth of the hospitality he received must surely have owed something to the news that only days earlier four of the Ionian islands had fallen to the British.[4] Byron travelled freely to Constantinople, but three years previously the city had been under blockade by Admiral Duckworth, for Turkey was at war with Russia and Russia was an ally against Napoleon. Since then Napoleon had concluded the Treaty of Tilsit with the Tsar, and the Turks had no option but to accept an alliance with the British.

Harold travels to escape 'the crowd, the hum, the shock of men', he is led 'by pensive sadness' to seek in travel escape from a public world that seems to him hollow and trivial, but he travels through a Europe that allows no such refuge, where all private space has been secured very publicly, by force of arms. Harold affects indifference to military matters:

> Oft did he mark the scenes of vanish'd war,
> Actium, Lepanto, fatal Trafalgar;
> Mark them unmov'd, for he would not delight
> (Born beneath some remote inglorious star)
> In themes of bloody fray or gallant fight,
> But loath'd the bravo's trade, and laugh'd at martial wight.
>
> (2, 355–60)[5]

Scenes of battle leave him unmoved, but when he gazes on the crag from which Sappho plunged to her death in obedience to a passion that is pure because quite private, Harold felt 'no common glow': 'He felt, or deem'd he felt, no common glow'. The qualifying clause admits a suspicion of all claims to highfalutin emotion, but it betrays too a recognition that Harold's contemptuous indifference to 'the bravo's trade' is a vulnerable attitude in a man sailing in an armed frigate through waters that have been secured for the British by Nelson in the battle that Harold despises. The space within which Harold savours his literary emotions is a space that has been won for him by the 'well-reev'd guns' of the frigate that he is sailing on.

Harold travels without a goal, but he is accompanied on his travels by a poet, and the poet, unlike Harold, is a true pilgrim. He travels not to assuage his own ennui but to visit the holy places of his craft. His ultimate goal is Mount Parnassus, and he interrupts the account of Spain in the first canto to record that the goal has been achieved:

> Oh, thou Parnassus! whom I now survey,
> Not in the phrenzy of a dreamer's eye,
> Not in the fabled landscape of a lay,
> But soaring snow-clad through thy native sky,
> In the wild pomp of mountain majesty!
> (1, 612–16)

The journey to Parnassus signifies his quest for an authentic poetry, a poetry that will not 'shame' the Muse as have so many 'later lyres', and his journey is prompted by a recognition that he lives at a time when such a poetry has become all but impossible to write. The apostrophe to Mount Parnassus interrupts a tribute to Spanish women, women who have abandoned the 'unstrung guitar', and chosen to sing instead 'the loud song' of war. Byron records their dilemma sympathetically, for it is his own dilemma, too. *Childe Harold* was written at a time when poetry seemed condemned either to be loud or tinkling, either to promulgate shrilly the patriotic fervour of a nation at war or to retreat into a lyric voice fit only for the expression of private sentiment. Byron's prayer to Parnassus, his prayer that he be allowed to pluck 'one leaf of Daphne's deathless plant', is a plea that somehow he be allowed to escape this dilemma.

In his preface Byron insists that any similarities between his own poem and 'the different poems which have been written on Spanish subjects' are only casual. In the poem itself he is a good deal more aggressive. Wellington's victories are fit only to 'shine in worthless lays, the theme of transient song'. Since Croker's success with *The Battles of Talavera* in 1809, every allied victory, and especially any victory by Wellington, had prompted a poem.[6] In his review of Croker's poem, Scott had deplored 'the apparent apathy of our poets and rhymers to the events that are passing over them',[7] but it was an apathy that did not last. In 1811 *The Battles of the Danube and Barrossa*, published by Murray, and *The Battle of Albuera, A Poem, with an Epistle dedicated to Lord Wellington* both appeared, and Scott produced his own contribution to the war effort, *A Vision of Don Roderick*. The appearance of a poem on Spain, written in Spenserian stanzas, by the most popular poet of the day must have impressed Byron forcibly as he set about preparing his own poem for publication. But Scott had, one suspects, been in his mind from the first.[8] According to Lockhart, it was the publication of *Marmion* that had established Scott's character as 'the mighty minstrel of the Antigallican war'.[9] In his early narrative poems Scott's concern is to re-create the martial, chivalric values that were needed to sustain his country in its struggle against Napoleon. Croker's decision to write his poem on Talavera in the *Marmion* stanza would have seemed to him obvious enough for his poem is a continuation of Scott's enterprise by other, more direct, means. Both are concerned to develop a style, derived from the ballad, in which individual sentiment is subordinated to the communal and introspection is absorbed into patriotism, the large sense of the self as embodied within the nation.

The first appearance of *Childe Harold* immediately prompted comparison with Scott.[10] Byron's poem came equipped with notes, some of them elaborate and displaying curious pieces of learning: specimens of Albanian folk songs, a bibliography of modern Greek authors. Byron, it was clear, was appropriating the form that Scott had made his own, but with crucial differences. The historical cast of Scott's learning becomes, in Byron's adaptation, resolutely contemporary, and whereas Scott's notes claim disinterested scholarly authority Byron's are characteristically partisan and controversial. *Childe Harold* is best seen as an attempt to rewrite the poetic romance that had become, in Scott's hands, the most powerful literary expression of the unity of Britain in its struggle against Napoleon.

Scott's whole enterprise is founded on his success in forging a powerfully anachronistic rhetoric, a rhetoric that allows his celebration of the warrior virtues of a feudal society to pass smoothly over the centuries and become a eulogy to the kind of virtue demanded of Britain in the early nineteenth century. Byron takes Scott's anachronism, exposes it, and makes it comic by the simple device of attaching a pastiche archaic language to the utterly modern character of his hero:

> Childe Harold was he hight: – but whence his name
> And lineage long, it suits me not to say;
> Suffice it, that perchance they were of fame,

> And had been glorious in another day:
> But one sad losel spoils a name for aye,
> However mighty in the olden time...
> (1, 19–24)

The comedy exposes Harold as a degenerate representative of the chivalric tradition, and, more significantly, points the absurdity of the attempt by Scott to construe Burke's rhetoric literally, and resurrect the age of chivalry three centuries after the event.[11] But the archaic language is largely confined to the opening stanzas of the poem. Byron's decision to choose as a hero a man alienated from his family, his friends, and his nation serves a wider function: it allows the whole poem to bear witness to a fact of modern experience that it is in Scott's interest to deny, the fact of self-consciousness, the existence of a self that cannot be subsumed within any larger affiliation to a group or to a nation.

Contemporary reviewers noted this as the most striking characteristic of the poem. Scott's friend, George Ellis, reviewing the poem in the *Quarterly*, was enthusiastic, but noted 'faults arising from caprice, or from a disregard of general opinion'. Jeffreys in the *Edinburgh* was more intelligently alert to 'that singular turn of sentiment which we have doubted whether to rank among the defects or the attractions of this performance'.[12] Jerome McGann is the modern critic most sensitive to this aspect of the poem. For him, the true subject of the poem is to be found in the 'shifting sensibilities' of the narrator. His ideas as ideas, are 'strictly of secondary poetic importance: what matters is that they are his, and that in them we read the temper of his mind'.[13] All that is missing from McGann's account is a proper sense of the effrontery of a poet who conducts his reader to the Spanish peninsula, to the arena where the struggle for the whole of Europe was being most intensely contested, only to insist that these events are of strictly secondary importance relative to his own 'shifting sensibilities'. It is an effrontery that lends the poem the bravura dash that so impressed contemporary readers, but it does more than just confirm Byron's predilection for wilful self-display. In a debate on the conduct of the Peninsular war early in 1812 Lord Jocelyn took the opportunity to rehearse an opinion that had become the merest commonplace: 'Unanimity', he said 'was at all times desirable, but particularly when engaged in our own defence as a nation, and still more as a free nation.'[14] The need to preserve freedom requires the suppression of all difference, all dissent, and by 1812 the thought had become so hackneyed that Lord Jocelyn seems quite unaware that it involves a paradox. It was a cast of mind that infiltrated all areas of public life, not excepting literature. The pressures of the time demanded that notions of literary value, for example, be disregarded in favour of an appreciation of the public utility of literary production. The *Quarterly* welcomed all patriotic poems on Spain 'however deficient these effusions may be in poetical merit', for 'if they be not calculated to excite the public feeling, they may at least be admitted as evidence of it'.[15] *Childe Harold* with its misanthropic, self-absorbed hero, presented within a narrative remarkable for the variousness rather than the consistency of its opinions, is designed as a calculated affront to any demand that the individual surrender to a national 'unanimity', or that the private voice subordinate itself to the voice of 'public feeling'.

At the beginning of the poem there seems a clear enough distinction between the frame of mind attributed to Harold and the frame of mind embodied in the narrative. The attitude towards Harold veers between sympathy and disapproval, but both responses are subsumed within a ground tone of amused indulgence. Harold represents himself flamboyantly as a man without human ties, but the narrator seems staunchly aware of himself as an Englishman abroad. The 'thousand keels' in Lisbon harbour prompt a swell of pride at such a demonstration of Britain's naval power. Ponderous facetiousness fails to mask a very British distrust of the personal hygiene of foreigners:

>Ne personage of high or mean degree
>Doth care for cleanness of surtout or shirt...
>(1, 231–2)

An unsuspicious faith in the rightness of British constitutional arrangements secures the charge that Portugal is a land where 'law secures not life', and a note appended to the stanza records as 'a well-known fact' the surprising information that in 1809 Englishmen were 'daily butchered' by Portuguese assassins, murders that were connived at by British ministers cravenly anxious to avoid antagonizing an allied country. This has the unmistakable ring of an authentic expatriate myth. The church at Mafra prompts reflex references to the Inquisition and 'the Babylonian whore'. The Portuguese are consistently regarded with the contempt that powerful nations have always reserved for their weaker allies. They 'lick yet loath the hand that wields the sword', their virulence checked only by their cowardice. At this point in the poem, the narrator, bristling with English prejudice, seems an embodiment of exactly those qualities that Harold is seeking to escape:

>With thee, my bark, I'll swiftly go
>Athwart the foaming brine;

> Nor care what land thou bear'st me to,
> So not again to mine.
>
> (1, 190–3)

But rather soon the responses of Harold and the narrator become a good deal harder to disentangle, until, by the end of the second canto, the two are united in a tolerant cosmopolitanism born of a measured judgement that the inhabitants of one nation are not markedly wiser, kinder and less corrupt than the inhabitants of any other.

The stanzas on Cintra are crucial in bringing about this change, for this is the first occasion when Byron employs a syntax that confuses his two characters. The thoughts on the Convention are presented as the narrator's until, at their conclusion, Byron adds, 'So deem'd the Childe'. It may seem an inconsequential confusion because the Convention of Cintra had the peculiar virtue of having provoked a national sense of outrage in which Tory, Whig and Radical seemed to join equally. Any treaty that united in indignation Wordsworth and Cobbett must be granted a rare power to unify national sentiment.[16] Nevertheless, it is in these stanzas that the 'singular turn of sentiment' that Jeffrey found so distinctive in *Childe Harold* first reveals itself:

> And ever since that martial synod met,
> Britannia sickens, Cintra! at thy name;
> And folks in office at the mention fret,
> And fain would blush, if blush they could, for shame.
>
> (1, 306–9)

The mode is satirical, but it is a satire in which anger is less apparent than a kind of levity. The clash between the high-sounding 'Britannia' and the 'folks' who misgovern her does not secure a distinction between the greatness of the nation and the paltriness of the ministers because Britannia herself is a comical figure, caught in one of her periodic fits of moral indignation. A calculated aristocratic hauteur has been developed until it seems to have embraced in its contempt the entire realm of public and political life. It is an attitude recurrent in the poem, though not sustained. But it does alert the reader to the problem that dominates the first canto of the poem.

In travelling through Spain and Portugal Byron was visiting the theatre in which the fate of Europe was being decided, but he travelled as a tourist, as a spectator rather than an actor. The problem that the canto addresses is not in the end the problem of what policy should be followed in the Peninsula, but the problem of how the events there should be looked at. This becomes clear enough in the stanzas that Jeffrey singled out for praise, the stanzas on Talavera, the site of Wellington's first great Spanish victory, and the site that had prompted Croker to write what had become the best-known poem on the Spanish war. This scene, like most scenes in *Childe Harold*, prompts reflections so various that they end in bewilderment. There is the shame of the non-participant who can only watch helplessly while his 'brethren' die, there is an excited sense that modern warfare with its muskets and cannon has generated a new and terrible sublime, as well as a recognition that such a war in which 'thousands cease to breathe' at each volley has robbed death in battle of all distinction, there is hatred of the 'tyrants' at whose behest such battles are fought, and there is a response to the soldiers themselves compounded oddly of wonderment and contempt. The soldiers of three nations:

> Are met – as if at home they could not die –
> To feed the crow on Talavera's plain,
> And fertilize the field that each pretends to gain.
> (1, 447–9)

In the end, the point about Talavera is that there is no way of looking at it:

> By Heaven! it is a splendid sight to see
> (For one who hath no friend, no brother there)
> Their rival scarfs of mix'd embroidery,
> Their various arms that glitter in the air!
> (1, 432–5)

To respond to such splendour is to be inhuman, to fail to respond to it is to be blind. In the face of such scenes the poet's heroic aspirations are in irremediable conflict with his moral sense, and at that moment the central theme of the first canto is revealed.

As he tours the field, imagining the battle in which so many died, Byron becomes the representative of all those countrymen of his who eagerly scanned their newspapers for the latest bulletin from the Peninsula, who triumphed in the news of each victory and grieved over every fresh defeat; of Scott, for example, who kept a map of Europe on his study wall, marking with flags the positions of the armies, and grounded his faith that Napoleon would ultimately be defeated on Wellington and the Peninsular army. Byron did not simply travel through Spain, he travelled through the map of his countrymen's imaginings. Like them he is an observer of war, not a participant, and it is his own position as an uninvolved spectator that he eventually turns to scrutinize.

The one extended digression in the first canto is the description of the cockney pleasures of a London Sunday, when the 'spruce citizen, wash'd artizan, / And smug apprentice gulp their weekly air'. Their pastimes seem humdrum but innocent in comparison with the sabbath recreation at Seville, the bull-fight. But Robert Gleckner has suggested that we ought to be more struck by the similarity than the differences: 'The same corruption sits in both societies, and in each it is finally love, the human heart, that is its victim.'[17] But Byron's point is surely more specific. The bull-fight unites the inhabitants of Seville – 'Young, old, high, low, at once the same diversion share' – and it is appalling that any society should find its cohesion in a common relish for witnessed pain, but it is not clear how, in this, Seville is distinct from Britain, where the spruce citizens and the 'ribbon'd fair' of London have found their community in a shared fascination with the carnage on the battlefields of Spain.

Canto 1 is set for the most part on the European mainland, Canto 2 is a sea canto. In Canto 1 the poem is confined to the peripheries of a Europe over which Napoleon's armies held sway, but in Canto 2 Byron records how he travelled freely through the Mediterranean, for Nelson's victory at Trafalgar had made the Mediterranean a British sea, and confirmed Britain's status as the 'ocean queen'. But a more important difference is that in the second canto the focus shifts from violence to power, from war to empire. The salient fact about the Europe through which Byron travelled was that its map had simplified. The old map with its chequerboard of national boundaries had been rendered obsolete by a war in which Europe had been divided into two competing spheres of influence, a state of affairs that is only rendered more apparent by the fact that Byron's travels took place largely within the dominions of a third empire, the Ottoman. Turkey was already the sick man of Europe, enfeebled by long years of war with Russia, and forced to rely for its security on a defensive alliance with either Britain or France, aware that both these powers would sacrifice Turkish interests if the opportunity should arise to secure the more important prize of an alliance with the Russians. The Ottoman empire remained largely intact, but it was preserved not by its own strength but by the refusal of either of the great powers to countenance the Turkish dominions being yielded to the other. Canto 2 is a meditation on the imperial ambitions of Britain and of France, of the two powers competing to be the dominant force in Europe.

Byron's crucial tactic is to place contemporary history within a vast historical panorama. The imperial pretensions of Britain and of France are seen from the perspective of the debilitated fading empire of the Ottomans and the long ago extinguished empire of Athens. The monuments of Ancient Greece prompt Byron, as they had prompted almost every traveller before him, to ask, 'Where are thy men of might? thy grand in soul?', and to answer 'Gone – glimmering through the dream of things that were'.[18] Greece is for him, as it was for others, a nation shrunk into a memento mori, its ruined temples an emblem of the mortality of the temple of reason, the human skull:

> Look on its broken arch, its ruin'd wall,
> Its chambers desolate, and portals foul:
> Yes, this was once Ambition's airy hall,
> The dome of Thought, the palace of the Soul...
> (2, 46–9)

But Byron's meditation is given extra point by all the bodies that 'feed the crow on Talavera's plain' in order that some general can claim a tract of land, when the truth is that no one can:

> call with truth one span of earth their own,
> Save that wherein at last they crumble bone by bone.
> (1, 457–8)

And similarly the fate that has befallen the Greeks and that is slowly but certainly befalling the Turks, the thought that strikes Byron as he gazes at the Parthenon, gains a sharper relevance in a Europe that is being torn apart by the rival imperial ambitions of Britain and France:

> 'Twas Jove's – 'tis Mahomet's – and other creeds
> Will rise with other years...

In the end, Byron's meditations have less in common with the similar reflections that Greece prompted in almost all classically educated travellers than with Mrs Barbauld's reflections in her poem, *Eighteen Hundred and Eleven*.[19] For Mrs Barbauld England is a nation exhausted by war and polluted by greed, its place amongst the nations of the world about to be usurped by younger, more vigorous states. She imagines how some day, in the not too distant future, a pilgrimage to London will inspire in the traveller the same emotions that are aroused by a tour amidst the dilapidated monuments of Ancient Greece:

> Pensive and thoughtful shall the wanderers greet
> Each splendid square, and still, untrodden street,
> Or of some broken turret, mined by time,
> The broken stairs with perilous steps shall climb,
> Thence stretch their view the wide horizon round,
> By scattered hamlets trace its ancient bound,
> And, choked no more by fleets, fair Thames survey
> Through reeds and sedge pursue his idle way.

The second canto of *Childe Harold* is a meditation on the transience of all empires, and hence on the futility of the wars that are fought to secure them.

It is in Greece, too, that Byron finds, as he rides across the plain of Marathon, his type of the just war, the only war to which he can give a wholehearted assent, the war fought by a nation to preserve its own independence. He urges such a war on the citizens of modern Greece:

> Hereditary bondsmen! know ye not
> Who would be free themselves must strike the blow?
>   (2, 721–2)

But, even as it is announced, the stirring sentiment rings disquietingly hollow, and it is soon countered by a weary acceptance that the process of historical decline is all but irreversible:

> A thousand years scarce serves to form a state;
> An hour may lay it in the dust: and when
> Can man its shatter'd splendour renovate,
> Recall its virtues back, and vanquish Time and Fate?
>   (2, 797–800)

It is not only, not even primarily, the degradation of the modern Greek character that will prevent the Greeks from reasserting their independence. In the sober medium of a prose note, Byron's optimism extends no further than a hope that the Greeks 'may be subjects without being slaves'. Significantly, he limits his aspirations for Greece to a wish that it may be granted the status of the British colonies, which 'are not independent, but they are free and industrious'. In 1811, the ideal of nationhood, of Europe as a confederation of free and independent states – the ideal on which Byron's political thought, like the thought of all those who called themselves Whigs and looked back to Fox as their political father, relied for its coherence – seemed already obsolete, an ideal that had become irrelevant in a Europe that was no longer made up of nations, but divided between empires.

If Greece remained for Byron 'haunted, holy ground' it was in part because it was in Greece that his own political ideal of republican independence had first been embodied, but it was also, and more importantly, because Greece was peculiarly the country of poetry, the land of Parnassus. The ideal of art, unlike the ideal of national independence, might seem immune from the war between Britain and France. Lord Elgin's function within the poem is to demonstrate that this is not the case. In stripping the Parthenon of its friezes, Elgin offered a lively demonstration that art offers no sanctuary from a world of power. In Greece Elgin did no more than imitate what Napoleon had done in Italy. The Porte in Constantinople was too reliant on the power of British arms to deny Elgin the permission he needed. Elgin's excuse was that it was necessary to remove the sculptures to preserve them, his motive was that the sculptures might inspire a new school of British art, but he justified his action on the simple ground that if the sculptures had not been seized by him, they would inevitably have been seized by the French. Lord Elgin's activities, the fact itself that the marbles were transported to Britain by British warships, afforded an ample proof that art could no longer claim to transcend politics in a world in which the work of art had become the most prized trophy of success in war.[20]

If in Europe possession of works of art was contested between Britain and France, in Britain itself art, more particularly literature, became a site for the competition between parties. During the war years it seemed impossible to reflect on events in Europe without being accused of subordinating the exalted duty of the artist to the paltry interest of party. In his review of Scott's *Roderick*, Jeffrey began by insisting that it can never be the proper function of poetry 'to celebrate the heroes of the last Gazette'. Poetry, his implication is, should address the timeless and the universal, and therefore 'there can be no successful poetry upon subjects of this description'.[21] His view seems entirely opposed to the position of the reviewer in *The British Critic*, who welcomed *The Battle of Albuera*, a particularly feeble war poem, on the ground that it could not 'fail to please every true patriot and lover of poetry'.²² This reviewer seems so confident that love of country and love of poetry are compatible that he is scarcely prepared to distinguish between them. Scott, too, seems quite at odds with Jeffrey when he praised Croker for refusing to share 'the apparent apathy of our poets and rhymers to the events which are passing over them'. For Scott, the avoidance of the merely topical which Jeffrey believed essential if poetry was not to be degraded into a form of patriotic journalism in itself condemns poetry to triviality by preventing the poet from confronting the most important events of the time. But the debate about the proper subject matter of poetry always reveals itself as no more than a pretext for the real dispute, which is not between rival aesthetic principles but rival parties. Jeffrey's real objection to Scott's *Roderick* is not to its subject matter but to Scott's tactic of displaying his partisanship in the guise of simple patriotism. In reserving his praise for Wellington alone, and passing over in silence the heroic death of Sir John Moore at Corunna 'Scott has permitted the spirit of party to stand in the way, not only of poetical justice, but of patriotic and generous feeling'.²³ It was not only Whig reviewers who showed themselves painfully sensitive to 'the spirit of party' as it revealed itself in the work of Tory poets. Mrs Barbauld was roundly advised by *The Quarterly* reviewer who noticed her *Eighteen Hundred and Eleven* to go back to writing the children's verse for which a woman was qualified and to desist from writing party pamphlets.²⁴ Similarly, the *Quarterly* interrupted an exuberant demonstration that *Portugal*, a poem reflecting on the Peninsular war by the radical Whig Lord George Grenville, was utterly incomprehensible long enough to indicate that the reviewer had understood the poem very well, and that its defeatism was a lamentable example of how poetry might be degraded by placing it at the service of party.²⁵

Childe Harold was unmistakably a Whig poem. It would be possible to draw from its first two cantos a fairly full compendium of the opinions that defined the Whig party in the years after Fox's death: a distrust of professional armies, an acceptance of the right of each nation to determine its own form of government, religious tolerance verging on scepticism, a championing of Liberty more remarkable for the confidence of its rhetoric than for the precision with which Liberty is defined.²⁶ Byron had after all travelled in order to prepare himself to take his place in Parliament, and he seems to have timed the publication of *Childe Harold* so that it coincided with the beginning of his active political career.²⁷ Byron's publisher, Murray, was evidently concerned that the poem was too explicitly partisan. He urged Byron fruitlessly to alter 'some expressions concerning Spain and Portugal which...do not harmonize with the now prevalent feeling'.[28] Jeffrey evidently found the tenor of the poem's politics entirely congenial, but he, like Murray, thought the 'general strain of these sentiments...very little likely to attract popularity in the present temper of the country'. In particular, he noted that Byron spoke 'in a very slighting and sarcastic manner of wars, and victories, and military heroes in general'. George Ellis in the *Quarterly* was, as Jeffrey predicted, alert to the poem's failure to offer its support to the war effort. He quoted the lines expressing Harold's contempt for 'the bravo's trade', and was 'induced to ask, not without some anxiety and alarm, whether such are indeed the opinions which a British peer entertains of a British army'. Mrs Barbauld and Lord George Grenville had provoked virulent abuse by a rather less emphatic expression of similar sentiments, and yet, surprisingly, Ellis goes on to welcome Byron's poem very cordially. Byron's own response to the reviews of his poem was entirely just: 'it would ill become me to quarrel with their very slight degree of censure, when, perhaps, if they had been less kind they had been more candid.'[29] *Childe Harold*, so far as I have been able to discover, was the single example of a poem that addressed the large public issues of the time, and yet escaped being immediately categorized by reviews hostile to its political sentiments as a mere ebullition of party spirit. Even more strikingly, although its posture seemed, as Jeffrey himself felt called upon to admit, 'very little likely to attract popularity in the present temper of the country', the poem took so immediately that its success was an established fact even before many of the reviews had appeared.

The reviewers chose to present *Childe Harold* as characterized by what Jeffrey calls 'singularity' and Ellis terms, slightly more astringently, 'caprice' rather than by partisanship, and in this they were surely properly responsive to the poem. For Jerome McGann, in the most persuasive account of *Childe Harold* yet to appear, that 'singularity' is the poem's true subject, for in *Childe Harold* opinions function only to map a private space. The poem ends when the death of Edleston unites the narrator and his hero in a bitter misanthropy that accepts the public world merely as a contemptible masquerade, of use only to disguise the unbearable tenderness of an inner life given over to the nurturing of a quite private grief. If, as I have argued, the poem is a pilgrimage to Parnassus, a quest for a stance from which the poet can address the public world in a true poem rather than a 'worthless lay' or 'transient song', then the poem would seem to end in a confession of utter failure. The defining condition of human life is to 'be alone on earth, as I am now', and the poet can have no other function than to speak out of his own privacy and to find a response, perhaps, from the privacy of his reader. The first canto ends with an elegy for the death of Byron's schoolfriend, John Wingfield, who died in Spain as a soldier, but of disease rather than in battle. Byron honours his 'unlaurel'd death' in a quiet, troubled stanza that recognizes Wingfield both as a friend and as a compatriot, and finds a precarious relationship between the two. But with Edleston's death no such connection is possible. The poem, it seems, has conducted its readers through much of Europe, from Portugal to Spain, Malta, Albania, Greece and Turkey, only to remind them at the last that public affairs are utterly insignificant in comparison with private grief.

It was an accident that Byron, on his return to England, was afflicted by the deaths of three people close to him, 'the parent, friend', and Edleston, 'the more than friend'. His poem can end so appropriately in mourning for those deaths because the tour through Europe has not yielded the firm grasp of international affairs that Byron had hoped to gain: it has resulted only in confusion. McGann prizes the poem's inconsistencies of opinion, because inconsistency is more capable than coherence of charting an idiosyncratic temperament. But Byron's inconsistencies are at least as characteristic of his party as they are of himself: he is never more truly a Whig than in his bewilderment. It was not simply that the Whigs were divided between those like Lord Holland who, following his tour through Spain and Portugal, had become an enthusiastic advocate of the Peninsular campaign,[30] and those like Samuel Whitbread who had demanded ever since 1808 that peace negotiations be entered into at once. It was more significant that such divisions arose because Foxite principles gave no clue as to what European policy the Whigs should recommend. It was unclear whether the presence of the British army on the Peninsula was an unwarrantable interference in the internal affairs of another country or a proper use of British arms to secure the freedom of the Spanish and Portuguese to choose their own governments. A good Whig might plausibly take either view, and the party could maintain whatever unity it had only by seeming to entertain both positions.[31] Nor was this merely a political stratagem. The Whig leader Lord Grey allowed Ponsonby to exercise nominal leadership of the Whig party in Parliament during these years, and chose himself to retire to his estates. Only rarely could he be cajoled into visiting London. His disillusion seems to have arisen less from despair of ever achieving power as despair at the impossibility of finding a foreign policy.

It is not a coincidence that the trajectory of Grey's career in these years, his virtual retreat from public to private life, is reflected in the trajectory of Byron's poem, for Byron's poem frankly displays the humane, intelligent and ultimately incoherent responses to the European situation that Grey despaired of formulating as a policy. *Childe Harold* is a Whig poem that recognizes bitterly that Whig principles cannot be coherently applied to the Europe through which Byron conducts his reader, a Whig poem that fails to find a relation between its Whig principles and any possible exercise of real power. Hence the appropriateness of the poem's hero who travels in a futile attempt to escape himself, and whose travels serve only to confirm him in his own gloom. It was not to be expected that a staunch Tory such as George Ellis would be prompted to any very extreme indignation by a poem that acknowledges so frankly the impotence of the principles that it espouses. In *Childe Harold*, Whiggism has become what Jeffrey recognizes as a 'singularity' and Ellis as 'caprice'. It seems an unpromising accomplishment, but it was the achievement that secured the poem's extraordinary success.

Shortly after the poem's publication, the Duchess of Devonshire wrote to a friend giving the latest London news: 'The subject of conversation, of curiosity, of enthusiasm almost, one might say, of the moment is not Spain or Portugal, Warriors or Patriots, but Lord Byron.'[32] She chose her alternatives carefully. The 'singularity' that Jeffrey 'doubted whether to rank among the defects or the attractions' of the poem secured its success not in spite but because of its failure to 'harmonise', as Murray put it, 'with the now prevalent feeling'. *Childe Harold* offered its first readers an opportunity to escape from communal sentiment, it offered release from the patriotic demand that the nation in wartime consent to an impersonal unanimity. In Scott's hands the romance had become the most powerful expression of the unity of national sentiment. Byron rewrote the romance in a manner that, by removing his readers from the 'crowd' and reminding them that each stands 'alone on earth', bestowed on them once more their own irreducible individuality. It was an achievement born out of despair. A Europe that no longer seemed to admit the possibility of being formed into a confederation of free nations might at least allow the freedom of the individual self.

Childe Harold was prompted by Byron's bleak recognition of the impotence of his own political principles and by weariness of a war that seemed as if it would never end.[33] Within a year of the publication of the poem, Napoleon was embarked on his disastrous retreat from

Moscow, and Wellington was preparing to mount the final assault that would end with his army driving into south-western France. The victory of the British and their allies was no longer in doubt, and all that remained to be decided was its extent. But the stance that Byron had developed in response to war, his subordination of public sentiment to individual feeling, proved equally fascinating to a nation at peace. It was Scott's poetry, and the poetry of his imitators, that lost its hold on the public. Scott was himself one of the first to recognize it. In his 1830 introduction to *Rokeby* he recalls how he had been 'astonished at the power' of the first two cantos of *Childe Harold* in their expression of 'those passions which agitate the human heart with most violence'. The time had passed when what was needed was to steel the heart, and to persuade his readers that their individual passions must be subsumed within the expression of a single, all-important national purpose, and, recognizing this, Scott abandoned poetry for the novel, abdicating his position as 'the Monarch of Parnassus' in favour of the man who had dubbed him with that title[34]: 'There would have been little wisdom in measuring my forces with so formidable an antagonist.'[35]

Part Three
England in 1819

Introduction
Peter Bell the Third

On 16 August 1819, a gathering of some 30 000 people met at St Peter's Field in Manchester to petition for reform, and to hear an address from the radical orator, Henry Hunt. They were attacked by the local militia. Eleven of the demonstrators were killed, and several hundred injured. After the attack two of the militia men walked over the field, looking with some satisfaction at the results of their action. 'This was our Waterloo', said one, and was overheard by a *Times* reporter, supplying the name by which the events of that day have been remembered, the Peterloo massacre. It was one of those events, like the Amritsar massacre, the Sharpeville killings in South Africa, the killings on the campus of Kent State, and Bloody Sunday in Londonderry, that achieved from the very first a symbolic status. Such events have the power to polarize the politics of a nation.

'It is no longer a question between Ins and Outs, nor between Whigs and Tories. It is between those who have something to lose, and those who have everything to gain by a dissolution of society', wrote Southey.[1] Keats, who had less to lose than many, shared Southey's analysis however much he differed from him in his sympathies: 'This is no contest between whig and tory – but between right and wrong.'[2] At moments like this the distinction between poetry and politics disappears. In his very first report of the Peterloo massacre Leigh Hunt quoted the most notorious line from Wordworth's 'Thanksgiving Ode', 'carnage is [God's] daughter', ascribing the sentiment to 'a pathetic court poet'.[3] *Blackwood's* responded with a tastelessly jocose little piece by Christopher North based on the pretence that Henry and Leigh Hunt were near relations. 'No-one', we are told, 'can listen for five minutes to the oral eloquence of Henry Hunt without being reminded of the written wisdom of Leigh', and this is to be expected, for 'the

Cockney School of Politics...is so intimately connected with the Cockney School of Poetry, that it is almost impossible to describe the one without using many expressions equally applicable to the other'.[4] The *Edinburgh* allowed space for its usual diatribe against Cobbett and the other purveyors of twopenny trash, the 'wicked and contemptible set of public writers' who had undermined the confidence of the people in the Whigs as their natural leaders, but its attack is principally directed against 'those unhappy alarmists who see a civil war in every provincial tumult', and singled out from amongst this group are 'the Laureate and his tuneful friends'.[5]

It might seem that one of the effects of Peterloo was to divide the literary world along party lines more emphatically than at any time since the pamphlet war of the 1790s. But, in fact, the two situations were very different. The 'radical', the 'Tory', and the 'Whig' reviews were forced by Peterloo to confront a new politics, the chief architect of which was Cobbett. It was a politics that could not easily be accommodated by the old political groupings, because in the new politics ideological differences, differences of opinion, were subordinated to differences of class. Whigs might, when it seemed opportune, dignify the unrepresented majority of the nation as 'the people', Tories might recall Burke's description of that same group as 'the swinish multitude', but Whig and Tory alike assumed their own distance from the uneducated and propertyless populace. The new politics was not so great an embarrassment to them as it was to the small group of radicals or reformers whose authority derived from their claim to represent the interests of those who, as yet, had no vote of their own. Cobbett and Henry Hunt, as they well knew, posed a less immediate threat to the Tory government than they did to the status of the reformers who grouped themselves under the leadership of Sir Francis Burdett. It was this uncomfortable fact that Christopher North gleefully seized on in *Blackwood's*. Why was it, he asked, that Leigh Hunt could never mention Henry Hunt without giving vent to 'some malicious sarcasm against that worthy kinsman of his', whereas, 'He talks at times of the Wolseleys, the Burdetts and the Shellys [sic], in terms which would almost persuade one that he really entertained some feelings of decent reverence for the old phylarchic aristocracies of England'?

Leigh Hunt had established *The Examiner* at a time when his claim to political authority required him to assert his own gentlemanly status. He developed a journalistic manner that, however its pretensions might be mocked, insisted on his own cultural qualifications to enter the political debate. By 1819, Cobbett in particular had developed a quite different political prose which gained its authority precisely by jettisoning all the cultural baggage that might serve to implicate him with the modes of thinking of his political enemies. That is surely why by 1819 Leigh Hunt cannot allude to matters of class without betraying his embarrassment. He wishes that Henry Hunt would be 'a little less coarse' and immediately and inconsequentially adds that 'the charge of coarseness itself is contemptible from the mouths of his aristocratical enemies'. He upbraids the editor of the *Courier* for believing that he discredits the reformers by referring to them as 'tradesmen', but himself cannot mention the *Courier* without adding that its owner began life as a tailor, or the *Quarterly* without repeating that its editor, Gifford, had been an apprentice shoemaker.[6] Hunt consistently exposes his unhappy sensitivity to the social distinctions that he affects to despise.

In Hunt's first report of Peterloo Wordsworth is angrily dismissed as 'a pathetic court poet', a poet who had once championed the poor, but had since sold his principles for a pension, and, just the year before, had busied himself in assisting the Lansdowne interest to retain their hold on his Westmorland constituency against the challenge of the reformer, Brougham. But the poem Wordsworth had chosen to publish in 1819, the ballad, *Peter Bell*, could scarcely have been less 'courtly'. His decision at last to publish a poem, which, as he pointed out in his preface, he had first conceived in 1798, the year of *Lyrical Ballads*, was evidently a defiant gesture directed at the growing number of those, like Hunt, who accused him of having betrayed the principles on which his early poetry was written, and it succeeded in wrong-footing his assailants. Keats's friend, Reynolds, for example, who contrived to publish his parody of Wordsworth's poem before the poem itself had yet appeared, is reduced to poking vulgar fun at Wordsworth's habit of writing poems about people with plebeian, unliterary names. *Peter Bell* is associated in his derision with early poems such as *Goody Blake* and *Harry Gill* and *The Idiot Boy*, with the odd result that the young London Radical seems trivially snobbish in comparison with the poet he is attempting to ridicule.

Leigh Hunt did not find *Peter Bell* funny. Unlike Reynolds, he seems to have recognized the publication as an aggressive as well as a defensive act, and he was provoked by it to his most savage review of a poem by Wordsworth. For him, the poem was a 'didactic little horror', a 'Methodistical nightmare', the story of a man brought to 'a proper united sense of hare-bells and hell-fire', when he happens to overhear 'a Damnation Sermon, which a Methodist is vociferating'. Throughout the first half of 1819, *The Examiner* led a campaign for the defence of

Richard Carlile, the radical publisher of Tom Paine's *Age of Reason*, who was facing a series of blasphemy charges that had been brought against him by the Society for the Suppression of Vice. The defence of Carlile was accompanied by a series of articles attacking Methodism.[7] This was no coincidence. In 1819 the campaign for parliamentary reform had finally established itself as a mass popular movement. Reform meetings attracted huge numbers, culminating in the 30 000 who gathered in Manchester. But another popular movement was growing still faster, a movement founded by John Wesley, a High Tory, that demanded of its members absolute political quiescence. In Manchester, for example, the Methodist leadership expelled any of their congregation found to be active in reform politics. Methodism and Parliamentary reform were the two great popular movements of 1819, and they were rival movements.[8] Southey was at work on a sympathetic biography of Wesley, finally published in 1820. Wordsworth's decision to publish *Peter Bell* must have seemed to Leigh Hunt confirming evidence that the Lake Poets had joined in a conspiracy to lend their support to one popular movement as a means of assisting in the suppression of the other, as a way of substituting for Henry Hunt vociferating his demands for reform a Methodist vociferating a damnation sermon.

In 1819 Leigh Hunt found himself in an uncomfortable position, his politics usurped by a group of Radicals, foremost amongst them Henry Hunt and Cobbett, who seemed to him dangerous and vulgar demagogues, and his own brand of genially tolerant deism in flat contradiction to the most popular religious movement of his time. It is a position most comprehensively summarized not in any of his own writings, but in his friend, Shelley's, *Peter Bell the Third*. Shelley sent the poem to Hunt in November, 1819, asking him to arrange for it to be published anonymously by Ollier.[9] Hunt seems not to have approached any publisher. In September, he had sent Hunt *The Mask of Anarchy* hoping that Hunt would publish it in *The Examiner*,[10] but Hunt declined. When he finally released it, in 1832, he explained that he had judged it too inflammatory to publish at the time. It seems unlikely that he could have had a similar motive for suppressing *Peter Bell the Third*. More probably, Hunt thought it unwise to arrange for the publication of an anonymous poem inspired, as its preface admitted, by the reviews of Wordsworth's and Reynolds's poems in *The Examiner*, dedicated to Hunt's friend, Thomas Moore, centrally concerned with London social life and London politics, and preoccupied with precisely those issues that had dominated *The Examiner* in 1819. The preface with its playful descriptions of 'Mr Examiner Hunt' as a 'murderous & smiling villain', and an 'odious thief, liar, scoundrel, coxcomb & monster' would surely only have confirmed Hunt's fear that if the poem had been published it would have been widely assumed to be by Hunt himself.

Nothing brings *Peter Bell the Third* closer to Hunt than the acute and troubled awareness of social distinctions that the poem repeatedly registers.[11] We are reminded that dandies share with evangelicals the habit of oiling their hair, and are invited to savour the distinction made by the difference between the variety of oil that each group favours. Wordsworth is ridiculed by being represented as a footman humbly waiting behind his master's chair at table. The comedy of his being placed in this menial station is heightened by the presence of Coleridge sitting at the table as an invited guest. Like Reynolds, Shelley makes play of the disparity between Peter's 'individual mind', to which he pays noble tribute, and the comically humdrum materials on which it feeds: ditches, fences, milk pans, pedlars and old parsons. Rydal Mount is the reward Wordsworth has earned by his political apostasy, but Shelley's description of the house with its 'genteel drive' neatly laid with 'sifted gravel' swithers uncertainly between radical contempt for the earnings of placemen and aristocratic scorn of bourgeois gentrification.

Shelley shared with Hunt a dislike of the puritanical asceticism that they detected in the Lake Poets, hence the attack on Wordsworth as 'unsexual'. But again the attack is uneasy in its direction. Shelley is eager to distinguish the frank sexuality that he espouses from the behaviour of fashionable rakes, 'Things whose trade is, over ladies / To lean, and flirt, and stare, and simper', but he cannot avoid exposing the hint of gentlemanly prejudice that glints from the word 'trade'. When Wordsworth is represented as comically reverent in his dealings with nature, daring to do no more than touch 'the hem of Nature's shift', his timidity is laughed at with the kind of hearty masculinity that one associates with Fielding. 'Tempt not again my deepest bliss', says Nature. Burns makes an appearance as a sort of poetic Tom Jones next to whom Wordsworth is revealed as a Blifil, and finally Wordsworth is categorized, with schoolboy relish, as 'a male prude', that is, an embodiment of an unpleasant and female type. *Peter Bell the Third* is one of Shelley's few genuinely funny poems, but its humour is a product of exactly those things that made Shelley distrust comedy: it is a humour that exploits the distinctions – between men and women, rich and poor, the educated and the uneducated – that in his other writings Shelley is at pains to deny.[12]

Shelley silently borrows from Cobbett his understanding of 'paper money' as a 'scheme' devised to service the National Debt, but his explicit references to Cobbett are, like Hunt's, primly disapproving, warning against any indulgence in 'Cobbett's snuff, revenge'. His central tactic is an entirely conventional one:

> There is a Castles and a Canning,
> A Cobbett and a Castlereagh...
> (152–3)

The informant and agent provocateur, Castles, properly Castle,[13] Cobbett, and the government ministers are, the alliteration suggests, morally equivalent and practically in league, engaged in a single conspiracy against the peace of the nation.

Shelley follows Hunt again in associating Wordsworth with Methodism. The whole of *Peter Bell the Third* parodies Wordsworth's 'damnation sermon' in *Peter Bell*, but substitutes for the Methodist emphasis on divine retribution a humanist theology in which we are 'damned by one another' rather than by God. Wordsworthian imagination is characterized as a variant form of the 'inner illumination' demanded by Methodists, and Wordsworth himself 'dies' to be reborn in his imagination as a countryman of Wesley's, a Lincolnshireman:

> Peter thought he had cronies dear,
> Brothers, sisters, cousins, cronies,
> In the fens of Lincolnshire...
> (111–13)

By categorizing Wordsworth as a Methodist, Shelley makes him the representative poet of popular Toryism. But when Shelley parodies the notorious lines from the 'Thanksgiving Ode', Wordsworth becomes a colleague of Cobbett's. 'It is curious to observe', Shelley adds in a note, 'how often extremes meet', and goes on to claim that Wordsworth, because he sanctions the use of violence 'is indeed a sort of metrical Cobbett' (note to 652).

Shelley described *Peter Bell the Third* as a 'party squib',[14] a poem written directly into the polarized politics of England in 1819. It is odd, then, that it should work not to expose but to collapse distinctions between parties, to argue, somewhat feebly, that the political differences between Wordsworth, Cobbett and Castlereagh are apparent rather than real. 1819 was, Shelley knew, a dark time, and when darkness falls differences are obliterated:

> when day begins to thicken,
> None knows a pigeon from a crow...
> (250-1)

Wordsworth is the representative man of such a year precisely because he is indecipherable, 'a walking paradox', a 'pathetic court poet' who could choose that moment to publish a ballad as defiantly unadorned as *Peter Bell*. Shelley's poem may begin as 'a party squib', but it makes the sad discovery that the events of the year have left Shelley, like Leigh Hunt, like all the 'genteel reformers', with no party that he can call his own, as the spokesman only of a powerless 'few':

> And some few, like we know who,
> Damned – but God alone knows why –
> To believe their minds are given
> To make this ugly Hell a Heaven;
> In which faith they live and die.
> (242-6)

So it is that a poem that begins by engaging in the war between the poets ends like *Adonais*, mournfully surveying a world in which to be a poet at all is to expose oneself to the slanders of a vicious public opinion, a world in which all poets are united as victims. In the poem's sixth part Peter Bell is driven mad by the reviewers, charged with a catalogue of grotesque offences that seem to have in common only their comic outrageousness. Wordsworth was, of course, notoriously sensitive to criticism, but consider the mildest of the charges:

> What does the rascal mean or hope,
> No longer imitating Pope,
> In that barbarian Shakespeare poking?
> (475-7)

This is an imaginary accusation as levelled at Wordsworth, but an accurate summary of the kind of ridicule that Leigh Hunt, Wordsworth's antagonist, had exposed himself to by his prefaces. A stanza that Shelley thought better of tells how Peter was hailed as an 'impious libertine', who 'commits incest with his sister / In ruined Abbies'. Shelley scored out this stanza, surely, because he feared that Byron might not be amused by it.¹⁵ Another reviewer exclaims:

> Is incest not enough,
> And must there be adultery too?
> Grace after meat?
> (478–80)

The lines closely echo a passage from the *Quarterly*'s review of Hunt's *Foliage*, that evidently refer to Shelley's *Laon and Cythna*: 'he, if such there be, who thinks even adultery vapid unless he can render it more exquisitely poignant by adding incest to it'.¹⁶ In that same review, the reviewer hinted at his knowledge of the painful personal events that had led to Shelley's leaving England. It is hard not to think that those same events were in Shelley's mind when he devised the most fantastic of all the reviewers' charges:

> Peter seduced Mrs. Foy's daughter,
> Then drowned the Mother in Ullswater,
> The last thing as he went to bed.
> (470–2)

It is hard to believe that Shelley could have written those lines without thinking of the daughter of another famous woman, and of a mother, drowned not in Ullswater but the Serpentine, and to think of such things is to transform the lines – comic high spirits evaporate leaving a residue of hysterical bitterness. Wordsworth is no longer the butt of Shelley's attack, but a fellow victim, as much a casualty of a national mood in which taste in poetry had become simply an expression of political partisanship as Leigh Hunt, Keats, Byron, and Shelley himself.

In this, the third and final section of the book, I will focus on England in 1819, first as it is represented in the work of Byron and Shelley, and then in the work of Hunt and Keats. It was a year that culminated in the killings at Manchester that prompted Keats to write, 'This is no contest between whig and tory – but between right and wrong.' But 1819 was also the year in which the character of English politics was shown to have changed, the year in which it became apparent that political differences could no longer be disentangled from differences of class. It is a story appropriately introduced by *Peter Bell the Third*, a poem in which Shelley is forced at the last to register that his political differences from Wordsworth are in the end less important than what they have in common; a poem that begins by pillorying Wordsworth as an apostate and ends by expressing solidarity with a fellow member of the class of poets. When I speak of class politics and of the class of poets, I am, of course, using the word in two very different senses. I shall argue in this chapter that 1819 was the year in which the the one sense of the word decisively displaced the other. This section shares a title with James Chandler's recent monumental study,[17] but it shares very little else. My business in the chapters that follow is to make a single point: that in England in 1819 literature and class converged, and that they did so in the field of style.

7
Asleep in Italy: Byron and Shelley in 1819

It is an oddity that the two English poets who responded most directly to the politics of England in 1819 wrote from abroad. By the autumn of 1819, Shelley had been resident in Italy for eighteen months. Byron had been absent from England for almost half his adult life, and had not set foot on English soil since the spring of 1816. It is a fact that he muses on frequently in his letters, and almost always it prompts in him a mixed emotion. There is a proud consciousness that his residence abroad has equipped him with a wisdom unavailable to his less mobile English friends: 'L'univers est une espèce de livre, dont on n'a lu que le première page quand on n'a vu que son pays.'[1] But there is also a sad sense that England and its ways have themselves become foreign to him. In the year from 1819 to 1820 both emotions were unusually intense. Byron was actively involved with his Italian friends in the attempt to orchestrate a revolt against the Austrian occupation. His guarded references to his activities in his letters home are inflected by a heady sense of the difference between a nationalist uprising and the 'miserable squabbles'[2] that dominated English politics: 'Here you may believe there will be cutting of thrapples and something *like* a civil buffeting' (7, 76). But in England his friends and school contemporaries were making their mark in the public world. Robert Peel was already a power in the land. Douglas Kinnaird had taken his seat in Parliament. Hobhouse, by being called before the bar of the House and committed to Newgate, had established himself as a radical hero, and gained his reward when, very soon after his release, he was triumphantly returned for Westminster. He quickly became one of Queen Caroline's closest advisers in the marital dispute that dominated English politics in 1820. Byron had made his flamboyant entry into the public world before any of them, in 1812, when he made his speeches in the Lords, but by 1819 it must have been clear that the public career that seemed to lay open before Hobhouse was no longer available to him. Any such reflection would have been the more poignant at a time when English politics seemed newly volatile. The mass campaign for Parliamentary reform that culminated with Peterloo, the death of the old king, the coronation of the new, the Cato Street conspiracy and the trial of the Queen gave to political life a dramatic character that it had not assumed for many years, but it was a drama in which Byron had no part. Hence the wistfulness behind the bravado in his repeated suggestions that he might one of these days 'come amongst you'.

Had he ever carried out his promise, he would, he knew, have entered a political landscape with which he was no longer familiar. 'Radical', he wrote to Hobhouse in April 1820, 'is a new word since my time – it was not in the political vocabulary in 1816 – when I left England – and I don't know what it means – is it uprooting?' (7, 81). Byron still considered himself a Whig. He was a member of the Whig club that Hobhouse had formed at Cambridge and he remained happy until the end of his life to 'retain', as he puts it in the Dedication of *Don Juan*, his 'buff and blue'. His political heroes were Fox and Sheridan, and his political allegiances were to Lord Holland, Fox's nephew, and Sir Francis Burdett, who had inherited Fox's Westminster seat. Holland House remained the spiritual home of the Foxite Whigs, but Burdett, whose vociferous campaigning for Parliamentary reform had separated him from the Whig party, also claimed to speak as Fox's true heir. In 1816 Byron had found it possible to side with both: he could be 'a friend to and a Voter for reform' (7, 44) without cutting his ties with his 'friends, the Whigs' (*Don Juan*, 11, 79), because the political world with which he was familiar was a world in which political differences were softened by, and subordinate to, social relationships. A Reformer like Burdett, a Whig like Lord Holland, and a Tory like Robert Peel differed in their politics, but each recognized that they shared a more important kinship, they were all gentlemen: they might be separated by the floor of the House of Commons, but they were happy to share dinner tables. Hence Byron's response to the Cato Street conspiracy, the muddle-headed plot to blow up the greater part of the Tory Cabinet at a private dinner party: 'And if they had killed poor Harrowby – in whose house I have been five hundred times – at dinners and parties – his wife is one of "the Exquisites" – and t'other fellows – what end would it have answered?' (7, 62).

Byron refers to Thistlewood and his confederates as 'these Utican conspirators'.[3] The little joke is revealing in its very feebleness.

Perturbed by such events, Byron's impulse is to invoke the education that he and Hobhouse and Harrowby and Peel had shared, the culture that they held in common, and that ought to distinguish them from the likes of Thistlewood. But by the end of March 1820, when he wrote this letter, he was already aware that English political life had changed dramatically, and it was John Cam Hobhouse, its recipient, who had done most to educate him in the new political realities. The easiest way to understand the new state of affairs is to survey the three elections held in the Westminster seat in the years from 1818 to 1820. Westminster, in which every male householder was a voter, had an unusually wide electorate. It was represented by two members. Burdett's position was unchallengeable, and it was his habit to choose his own running-mate. Since each elector had two votes, the result should have been the election of two members favourable to reform. In 1818, Burdett nominated Douglas Kinnaird, Byron's friend and banker, and the issue was almost disastrous. Cobbett furiously accused Burdett of treating Westminster as if it was his own rotten borough. At his instigation, two rival candidates were put up, Major Cartwright, the veteran campaigner for Parliamentary reform, and Henry Hunt. The Whigs saw their opportunity in this split between the reformers, and fielded not one but two Whig candidates. It seemed for a while as if Burdett himself was in danger of losing his seat. His election was only secured when Kinnaird agreed to stand down. In the end Burdett was elected safely enough, together with the Whig, Sir Samuel Romilly. The next year, following Romilly's suicide, there was a by-election. Burdett nominated Hobhouse, but again his nominee was furiously opposed in print by Cobbett and in person by Hunt and Cartwright, and the result was that Hobhouse was defeated by the Whig George Lamb, Lady Caroline's brother-in-law. As Byron remarked: 'With the Burdettites divided – and the Whigs & Tories united – what else could be expected?' (6, 107). But to Hunt and Cobbett the exercise had been entirely successful. Their interest, it is clear, was not to secure the election of two reform candidates for Westminster, but to challenge Burdett's claim to the leadership of the reform movement. In orchestrating the defeats of Kinnaird and Hobhouse they proved their power. Hobhouse succeeded in the election of 1820, but only after he had spent the intervening months forging an alliance with Hunt, Cobbett and Cartwright, the very men who had vilified him in the election of the preceding year.

Burdett had split with the Whigs over the issue of Parliamentary reform. In policy he was closer to Cobbett, closer to Henry Hunt, than he was to Lord Grey, but in one respect, and for Hunt and Cobbett it was crucial, he remained a Whig. That is, he saw himself as the true heir of Fox, his duty being to represent the unrepresented, to speak for those who could not speak for themselves – or, as Cobbett saw it, he arrogated to himself the right to act as the chief spokesman for a class with which, by his possession of immense wealth, by his education, and by his haughty aristocratic demeanour, he disclaimed any affinity. For Byron, Burdett was the chief of 'the genteel part of the reformers', a group that included of course his friends, Kinnaird and Hobhouse, who 'were all men of education – and courteous deportment' (7, 44–5), and were to be distinguished sharply from the 'pack of blackguards' led by Hunt and Cobbett. Cobbett was as sensitive as Byron to the distinction, but to him it indicated only that it was time to have done with reformers who claimed to represent the interests of those whose persons they despised. In the summer of 1819, Samuel Bamford, the weaver poet and an organizer of the Peterloo demonstration, was one of a small deputation of working men who were received by Burdett in his London house. Bamford recalls: 'His manner was dignified and civilly familiar, submitting to rather than seeking conversation with men of our class.'[4] The choice of word – class – is significant. Hunt and Cobbett were busy in these years trying to put an end to political life as Byron understood it, a life conducted by men who differed in their views but shared the same manners. For them, politics was not a conflict between opinions but a conflict between classes.

In the year that intervened between his defeat and his victory in the Westminster elections, Hobhouse worked hard to unite in his own person the two reform factions. He attended the dinner to congratulate Hunt on his return to London after Peterloo, and he orchestrated his own imprisonment by writing an inflammatory pamphlet that asked: 'What prevents the people from walking down to the House, and pulling out the members by the ears, locking up their doors, and flinging the key into the Thames?'[5] Finally, he seized the opportunity of the Queen's trial to associate himself with the broadly based coalition that came together to defend her, a coalition in which the Whig Brougham, her chief Parliamentary defender, worked together with Cobbett, who orchestrated the propaganda on her behalf in the country. The Westminster seat was his hard-earned reward. Hobhouse, like Byron, had been brought up to a quite different political life, a life that still survived for most public men. Even after he had been committed to Newgate, Peel passed him a consolatory message: 'We'll let him out at Xmas can't he contrive to say he's ill'.[6] But there was no chance of that. Hobhouse had realized that his chances of political success depended on him carefully preserving the appearance that he had, as he put it in his pamphlet, 'an instinctive horror and disgust at the very abstract idea of a borough-monger', that would necessarily prevent him from engaging in social civilities with a Tory minister.

Byron witnessed Hobhouse's manoeuvres from afar. He was at first puzzled, then angry and derisive, until at the last he seems to have arrived at the glum conviction that between him and his friend there had developed an irreconcilable political difference. 'What had you to do with those blackguard Reformers? who made you defy & leave the Whigs, and make you lose your Election' (6, 165), he asks after Hobhouse's first campaign. Hobhouse's imprisonment prompted a witty lampoon in which Hobhouse, Hobby O, found himself associated with the mob and with Cobbett, Mobby O and Cobby O. Hobhouse was offended, but Byron did not seem to grasp that Hobhouse objected not so much to Byron's rough humour as to his sending the squib to Murray, publisher of the *Quarterly* and a man always anxious to please the Tory ministry. Murray promptly had it published in the *Morning Post*, just before Hobhouse's election, as the comment of 'a noble poet...on *his quondam friend* and annotator'.[7] The thought that his friend was associating with Hunt and Cobbett more often provoked Byron's fury than his laughter. He gave Hobhouse as his considered opinion that at Peterloo the Manchester yeomanry had been guilty of murder on two counts, 'in butchering the weak', and in failing to 'cut down *Hunt*' (7, 81). Even Castlereagh was to be preferred to Hunt on the ground that 'a Gentleman scoundrel is always preferable to a vulgar one' (6, 229). Byron still occasionally entertained thoughts that he might come home and attempt to resuscitate his political career, but he was no longer sure what side he would be on: 'If I came home (which I never shall) I should take a *decided* part in politics...but am not yet quite sure *what* part' (8, 240). In the year from 1819 to 1820 Byron was forced to recognize that his support for 'reform' had come to contradict his 'contempt and abhorrence' of 'the people calling themselves reformers', and that his loyalty to his principles was now in flat contradiction to his loyalty to his class. It was a recognition that disqualified him from taking any active part in English politics, and confined his political activities to Italy and Greece, where it remained possible to champion the rights of the people without compromising his social status.

It has long been recognized, of course, that Byron's political principles were at odds with his class prejudices,[8] but it is important to make two more points. First, it was a contradiction that forced itself on his awareness quite suddenly, in the closing months of 1819, not as the consequence of a sudden access of self-knowledge, but rather of his recognition that Henry Hunt and Cobbett between them had changed the nature of English politics. Secondly, it prompted Byron to rethink both his political and his poetic principles. Hunt, Cobbett, and their associates are 'awkward butchers', 'infamous scoundrels', 'ragamuffins', 'dirty levellers' (7, pp. 62, 63, 99). But from this impressively energetic vocabulary of abuse one term emerges as dominant: they are 'blackguards', proponents of a democracy that is, truth to be told, no more than an 'Aristocracy of Blackguards' (7, pp. 44, 81, 86, 99, 107). In this period only one other public figure provokes in Byron a response so venomously intemperate, the 'little dirty blackguard KEATES' (7, 229). The coincidence in the favoured term of abuse betrays, I suspect, Byron's belief that the poetic outrage of Keats's poetry shared an origin with the political outrage of Hunt's oratory, that Cockney politics and Cockney poetry were two manifestations of the same intellectual disease.[9] The attack on Pope in which Keats had joined was an attempt to 'level' the reputation of a great poet, an expression of the same disposition that had induced Hunt to subject his friend Hobhouse to crude verbal abuse (7, 86). Hunt's and Cobbett's politics and Keats's poetry were both attempts to break down the social distinctions on which polite society and polite literature alike depended. Hence the vigour with which Byron rushed to Pope's defence in his two letters to Murray, and hence, too, their manner, in which, as Hazlitt shrewdly noticed, critical argument is almost wholly subordinated to an expansive display by Byron of his own lordliness.[10]

Byron's defence of Pope is the more impassioned because he holds himself responsible for the creation of the degraded taste that fails to reverence Pope's achievement. He is, he confesses, one of the builders of the 'Babel' tower of modern poetry, and can claim only that, despite this, he never faltered in his admiration of 'the classic temple' of Pope's verse. He explicitly associates Pope's detractors with 'Mr Cobbett', and the effect is to suggest once again the entanglement of politics and poetry, as if he is now tempted to view his own advocacy of reform in the same light as his early romances: the one preparing the way for a 'blackguard' such as Henry Hunt, the other for a 'blackguard' such as Keats. Byron's present concern is to re-establish the cultural barriers that he feels himself to have assisted in demolishing, both by aligning himself with 'the genteel part of the reformers' and thus giving his countenance to a campaign that in the hands of Hunt and Cobbett was threatening the very survival of gentility, and by having contributed, despite his reverence for Pope, to the currency of 'the trashy jingle', which, in the hands of 'upstarts' such as Keats, was deployed in an attempt to tear the laurels from the head of 'that illustrious man'. So it is that Byron can voice his contempt of Henry Hunt and Cobbett by invoking the same standard on which Lockhart had founded his contempt for Leigh Hunt and Keats: 'Why our classical education alone – should teach us to trample on such unredeemed dirt' (7, 81).

Byron composed his responses to the new politics, to Peterloo, the Cato Street conspiracy, and the trial of the Queen in his play *Marino Faliero*, and it was in that play, too, that he began his attempt to revive the classical drama by repudiating the influence of the Elizabethan and Jacobean dramatists – 'always excepting B. Jonson – who was a Scholar & a Classic' (8, 57). As has become clear, the two aspects of the play are closely related. Shelley responded to these same events a good deal more voluminously, in his letter on Richard Carlile, in his unfinished essay 'A Philosophical View of Reform', in *Peter Bell the Third*, and *Swellfoot the Tyrant*, and in a group of topical poems, most famously in *The Mask of Anarchy*. From October 1818, until August 1821, Byron did not meet Shelley. The two men remained separated by the Apennines, but a comparison between *Marino Faliero* and *The Mask of Anarchy* would seem to suggest that more than geography kept the two apart.[11] Byron and Shelley shared the 'classical education' common to men of their class, but Byron's revival of the classical drama attempts to reimpose the social barriers that such an education erects; Shelley's broadside ballad attempts to dismantle them. The difference, it would seem, is symptomatic of political differences between the two men that the events of the year from 1819 to 1820 precipitated. Byron consistently and violently expresses his disgust for 'such infamous Scoundrels as Hunt and Cobbett'. In July 1819, Shelley told Peacock, 'Cobbett still more and more delights me', and after Peterloo, 'H. Hunt has behaved I think with great spirit and coolness in the whole affair'.[12] He wrote an impassioned letter to Leigh Hunt in his capacity as editor of *The Examiner* in defence of what Byron calls 'that fool Carlile and his trash' (6, 256). Byron's first response to the Cato Street affair is to the threat to his friends, Shelley's to the damaging effect it will have on the cause, 'Reform' (2, 176). Events in England led Byron to question whether he could, given the nature of the 'reformers', sustain his support for reform. They led Shelley to write his most substantial political essay, which he intended as 'a kind of standard book for the philosophical reformers politically considered' (2, 165). But such a summary caricatures the relative positions of the two men.

Like Byron, Shelley was brought up as a Whig. Until his expulsion from Oxford, he imagined that he would succeed to his father's parliamentary seat. But within a few months of his expulsion he had married an inn-keeper's daughter, and forfeited his claim of entry to the exclusive Whig circles that welcomed Byron as soon as he had succeeded to his peerage. It was an accident that worked together with Shelley's particular cast of mind to determine the character of his political thought. His is an abstract Whiggism, bookish rather than social, reliant less on the wish to preserve the memory and example of Charles James Fox than a desire to maintain the philosophical heritage of the Enlightenment. In *Queen Mab* the world is viewed, and its renovation prophesied, from outer space, a scenario that nicely embodies Shelley's Enlightenment assumption that his philosophical radicalism offers him a vantage point from which social ills may be surveyed from the outside, by the application of a system of values that itself transcends the social world that it explicates. Liberty is the chief of these values, and it is characterized most commonly as a freedom of opinion, as an escape from systems of belief and social institutions that threaten to curtail the freedom of enquiry. It is a freedom that comfortably allows only negative definition, as in the lines that end the third act of *Prometheus Unbound*:

> The loathsome mask has fallen, the man remains
> Sceptreless, free, uncircumscribed, but man
> Equal, unclassed, tribeless, and nationless,
> Exempt from awe, worship, degree, the king
> Over himself; just, gentle, wise, but man
> Passionless? – no, yet free from guilt or pain...
> (3, 4, 193–8)

It seems very different from Byron's version of Liberty, which most characteristically hankers for the untrammelled possession of a private space, an area, like his Sardanapalus's palace, in which the individual is free to accommodate each movement of his ever mobile consciousness. But the two versions are less opposed than they may seem. Sardanapalus wishes well to the people he governs, but his own happiness is contingent on his removal from them. Similarly, Ianthe, or the Spirit of the Hour, or Prometheus and Asia in their cave are animated by a loving concern for a populus from which they are separated. Sardanapalus and Prometheus are both recognizably versions of the Whig aristocrat, who champions the rights of the people with a benevolence that is disinterested because the product of his detachment. Both are Whiggish, too, in their understanding of freedom as the absence of constraint, as the condition that allows the individual to exercise his own autonomy. The freedom that both celebrate is modelled on a social ideal that is distinctively gentlemanly and aristocratic, life given over to a perfect, because unimpeded, expression of the self.[13] Byron responded so violently to Cobbett, Henry Hunt, and to the new politics that they expounded because he correctly understood that they challenged the social foundation on which his own politics rested. They challenged Shelley's politics, too, and, like Byron, he struggled to come to terms with the new state of affairs.

Peacock regularly sent Shelley copies of Cobbett's *Political Register*. In January 1819, this only prompted a somewhat priggish lament: 'What a pity that so powerful a genius should be combined with the most odious moral qualities' (2, 75).[14] Like Byron, he blamed Cobbett for Hobhouse's defeat at Westminster (2, 94). But by June his attitude, like Leigh Hunt's,[15] had softened: 'Cobbett still more & more delights me', although he retained a horror of 'the sanguinary commonplaces of his creed' (2, 99). By 1820, the *Political Register* seems to have replaced *The Examiner* as Shelley's most trusted source of information on English affairs (2, 193), and yet, late in 1819, in *Peter Bell the Third*, Shelley was still capable of traducing Wordsworth as 'a sort of metrical Cobbett', presumably, because, despite the apparent political differences between the two, they had in common a passion for violence, 'Cobbett's snuff, revenge'.

The events of 1819 led Byron to distance himself from the likes of Cobbett, both in his politics and his style. Shelley's response was more like Hobhouse's. He entered into negotiations. In the major prose essay of the period, 'A Philosophical View of Reform', as K. N. Cameron has shown, Shelley's economic analysis depends heavily on Cobbett,[16] and this represents much more than a local borrowing. The whole essay shares Cobbett's premise that political reform is important as the necessary precondition to economic reform. The widest possible extension of the franchise is desirable as the means to secure the widest possible distribution of what Shelley calls the 'external materials of life'.[17] The measures of England's degradation are no longer the 'large codes' that work to constrain the citizen's religious, political and sexual freedom, but rather the fact that the mass of the population 'eat less bread' and 'wear worse clothes'. The earlier construction of liberty as an ideal of intellectual autonomy is modified by a new willingness to define freedom in terms of economic well-being. Shelley has allowed Cobbett to infiltrate his political thought, and, just as revealingly, to infiltrate, too, his prose style, so that the somewhat formal periods that characterize Shelley's discursive prose manner are repeatedly tightened to produce the sharp derisive epigrams that salt Cobbett's prose. Power, Shelley argues, has been transferred from the King to the fund-holders, from aristocrat to plutocrat: 'Monarchy is only the string that ties the robber's bundle.' 'A Philosophical View of Reform' is, in itself, evidence that Shelley had come to share Leigh Hunt's recognition of Cobbett's extraordinary talent, and yet his essay ends by issuing a warning against 'certain vulgar agitators' who demand 'Retribution', and Shelley, it is clear, regarded Cobbett as the chief amongst these.

It seems likely that Shelley's failure to finish the essay should be explained not simply, as Reiman suggests, by his failure to interest a publisher in it,[18] but because Shelley could find no way of resolving his own contradictory opinions. The confident sweep of the essay's historical and global survey subsides into tentativeness as soon as Shelley focuses on England in 1819. The programme of moderate reform that he proposes is lucid enough, but the problem of how to secure a reform if Parliament persists in rejecting it produces only vacillation. Shelley, like all good Whigs, allows to the people an ultimate right of resistance, and accepts that 'the last resort of resistance is undoubtedly insurrection', but even to state this central tenet of Whig ideology summons up for Shelley a baleful vision of the disastrous consequences of civil war. He is trapped between a clear-sighted recognition that violent revolutions inevitably contaminate the political ends which are their only justification, and an equally clear-sighted perception that the vested interests that sustain the present corrupt system of government are so powerful that they will never peacefully be persuaded to act against themselves. The campaign of passive resistance that he advocates does not, as some of Shelley's more enthusiastic commentators have suggested, prefigure a strategy successfully used more than a hundred years later by Gandhi and by Martin Luther King. It is a desperate attempt to resolve the contradiction between his recognition of the necessity for reform and his insistence on the evils attending violent revolution, and it is a proposal that he himself recognizes as futile, impossible to implement in the face of 'the inoperative and unconscious abjectness', the 'incurable supineness' of 'a considerable mass of the people'.

Shelley had intended his essay as 'a kind of standard book for the philosophical reformers politically considered'. In the end, he succeeded only in expressing his own bewilderment. On the one hand,

Shelley follows Cobbett in recognizing that the real political struggle is economic, that one small class has contrived to appropriate an undue proportion of the national wealth with the result that a much larger class is rendered destitute. Political power is at once the means by which this wealth was acquired and the means by which it continues to be secured. For this reason it is a power that the rich will never willingly surrender: 'So dear is power that the tyrants themselves neither then, nor now, nor ever, left or leave a path to freedom but through their own blood.' On the other hand, Shelley persists in his former assumption that politics is a branch of philosophy, and that the question of reform may be determined by the rational arguments of those Cobbett was apt to describe as the 'feelosofers'. If 'Godwin, Hazlitt, Bentham, and Hunt' were to address members of Parliament in a series of pamphlets, their arguments, 'radiant and irresistible like the meridian sun, would strike all but the eagles who dared to gaze upon its beams, with blindness and confusion'. It seems an unlikely scenario, but it is more important to note that Shelley's two positions are contradictory. The one represents 'old Corruption' as a powerful interest that must be overthrown, the other represents it as an argument that is vulnerable to refutation. If Shelley's first position reveals the influence of Cobbett, the second shows him still the pupil of Godwin. In the essay the two positions fall apart, it is in the poem, *The Mask of Anarchy*, that Shelley attempts to resolve them.

Byron insisted to Murray that *Marino Faliero* was 'not a political play', 'though', he added, 'it may look like it'. As contemporaries noted, it looked very like it.[19] The libel impugning the chastity of Angiolina, the Doge's wife, in a play written so soon after the trial of the Queen, carried a very obvious topical reference. Byron's response to the Cato Street conspiracy, and the threat to 'poor Harrowby – in whose house I have been five hundred times – at dinners and parties' is reflected in Faliero's response to the plot to massacre the patricians. Faliero insists on his difference from the plebeian conspirators by reminding them: 'You never brake their bread, nor shared their salt.' Most importantly, Byron's hysterically fierce rejection of the notion that, as a 'friend to reform', he might be supposed a friend to the likes of Hunt and Cobbett, and the angry scorn with which he received the news that Hobhouse had sat down to dinner with such people are preserved in Faliero's feeling that to enter into league with the likes of Bertuccio and Calendaro is to inflict upon himself a scarcely tolerable self-abasement: 'We! – We! – no matter – you have earned the right/ To talk of us.'

Marino Faliero began, Byron tells us, with a veil, the 'black veil' in the Ducal palace that obscured 'the place of Marino Faliero among the doges'. It is not enough for the patricians that Marino be executed as a traitor, his place in Venetian history must be erased:

> The place wherein as Doge thou shouldst be painted,
> With thine illustrious predecessors, is
> To be left vacant, with a dark black veil
> Flung over these dim words engraved beneath –
> 'This place is of Marino Faliero
> Decapitated for his crimes'.
>
> (5. 1. 496–501)

Byron's play is an attempt to supply the missing portrait, but not only that. The play attempts to recover the lost face of the Doge, and, in doing so, it tries to reconstruct Byron's own political identity in the aftermath of the events of the past year.

The first projects fails. The play ends with its bitterest irony. In the last moments of his life Marino stands at the head of the Giant's Staircase. The ducal bonnet is removed from his head, and he is at last free of the trappings of the state:

> So now the Doge is nothing, and at last
> I am again Marino Faliero.
>
> (5. 3. 1–2)

Moments later the axe descends, and he is, with savage literalness, defaced. Faliero at last peels away his public mask, sits for a true portrait, and finds that he has no head left to be painted. Byron's play fails to supply the place of the absent medallion in the Doge's palace: it finds its appropriate pictorial counterpart only later, in Delacroix's painting of the final scene of the play, with its swirl of faces surrounding a blank white staircase at the foot of which lies a headless corpse. I can count over fifty faces in that painting, but one face is brutally absent, the face of the executed man, of Marino Faliero.

Faliero is introduced in the first scene by Pietro, one of the palace officers:

> Placed at the ducal table, cover'd o'er
> With all the apparel of the state; petitions,

168 *England in 1819*

> Despatches, judgements, acts, reprieves, reports,
> He sits as rapt as duty.
>
> (1. 1. 7–10)

So Pietro describes him, and he is describing a portrait. Not, of course, an early Venetian, but a typical eighteenth or early nineteenth century portrait of a statesman, represented as Reynolds represents, say, Pulteney, attending to his papers, despatching the business of the state. The private man and his public importance are fused to create what Reynolds taught the English to think of as historical portraiture. But Faliero is waiting for the Council's verdict on Steno. Whenever he hears a door creak, or a footstep, or a voice:

> His quick eye wanders,
> And he will start up from his chair, then pause,
> And seat himself again, and fix his gaze
> Upon some edict.
>
> (1. 1. 13–66)

His darting eye and his jerky impatience are at war with his statesmanlike immobility. He is a portrait but he will not stay still within his frame, and he cannot do so because Steno has broken apart that union of himself and his public role on which his stability depends.

What Steno has done strikes us, struck most of Byron's contemporaries, struck even Marino's wife Angiolina, as fairly trivial. He has scribbled on the ducal throne a coarse insult: 'Marino Faliero, the husband of the fair wife: others kiss her, but he keeps her.' No-one believes it, and Marino himself has an absolute and justified faith in his wife's fidelity. But for Faliero that is not the point. He is the Doge and he is Marino Faliero. When he mounts the ducal throne these two identities merge, and he becomes, so to speak, a historical portrait of himself. Steno has scribbled a coarse insult on the throne, on the frame of his portrait, and, for the Doge, to scrawl such graffiti is a kind of murder, punishable only by death. When the Council takes a lenient view of the offence, Faliero takes off his ducal bonnet and stamps on it. His action is symbolic. It marks the fact that he can never again feel at one with his public office. From now on his ducal costume is no longer, as in all state portraits uniforms must be, unified with its wearer. He feels like a player king, or a 'puppet', or, in his most striking rendition of the thought:

> A thing of robes and trinkets, dizen'd out
> To sit in state as for a sovereign's picture...
> (3. 2. 309-10)

He no longer feels himself to be a living portrait of himself, but rather like an artist's lay model, tricked out to look like a king.

I have described the condition of Faliero's sense of identity as the fusion between his private self and his public role, but to speak strictly this is not so, for the play puts in doubt the existence of such a thing as a private self. In the play written by Byron immediately after *Marino Faliero*, the young Foscari says, 'my soul is social', and Faliero might say the same. Faliero's sense of himself is contained within his sense of his own lineage, his awareness of himself as an aristocrat. In rendering the state magnificent service, especially in war, as when he led the Venetians to glorious victory at Zara, he completes himself. Such acts of heroism are gestures through which Faliero can win at once the respect of his ancestors and the gratitude of the state. Faliero needs such gestures, for they lend his erratic human impulses shape and definition. In actions such as this he may become solid, statuesque – literally, like Verocchio's great equestrian statue in the Campo San Giovanni-Paolo:

> a tall warrior's statue
> Bestriding a proud steed in the dim light
> Of the dull moon.
> (3. 1. 87-9)

Faliero proudly, though anachronistically, identifies the warrior as his ancestor. The statue was decreed to him by the city in gratitude for twice rescuing it from foreign threat. Marino has lived his whole life in emulation of that ancestor, looking always for some action in which the self-assertion proper to the aristocrat might become one with the dutiful service of the state. In such actions he can find the marble or the bronze repose that he seeks. Steno's insult, once it is condoned by the Council, destroys Faliero's sense of his own identity. Not to revenge himself against the state is to lose his sense of honour, his right to boast proudly his family name. But to take revenge, to join the conspiracy, is scarcely less terrible, for in becoming a traitor he does violence to the tradition of serving the state, of defending it in its moments of peril, that is his family's proudest boast. To act or not to act are for him alike kinds of suicide.

The story of the play is the story of Marino's attempt to survive the loss of his old identity by constructing a new one. He tries to place himself within some alternative tradition of aristocratic conduct. He invokes Brutus, Cassius, Agis of Sparta. He tries to redefine the state, so that treason itself may be envisaged as a kind of state service. He even imagines an alternative ritual that will dignify him in the place of the state ceremonial of Venice – an annual procession of free Venetians winding to the conspirators' tombs, and children scattering flowers over the ashes of their deliverers. Bertuccio and Calendaro, the staunch conspirators, find all that they need in such visions. Faliero does not. He is torn between the old values that he has lived his life by, and the new values through which he seeks to forge his new identity. He feels for the patricians the loyalty one owes one's friends. He recognizes them as extensions of himself. He feels, too, that they must be massacred to the last man. Feeling both these things his moral universe disintegrates. In the play's second act he celebrates virtues as the force that sustains the order of the universe:

> virtue
> Stands like the sun, and all which rolls around
> Drinks light and life and glory from her aspect.
> (2. 1. 396–8)

The events of the play force on him the possibility that this may not be so: that rather than power deriving its authority from virtue, virtue may derive its authority from power. A man's moral character may be determined by 'the true touchstone of desert, success'. If the conspiracy succeeds he will be able to impose on Venice a recognition of his own heroism. If it fails then all that he can do is to wait in his tomb, until the tricks of history transform him from the villain to the hero of the piece.

'Were it not better to record the facts?', Faliero asks his judges, and the facts of the matter were important to Byron. His play, he tells Murray, is 'strictly historical, read the history – and judge' (8, 168). Like Faliero, Byron writes as if fact can determine judgement, but the play articulates a more unsettling insight, that perhaps it is the judgement that determines the facts. Bertuccio is struck across the face by one patrician, Faliero is grossly insulted by another. Both offences seem individual and erratic, but for Bertuccio and Faliero they are representative, and hence justify insurrection. The local offences were:

> a mere ebullition of the vice,
> The general corruption generated
> By the foul aristocracy.
>   (3. 2. 524–6)

Their representative character is vigorously asserted, but it is supported not by illustration but by metaphor. Most often the patricians are represented as a poison within the body politic. Even without Derrida, it is clear that such metaphors are inherently reversible.

In the trial scene the Doge and his fellow conspirators are condemned to death, and, in the last scene of all, the 'people' witness the Doge's execution. The play comes to its tragic resolution, but its politics remain quite unresolved. For Benintende and the Council of Ten, the case is clear. The Doge and his co-conspirators are traitors, and the Council's duty is to administer justice. But the conspirators are just as convinced that the true traitors to the state are the patricians, and that the justification for their revolt can be expressed in the same word that the patricians use to insist on the propriety of their verdict, 'Justice'. In the Shakespearean history play human conflict is accommodated within a world that itself remains morally stable. When Antony speaks his tribute over the body of the dead Brutus, he reassures us that though we may quarrel, may even fight to the death, yet we are all human, and can honour each in the other those virtues that transcend merely political conflict. In *Marino Faliero* Byron made his first attempt to break with the Shakespearean tradition of dramatic language and dramatic construction, but his formal experiment is given point by the manner in which his play questions a deeper-seated Shakespearean convention, the notion that human conflicts take place within a stable moral order that subsumes them, and that allows them to be calmly contemplated.[20] In Byron's play only one character achieves a stable moral character, Angiolina, Faliero's wife, and she is preserved from the moral flux by remaining fixed within her woman's sphere. To enter, like the men, the political world is to occupy a sphere in which all values are reversible. Benintende ends the play as convinced that the Doge is a monstrous traitor as is the Doge that Benintende is a vile tyrant. The plot is foiled because Bertram, one of the conspirators, tries to save a nobleman, Lioni, to whom he is bound by ties of affection and gratitude. His action either proves his humanity, or exposes him as what

Calendaro calls him, 'the coward Bertram'. Lioni's response to Bertram's warning is to drag Bertram before the Ten, an action that either proves his loyalty to the state or betrays his loyalty to a friend. The Signior of the Night, who would rather die in his duty than fail to carry out his order to arrest Faliero, shows himself to be either a staunch servant of the state or a hireling slave. The play consistently refuses any retreat to some stable position of moral judgement from which one can give to each of its characters their due. History gave the Ten the power to impose their own moral order on Marino and his fellow conspirators. The lapse of years has given Byron the opportunity to reverse their judgement. But he chooses not to do so. In the end what interests him is the riddle of it all. How can one decide what is right and then choose sides if it is only in the act of choosing sides that the rights and wrongs of the matter become fixed? Byron writes a play in which he removes the black veil that obscures the face of Marino Faliero only to reveal a quite new kind of portrait, a portrait in which the character of the face is established only by the perspective of the spectator.

Byron presents his attempt to reform the English drama as a boldly revisionary act. The Shakespearean tradition is to be rejected in favour of a variety of classicism for which Alfieri supplies Byron with his most significant modern precedent. Byron calls attention to the manner in which his play approaches conformity to the classical unities, and to his refusal to found his plot on erotic passion, but still more fundamental to Byron's classicism is his subordination of character to action. Action is not illustrative of character; rather, character is the product of action. When Faliero's conspiracy is exposed, he is deprived of the opportunity to act out his plot, and hence to define himself. His double sentence in which he is deprived both of his head and of the portrait of that head is, thus, supremely appropriate: it signals the tragedy of a man who has lost one identity and failed to find another, of a man who has, quite literally, lost his face. It is a theme that has its origin in Byron's response to the England of 1819–20, and in his recognition that in that England his own political identity, as aristocratic champion of the people, as gentlemanly radical, as the classically educated spokesman for an inarticulate populace, has been erased. The history of Byron's responses to the stage production, in which Byron swithers between a nervous ambition for theatrical success, and a bitter sense that to expose himself on the stage to the 'impertinence' and 'insolence' of the rabble who make up theatre audiences could only be an intolerable 'pollution' (8, 90) is in the end less interesting as an index of Byron's sensitivities than as a measure of his self-identification with his Doge.[21] Byron suffers his exposure to an audience as Marino suffers entering a league with plebeians. He repudiates that audience by refusing them the 'melodrame' that they crave, and by writing a play armoured by its classicism against 'popularity', and yet he anxiously awaits news of the play's success and its failure clearly wounds him. His drama, like its hero, remains suspended between two identities, as a 'poem' addressed solely to the 'solitary *reader*', and as a play designed for an audience, and it is by harnessing such self-destroying energies that it expresses so completely Byron's response to an England that he no longer recognized.

Byron pointed his claim that *Marino Faliero* had never been intended to appeal to the theatre-going public with a characteristic display of hauteur: 'Had I sought their favour it would have been by a Pantomime.' Steven Jones has convincingly argued that in *The Mask of Anarchy* the poem's plot is modelled rather precisely on those of pantomimes. In *Marino Faliero*, Byron protected himself against the popular by retreating into a classicist stronghold, by defiantly writing in a manner available to, and possibly appreciable by, only those who shared his own 'classical education'. Shelley, as Jones has shown, made a determined effort to open up his poem to precisely those popular forms that Byron's classicism resists: not only the pantomime, but the cartoon, the transparency, and, most obviously, the broadside ballad.[22] Byron took pride that his play was liked by Gifford, who praised its 'sterling genuine English' (7, 194), whereas Shelley devises for his poem an English that claims to be genuine by refusing to be 'sterling', that is, he chooses a language that repeatedly implies in its baldness, and in its willingness to incorporate awkward metrical irregularity that a socially neutral English that subsumes differences of class no longer represents a valid ideal. Both in their form and in their language the two poems could scarcely be more distinct.

There are crucial differences, too, in their politics. The liberty that Faliero pursues remains undefined. Neither he, nor the plebeian conspirators imagine anything more than a freedom from patrician tyranny, with the result that freedom remains within the play a personal rather than a political value, the calm self-possession that Faliero enjoyed before Steno committed his outrage. In *The Mask of Anarchy*, on the contrary, as in 'A Philosophical View of Reform', freedom is first defined in terms of the 'external materials of life':

> For the labourer thou art bread
> And a comely table spread,

> From his daily labour come
> To a neat and happy home.
>
> Thou art clothes and fire and food
> For the trampled multitude –
> No – in countries that are free
> Such starvation cannot be
> As in England now we see.
>
> (221–9)

The freedom that Shelley's poem espouses, unlike the freedom celebrated in his earlier poems, is both social and material. Faliero, the moment he joins the conspiracy, assumes the role to which his rank entitles him as its leader. Shelley's poem allows those whose station in life distances them from 'the murmur of distress' a presence in the 'great Assembly' that will constitute the true Parliament of the nation, but a place alongside those who live in huts, workhouses, prisons, 'the haunts of daily life', not at their head. Shelley's poem seems free from 'the canker of aristocracy' that he regretted in Byron (2, 345).

The Mask of Anarchy begins with the poet 'asleep in Italy'. It is an oddly ambivalent sleep, at once a guilty quiescence from which the poet is roused by the news from England and the sleep that in dream poems such as Shelley's own *Queen Mab* and *The Triumph of Life* must overtake the poet before he can 'walk in the visions of poesy', and it inaugurates a poem in which all the key terms are subject to a similar reversal of their meaning. The poem begins with a processional masque in which Murder wears 'a mask like Castlereagh', the Foreign Secretary, the minister whose special responsibility it is to maintain peace; in which Fraud dons the ermined gown that betokens the incorruptibility of the Lord Chancellor; and Hypocrisy, in the shape of the Home Secretary, Sidmouth, identifies himself by his enthusiasm for the Bible. It is a procession fitly led by a figure named 'Anarchy' who looks indistinguishable from Death but announces himself as 'GOD AND KING AND LAW', and it is interrupted by a young woman whose name is 'Hope', 'But she looked more like Despair'. Her action in lying down before the horses seems suicidal, but when a divine shape interposes, her gesture of despair becomes the means by which Anarchy and his followers are routed. The Shape itself has both an angel's wings and armour 'like a viper's scale'. It is at once benevolent and Satanic, in confirmation of which it wears on its helm a 'planet like the Morning's', either Venus or Lucifer.

The opening 146 lines of the poem are written in a language that is inherently oppositional, that is, a language in which antithetical terms are consistently presented as synonyms, in which Anarchy is a synonym of Law, and Hope of Despair. Shelley's own stance is not, of course, in doubt. Anarchy and his army arrive in London planning to 'seize upon the Bank and Tower'. The fierce joke consists in ascribing to the Government the plot hatched in December 1816 by Thistlewood, Watson, Preston and their ultra-Radical associates. They tried to lead a section of those gathered for a reform meeting at Spa Fields in an insurrection which had as its first object the seizure of the Tower of London and the Bank of England. Shelley's point is that these institutions have indeed been seized by a rebellious minority, consisting not of the Spenceans but of the Tory Cabinet.[23] This is just one instance of the presiding joke: that those institutions that represent themselves as defending God and King and Law against the activities of those who threaten a new reign of anarchy, the reformers, radicals and demagogues, are themselves the true anarchs. It is the Prince Regent, remarkably divested of all his flesh and transformed into a 'skeleton', rather than Henry Hunt, who wantonly risks plunging the nation into civil war. Thistlewood and Sidmouth, Henry Hunt and the Regent are defined by the poem's language as parodies of one another. Thistlewood may seem to be a wild insurrectionary, the poem indicates, but the true insurrectionary is Sidmouth. The opening section of Shelley's poem gains all its exuberant energy by deploying this fierce, parodic language of reversal, but it is in the nature of such a language that it permits, indeed almost invites, itself to be reversed. Parody invites counter-parody, as Steven Jones notes. He succinctly illustrates his point with George Cruikshank's 'Death or Liberty', a cartoon in which a skeleton leads an army of 'destructions' in an assault on an apparently helpless maid. A lion has been roused from slumber and is apparently rushing to her defence. But in Cruikshank's cartoon the skeleton is labelled 'Radical Reform' and the maid is 'Britannia', who embodies 'the Virtues of the Constitution'. Timothy Webb makes the same point when he offers as a commentary on *The Mask of Anarchy* both John Stafford's ballad 'Peterloo' and the 'Answer' to it. Stafford's poem begins:

> On the Sixteenth day of August it was held at Peterloo,
> A just and lawful meeting we knew it to be true...

The 'Answer' begins:

> On the sixteenth day of August, eighteen hundred and nineteen,
> All in the town of Manchester the REBELLY CREW were seen...[24]

The point is that events such as the Peterloo massacre almost immediately came to exist only in the opposed significances attached to them, so that to insist on one reading of such events was inevitably to summon its contrary. It is this distinctive political situation that produced *The Mask of Anarchy*, just as it produced Byron's play, in which the conspirators and the patricians confront each other, each claiming to uphold justice, each accusing the other of treason.

It is an impasse that reduces Byron to silence, the silence that he so movingly registers in his play's strange final scene, in which he restages the execution of the Doge, but views it now from the perspective of the citizenry, who watch the sentence being carried out but cannot hear anything of what is spoken. Shelley responds quite differently. He attempts to supersede the language of parody and counter-parody that controls the first half of his poem by introducing a new voice, 'an accent unwithstood', which will speak in a language that has the power to unite a divided nation. It is a prophetic voice, its speech an 'incantation', its project to summon the future into existence by announcing it. But it is also a memorial voice, a voice that restages the reform meeting at Peterloo and the helplessness of the demonstrators in the face of the yeomen who attacked them. It intervenes only to spare them the undignified panic that overtook the crowd in the face of that attack. They are allowed to be 'calm and resolute', but the result is just the same:

> And if then the tyrants dare,
> Let them ride among you there,
> Slash and stab and maim and hew –
> What they like, that let them do.
>
> (344–7)

The victims become heroic, but only by virtue of electing their fate rather than simply succumbing to it. Their calmly 'folded arms and looks' are 'weapons of unvanquished war', the means, that is, by which the people secure their moral victory, but it is a victory not only consistent with, but dependent on, their physical defeat.

This poem, like *Prometheus Unbound*, asserts that true strength lies in 'meekness'. It is a paradoxical strength anticipated in the heroism of the young woman who lies down in front of Anarchy and his army. But the poem also twice asserts that strength lies in numbers, in the irresistible power of the crowd against which even a troop of armed militiamen are helpless:

> Rise like lions after slumber
> In unvanquishable number,
> Shake your chains to earth like dew
> Which in sleep had fallen on you –
> Ye are many – they are few.
> (151–5 and 372–6)

The crowd should not respond to the violence inflicted on them, but look instead to the protection of the 'old laws of England' and to the power of public indignation. The 'old laws of England' were frequently invoked by Radicals who represented themselves as engaged in an attempt to restore a corrupted, but once benign, constitution. It was this myth that Sir Francis Burdett somewhat theatrically invoked in 1810 when he contrived to be arrested as he sat with his son, assisting him in his translation of the Magna Carta. Cobbett and Henry Hunt would themselves on occasion use the same myth, but far less confidently. Cobbett's most recent scheme, and one that delighted Shelley, was a plan to ruin the national economy by the random distribution of forged bank notes, and hence bring down the Government. This is rather far from an appeal to laws old or new. Even within Shelley's poem, the appeal to law is weakened by the earlier characterization of lawyers. The Lord Chancellor is Fraud personified, and lawyers and priests constitute, together with the standing army, anarchy's most devoted followers:

> Lawyers and priests, a motley crowd,
> To the Earth their pale brows bowed,
> Like a bad prayer nor overloud
> Whispering – 'Thou art Law and God.'
> (66–9)

There are other unlikely transformations. The standing army, already characterized as composed of 'hired Murderers', now seems to include 'bold, true warriors/Who have hugged Danger in wars'. They may be disarmed, it seems, just as Marius, in Godwin's famous example, disarmed the soldier sent to execute him, 'by the force of sentiment' alone.[25] The voice strenuously tries to define a means to achieve a non-violent revolution, or, to use Byron's phrase, to find a way of making 'revolutions out of rose water' (7, 63), but the voice never seems fully persuaded of the realism of its own programme. If the people were ever to summon their own truly representative parliament, it would be attacked:

> On those who first should violate
> Such sacred heralds in their state
> Rest the blood that must ensue...
> And it will not rest on you.
>
> (340–3)

It would be pointless to absolve the 'Men of England' of responsibility for bloodshed if the only blood to be shed was their own, but the poem has already established that to respond to violence with violence is not to win freedom but to remain a slave. One of the characteristics that defines slavery is the readiness 'to exchange / Blood for blood, and wrong for wrong'.

The speech that ends the poem begins with a ringingly confident contrast between slavery and freedom, but when, in the last hundred lines it attempts to bring those definitions to bear on the England of late 1819 and to sketch a programme by which freedom can be won, all clarity disappears. The voice prophesies that its words will ring through every heart, 'Heard again, again, again'. It attempts to make of those last three words a rising crescendo, but to do so requires an energy that few voices could sustain. In all but the most vigorous readings they would constitute a diminishing echo. The final stanza repeats the stanza with which the voice began its exhortation: the speech comes full circle to register the completeness of its argument, or, in a less optimistic reading, in a confession that it has not got anywhere, that we are left at its end in precisely the position that we were at its beginning.

The obscurity of what the voice says has its counterpart in the obscurity of its origins. The maniac maid's action in lying down before Anarchy seems to trigger the appearance of the 'Shape' who puts Anarchy and his army to flight, rather as Asia triggers Demogorgon's eruption. The Shape then passes over the heads of men awakening 'Thoughts'. There follows a 'rushing light of clouds and splendour', which awakens 'sense', and then 'words of joy and fear' are spoken:

> As if their own indignant Earth
> Which gave the Sons of England birth
> Had felt the blood upon her brow...
>
> (139–41)

The Shape, it seems, has the capacity, like Wordsworth in *Peter Bell the Third* of 'Wakening a sort of thought in sense', and these thoughts are articulated in a voice like, but not identified with, the voice of Mother Earth. The result of all this is that the voice seems to have three distinct origins: in the 'Shape' which is described in a manner that firmly associates it with the sky and the heavens, in 'the heads of men' which have been impregnated with new thoughts by this sky-god, and in the Earth, figured as a matriarchal presence, closely associated with Britannia and with Liberty, a sort of mother goddess whose kingdom has been usurped by the patriarchal embodiment of 'God and King and Law', Anarchy, but who is roused by the Peterloo massacre to regain her kingdom. The 'Shape', like Shelley's Prometheus, seems a mythopoeic version of the Whig aristocrat, authorized by his culture and moral refinement to act as the champion of the inarticulate masses, the 'heads of men' raise the possibility of an educated and morally sophisticated populace able to speak for itself, and Mother Earth suggests an appeal from culture to nature, from present slavery to the peace and justice of some lost age of gold. Each embodies a powerful myth, but the myths, it is evident, are inconsistent one with another, and in this they prove an apt introduction to the speech that follows, which functions at once to supply, as it were, the speech that Henry Hunt was prevented from delivering at Manchester, and to deliver a finger-wagging warning to the likes of Henry Hunt to refrain from exciting the indignant passions of their audience. For all its declamatory confidence *The Mask of Anarchy*, almost as much as *Marino Faliero*, reveals that the events of 1819 have left Shelley anxious as to whether or not he still has a voice in which he can address his countrymen.

For Shelley, *Marino Faliero* was written in obedience to 'a system of criticism' that served only to 'cramp and limit' Byron's powers (2, 317), a judgement that he supported by comparing the play with the fifth canto of *Don Juan* (2, 330). The riven but static grandeur of the Doge is produced by a verse which, in its neoclassical formality, refuses all the 'mobility' that Shelley recognized as the condition of Byron's most extraordinary achievements. The Doge is forced by the events of the play to league himself with a bunch of men in whose company he finds himself uneasy, and in this, too, he offers a distorted reflection of Byron himself, who was induced by the events of 1819 to assume for a time the guise of a curmudgeonly cultural reactionary, determined to guard the walls of a cultural sanctuary rightly entered only by those equipped with the appropriate educational and social qualifications. It is not a role that fits him comfortably. Shelley seems to respond quite differently, opening himself in *The Mask of Anarchy* to the popular culture that *Marino Faliero* scornfully excludes. Most readers have found Shelley's poem the more congenial, but it would surely be wrong to claim that the success of *The Mask of Anarchy* is achieved without cost. It proves impossible to incorporate within the ballad form that Shelley chooses much of what characterizes his major verse: its metrical delicacy, its eroticism, its ability to render the 'minute gradations of the human heart'. Both Shelley and Byron are impelled by the events of 1819 into acts of ventriloquism, into speaking in a voice not their own. The reason is plain enough. Both had developed from early youth a political voice that identified them with what Byron called 'the genteel part of the reformers', and it was a voice that the events of these months, from Peterloo to Cato Street, had silenced.

8
Leigh Hunt, Keats and the Politics of Cockney Poetry

On the evidence of the poems it might seem that Keats's recent critics are a good deal more interested in politics than he was himself.[1] 'At Dilkes I fall foul of Politics',[2] Keats told his sister-in-law, representing it as a social danger on a level with Hunt's puns and the sentimentalism of Reynolds's sisters. But if his poems have similarly fallen foul of their modern readers, then there is at least good precedent for it. Contemporary reviewers shared with modern critics a sensitivity to the radical import of the poems curiously out of proportion to the provocation that the poems seem to offer. The opening of Book III of *Endymion* in which all the regalia of monarchy is dismissed as so much 'tinsel', and the references to Isabella's brothers as 'ledger-men' and 'money-bags' were passages repeatedly cited as evidence that Keats was as Cockney in his politics as his poetry. But the repetition works to undermine rather than to substantiate the charge. Tory reviewers had no need to characterize the politics of Shelley and Byron on the basis of two passages.

Geoffrey Matthews sensibly explains the reception of Keats by pointing out that Keats's literary career coincided with a period in which the rival reviews had worked so to blur 'literary and political opinion' that 'it was hardly possible for a creative writer associated with one side to obtain fair treatment from a reviewer employed by the other'.[3] Keats was championed by Hunt, Hunt was the editor of *The Examiner*, and the reviewers needed no more to convince them that Keats's poems must be deeply tainted by his patron's politics. For the reviewers Keats was guilty by association, and the damning association was with Hunt. But Geoffrey Matthews, like Keats's friend, Benjamin Bailey, assumes that the detestation in which Hunt was held by *The Quarterly* and by *Blackwood's* can be explained simply by reference to Hunt's being 'so decidedly a party-man',[4] whereas all the evidence suggests that it was a detestation prompted more forcibly by Hunt's poetry than his politics, and by one poem in particular, *The Story of Rimini*, a poem almost entirely without political reference.[5]

My dear Byron

It has become conventional in modern criticism to insist on the relationship between Cockney poetry and politics, to represent the attack on the closed couplet of the Augustans as an inflection of the political assault on a closed society. As William Keach, the most scrupulous of such critics, puts it, Hunt's claim in the Preface to *The Story of Rimini* that he had attempted 'a freer spirit of versification' is of a piece with his desire for a freer society. But it is Keach's special virtue that he advances such claims only to put them into question. It may be that Hunt's 'effort to reform the heroic couplet is an exact image of his reformist politics', but Keach is rightly chary of drawing the conclusion that Keats's far more radical experiments on the couplet form, from *Sleep and Poetry* to *Endymion*, indicate an analogous difference between Keats's politics and Hunt's liberal reformism.[6]

From 1815 to 1819, *The Examiner* was a journal divided between literature and politics, and throughout those years it became increasingly difficult to reconcile its two dominant interests, with the result that in 1819 Hunt launched *The Indicator*, a move that amounts almost to a confession that the languages of literature and of politics could no longer be accommodated together within the same publication. Hunt devoted his own energies to *The Indicator*, as if in recognition that the political language that he had developed, a language that continued to invoke Fox as the ultimate political authority, and that found in Sir Francis Burdett its most congenial parliamentary spokesman, had become outmoded. It had been usurped by the quite different language spoken by Henry Hunt, and written by Cobbett and the group of radical journalists that Cobbett had inspired. Given this, it was natural that Hunt should respond by turning to the other language in which he was proficient, the language of literature. Keach asks what political statement can be deduced from Keats's habit in *Endymion* of allowing the exigencies of rhyme to determine the sequence of thought, and the value of his question is that it reveals on one level what Hunt's decision to establish *The Indicator* reveals on another. It shows that the languages of Cockney politics and poetry were not one language but two. Hunt's political language was developed in the years of the Napoleonic wars. By 1810, in the series of articles that led to his imprisonment, it is fully formed. The language of Cockney poetry, on the other hand, was a product of the peace. It was fully embodied for the first time in *The Story of Rimini*, published in 1816.[7]

Cockney poetry is most easily defined not as a style but as a relationship between a style and a subject matter. Hunt's poem tells the story of the ill-fated marriage between Francesca, daughter of Guido Novello da Polenta, Duke of Ravenna, and Giovanni Malatesta, Duke of Rimini. The bridegroom's procession with which it begins and the funeral procession with which it ends frame the tale within two pageants which embody the elaborate social hierarchy that establishes the place of the poem's chief characters at its apex. It is not a continuous but a fractured hierarchy. The nobility of Ravenna assembles in the palace square to welcome the bridegroom, while the townspeople, barred by the palace guards from entering the square, throng the doorways to catch a glimpse of the procession. But a single mood of joyful expectancy unites the nobles gracefully seated on the lawn with the 'tip-toe' populace. The poet, Guy Cavalcanti, 'the young father of Italian song', is one of the privileged, the centre of an admiring circle amongst whom he dispenses courtly witticisms. Giovanni has agreed to marry by proxy, represented at the ceremony by his younger brother, Paulo, and when Paulo enters the courtyard he secures himself in the good graces of the bride and of all Ravenna by dropping into the hand of a follower a rich jewel, a gift for Cavalcanti. There is an obvious ironic discrepancy between Cavalcanti, blushingly and with a 'lowly grace', accepting his princely gift, and Hunt, who wrote his poem as the autumn rains 'Wash[ed] the dull bars' of the prison cell where he was imprisoned for his libel on the Prince Regent, but it is an irony that Hunt chooses not to point. He distinguishes himself from Cavalcanti more quietly, by surveying the bridal procession from the doorway, from amidst the 'rude heave' of the populace.

At the climax of *The Story of Rimini* is an act of transgression, an act which disrupts the ideal chivalric order figured in the poem's processions. Paulo commits adultery with his sister-in-law. But in the funeral procession which closes the poem the transgressive act is accommodated. Giovanni's jealous rage does not survive his brother's death, he arranges for Paulo and Francesca to be interred together, and by finding within himself this generosity of spirit he reinstitutes the ideal order that the events of the poem had threatened. It is in his style not in his story that Hunt overpowers the palace guards who prevent the common folk from mixing with the aristocratic wedding guests, and he does so by developing the poetic style that its detractors categorized as Cockney.

On her journey to Rimini the newly married Francesca travels through a forest. The forest itself is a typically Huntian hybrid of wild wood and cottage garden, made up of pear trees, juniper, and oak, intermingled with briony, honeysuckle and ivy, but over it all towers the pine, 'In lordly right, predominant o'er all'. Hunt blandly overthrows what Keats calls the 'grand democracy of Forest Trees' (*Letters*, 1, p. 232), and establishes in its stead a woody hierarchy that exactly reflects the feudal order of the human society that he depicts. But as soon as he establishes the dominance of the pine, he diverts the attention from the tree to its cones, its 'fruit with rough Mosaic rind'. The epithets are at once awkward and exact, and the effect is to allow the claims of the large, 'lordly right', to be challenged by the indecorous demand for attention made by the small. *The Story of Rimini* refuses in its style that graceful subordination of part to whole, and of the less to the more important that secures the economy of classical narrative. Similar effects are dispersed throughout the poem. In the square at Ravenna there is a fountain, and Hunt, characteristically, captures it at the point when the jets of water lose their shape and disintegrate into droplets, the moment at which the fountain begins to 'shake its loosening silver in the sun'. All through the tale there is a similar 'loosening', as Hunt allows the narrative momentum to dissipate by removing attention from the story to details, from his characters to their appurtenances. When they emerge, as light fades, into a grassy clearing in the forest, the horsemen pause, and allow their mounts to graze, to 'dip their warm mouths into the freshening grass'. The steaming horses and the dew-cooled grass conspire to make an appeal to the sympathetic imagination stronger than seems the right of such incidental figures.

Hunt always looks at horses closely, imitating, I suppose, the connoisseurship natural to characters devoted to the pleasures of the chase and the tournament. But the effect is to mimic rather than to share their culture. Paulo brings with him, as a gift for the Duke of Ravenna, a troop of Arabian steeds: 'with quoit-like drop their steps they bear'. This is exact – it works hard to capture the delicately vertical fall of the thoroughbred's hoof – but its awkwardness establishes Hunt's remove from any society where the finer points of horses are easily discussed. It establishes his role in relation to the society he writes about as that of the encroacher. Hunt has a clear sense of the manner of address that defines the gentleman. He knows that it is the product of a social confidence that the gentleman can transmit to all those who come into his presence. Paulo has it to perfection, the gentlemanly aura:

> That air, in short, which sets you at your ease,
> Without implying your perplexities...

Hunt's style is remarkably easy, but its distinctive, its definingly cockney, characteristic is that it is an ease that always implies the perplexities of its reader.

Most reviewers located the origins of their perplexity in the poem's diction, in Hunt's strange habits of word formation. A waist is 'clipsome', horsemen travel at a 'pranksome' speed, trees are 'darksome', and 'lightsome' does for the sit of a cap, the fall of a man's back, the slope of his nose, and for the morning star. Items in the poem may be 'streaky', 'mellowy', 'glary', 'scattery'. There are unusual comparatives: 'martialler', 'franklier', 'tastefuller'. Hunt likes adjectives formed from present participles: light conversation becomes 'fluttering talk', the happy earth is rendered as the 'warbling sphere'. Some words just seem odd, as when the hindquarters of horses are praised for their 'jauntiness'.[8] These Cockneyisms are not best defined linguistically, by calling attention, for example, to Hunt's habit of moving a word from one part of speech to another, so that sunlit patches become 'flings of sunshine'. Rather they are defined socially, by the perplexities, the awkward embarrassment, that they provoke in the reader. Hunt writes as if he had the freedom of an earlier poet, of Spenser, say, to invent his own poetic diction, as if he were unaware that poetic diction could no longer be defined by the character of the words used but by the cultural authority that had been invested in them, an authority that allows 'finny tribe' to remain unobtrusive, but exposes 'glary yellow' as ludicrously affected.

But Hunt writes only 'as if' he were unaware of these matters. His is always a knowing innocence, an 'affectation of a bright-eyed ease'. The character of the poem's style is fixed by a whole series of linguistic swoops, in which Hunt plunges from a precariously, even affectedly 'poetic' diction towards a diction that is daringly colloquial. In the Preface he defends the habit in formulations that echo Wordsworth's Preface to *Lyrical Ballads*. 'The proper language of poetry', Hunt claims, 'is in fact nothing different from that of real life.' He positions his own 'free and idiomatic cast of language' between the 'cant of art' and 'the cant of ordinary discourse', but the language of his poem reveals that between these two varieties of cant there is no longer any space. Wordsworth claims for the language of his own poems, the language of 'low and rustic life', a natural authority. It may be a language that survives in the speech of a particular class, but that is because rustic speakers use a language that is protected from contamination by 'arbitrary and capricious habits of expression'. Wordsworth values their language not because it is the expression of a particular locality and a particular social station, but, on the contrary, because it is 'a far more philosophical language' than that often used by poets, and hence retains an affinity with the 'pure and universally intelligible' language of Chaucer.

Hunt replaces Wordsworth's key word, 'natural', with the word 'rural'. The refinement of Francesca's sensibility is shown by her 'books, her flowers, her taste for rural sights'. Paulo is her proper mate because his taste can be summarized in the poem's most notorious couplet:

> The two divinest things this world has got,
> A lovely woman in a rural spot!

Hunt's 'rural' is Wordsworth's 'natural' debased from the status of moral principle to that of a variety of taste. ' 'Twas but the taste for what was natural', and the 'taste for rural sights' is developed in the city rather than in the countryside. It has its origins in a childhood spent, not in wandering 'like a breeze' over the mountains, but in reading. Hence the propriety of Hunt's prefacing Francesca's enjoyment of 'rural sights' by a reference to her 'books', and hence the special potency for him of a story in which the entry into the aristocratic world of high, forbidden passion comes through a book, when Paulo joins Francesca as she reaches that point in the tale of Launcelot when he begins to feel a guilty passion for the Queen, at the moment when Francesca begins to feel 'a growing interest in her reading'.

That phrase does more to define Cockney style than an expression such as 'scattery light'. It is 'free and idiomatic', and yet it remains redolent of the 'cant of ordinary discourse'; that is, it is an expression that betrays the social class of its user. Whenever the word 'taste' is used in the poem, it carries the special charge that it has for a class who is always anxious that it may be betrayed by its predilections, the class that Moore sums up in his Fudge family. But Leigh Hunt relocates the Fudges in the palaces of thirteenth-century Italy, crediting the Duke of Rimini with an ambition that his wife should 'haunt his eye, like taste personified', or admiring a troop of knights with the kind of simper that Miss Biddy Fudge reserves for a particularly fashionable beau:

> But what is of the most accomplished air,
> All wear memorials of their lady's love,
> A ribbon, or a scarf, or silken glove...

The result is to superimpose Hampstead on Rimini, so that Francesca's falcon responds to her for all the world as if it had been a canary: he 'sidled on his stand,/And twined his neck against her trembling hand'. Paulo, meanwhile, trying to shrug off his suspicion that Francesca might have more than sisterly feelings for him, exerts himself to 'look/About him for his falcon or his book'. The courtly appurtenances, the falcon, for example, survive, but they are overpowered by a syntax that transforms the palace chamber into a suburban sitting-room.

In *The Story of Rimini* Hunt invents cockney poetry as an inverted pastoral. Instead of courtly poets appropriating the language and sentiments of rustics, Hampstead poets appropriate the manners of the court, and infect its language with the cant terms of their own ordinary discourse: rural, tasteful, accomplished. To Lockhart the effect seemed self-evidently ridiculous, as it seems still to most modern readers. But for Lockhart laughter is not enough to dissolve the perplexities that the poem implies. Hunt's failure to find a style appropriate to his subject matter strikes him in the end not as a comedy of self-exposure but as a moral outrage. Hunt's theme, the incestuous love of a brother for his sister-in-law, stimulates a hysterically violent denunciation that Lockhart is never able fully to explain.[9] In *Parisina*, Byron himself had, as Lockhart knew, chosen a similar topic, incest between a son and a stepmother, and Byron's poem, although Lockhart did not admit it, may have been indebted to Hunt's.[10] Lockhart tries to secure a distinction between the two by insisting that Byron, unlike Hunt, preserves a reverential horror at the breaking of the incest taboo. But his case seems thin. Byron is protected from Lockhart's indignation not by the soundness of his morals but by the soundness of his style, by an ease that remains gentlemanly without ever descending to jauntiness.

Hazlitt was surely right to recognize that the judgements of the *Blackwood's* reviewers could be understood only by recognizing that for them the test of political opinion remained subordinate to a quite different test:

> It is name, it is title and influence that mollifies the tender-hearted Creatures of criticism... This is the reason why a certain Magazine praises Percy Bysshe Shelley, and vilifies 'Johnny Keats'.[11]

In other words, differences of political opinion might be more easily accommodated than differences of class. Hunt's political language remained firmly within an Enlightenment tradition that construed political difference as an opposition of ideas. In the years between 1815 and 1819 that language became increasingly irrelevant. Its place was usurped by the quite different language spoken by Henry Hunt and written by Cobbett, a language that construed political difference as the expression of class enmity. The politics that Hunt recognized, the battle between ideas, was being replaced by a different politics which hinged on the relationship between classes. Hunt found it all but impossible to address himself to this new phenomenon in his political prose. But in *The Story of Rimini* he had already developed a poetic style that had, as Lockhart's response reveals, a disruptive power precisely accommodated to the new politics of the peace.

In his Preface Hunt wrote the manifesto for the new poetry. The Preface recommends 'a freer spirit of versification', the use of a poetic language founded on 'an actual, existing language', and the repudiation of Pope as a model for versification in favour of Chaucer. But the radical import emerges from the social gestures that the Preface makes rather than the critical precepts that it lays down. The Preface parades a culture that is at once ostentatiously displayed and thin – 'Homer abounds' with 'exquisite specimens' of the 'natural' style, 'though, by the way, not in the translation'; 'with the Greek dramatists I am ashamed to say I am unacquainted'. The Preface simultaneously asserts a genial intimacy with the Western tradition of high culture, and exposes the fragile grounds on which that intimacy is claimed. It is at once an artistic credo, and a social gaffe, or, better, it is the social gaffe offered as itself embodying a poetic manifesto. The whole Preface is an elaboration of the address with which it begins, an address the temerity of which left Lockhart aghast, 'My Dear Byron', and it inaugurates a new school of poetry, defined, as Lockhart knew, by the class of its practitioners, a poetry that would at once lay claim to possession of a culture that had until then been the monopoly of the classically trained and university educated, and betray its lack of proper title to the culture that it claimed.

Johnny Keats

From early on in his career, from 1817, Keats made anxious efforts to free himself from Hunt's stylistic and social mannerisms, as many of his critics have noted.[12] By late 1818 he was able to write *Hyperion*, a poem as distant from any of Hunt's in its style as it is easy to imagine. But, in the wider sense in which I have defined the term, Keats remained throughout his career a Cockney poet. The narrative poems dramatize tales of encroachment. Lorenzo and Porphyro are interlopers, the one contriving entry into the domestic circle of his employers, the other into the castle of his enemies. Elsewhere, as in *Endymion* or *Lamia*, the plot threatens the boundary between species, between a mortal and a goddess or a serpent woman. In the lyric poems Keats confronts some item so heavily freighted with cultural associations that it can serve as a metonym for the whole tradition of high culture. Keats stands in contemplation of the Elgin marbles, a Grecian urn, a nightingale, or of Melancholy, the emotion that beyond all others the poetic tradition has dignified as a badge of cultural attainment. The poems chart the fluctuations by which Keats successively demands his right to a place within that culture, and betrays his bitter sense that its boundaries are patrolled by cultural monitors, such as Croker and Lockhart, whose function it is to preserve culture from the encroachments of those like Keats, whose education and social station do not qualify them for entry.

Of Keats's critics, only Marjorie Levinson has shown herself fully sensitive to the cultural predicament out of which the poems are produced; that is, Keats's intense consciousness of himself as belonging to a class that had no attributes other than its difference. On the one hand, there was the difference from Byron: '1 superfine! rich or noble poets – ut Byron. 2 common ut egomet' (*Letters*, 1, p. 368). On the other, there was the difference, that Keats insisted on, from the likes of Samuel Bamford, 'the weaver poet': 'I am a weaver boy to them', 'the literary fashionables' (*Letters*, 2, p. 186).[13] His was, as Levinson puts it, the 'neither/nor' position construed by the reviewers as 'monstrous'.[14] Levinson brilliantly offers 'On First Looking into Chapman's Homer' as an epitome of Keats's whole enterprise, for it is a poem that at once celebrates Keats's enfranchisement, and confesses his lack of title to the enfranchisement he claims. His reading has made him a free citizen of the Homeric world, able to breathe for the first time 'its pure serene', but the metaphor claims a natural ease that the poem's plot, with its ingenuous confession that Homer is available to Keats only in translation, denies. The poem's gestures cancel each other, so that it is predictable that the poem should end in silence. The wonder is that its silence should have been made eloquent, and it is in this that it prefigures Keats's whole achievement. He sought to inscribe his own name in the book of literature by the production of poems that betrayed the cultural disabilities that disqualified him from inclusion within it.

Levinson's book is important in part because it helps to explain the failure of those who have sought to address directly the question of Keats's political opinions. The evidence from the letters and the poems is clear: Keats placed himself firmly 'on the liberal side of the question' (*Letters*, 2, p. 176). He addresses politics at length in only two letters. In the letter of October, 1818, to his brother and sister-in-law, he repudiates at once Napoleon and 'the divine right Gentlemen'; 'All the departments of Government', and the 'Madmen' who would seek to overthrow them, men 'who would like to be beheaded on tower Hill merely for the sake of eclat'. Between these opposing groups, he recognizes only Leigh Hunt 'who from a principle of taste would like to see things go on better', and those 'like Sir F. Burdett who like to sit at the head of political dinners'. His own intervention is confined to expressions of nostalgia for the Commonwealth that seem rather too patly to echo Wordsworth: 'We have no Milton, no Algernon Sidney' (*Letters*,1, pp. 396–7). In the letter of September, 1819, he shares with the George Keatses an understanding of English history since Richard II that divides it into three stages. In the first the kings found common interest with the people in accomplishing 'the gradual annihilation of the tyranny of the nobles'. In the second, the kings turned on the people in an effort to 'destroy all popular privileges'. In the third, those privileges are reasserted. It is this third stage that has been 'put a stop to' by the 'unlucky termination' of the French Revolution, but Keats trusts that it will be no more than 'a temporry stop' (*Letters*, 2, pp. 192–4). This is the familiar Whig view of history, lucidly and sensibly rehearsed, and it bears not the faintest stamp of the delicate, exploratory intelligence that is scarcely ever absent when Keats is thinking about poets, or poetry, or his own compositional processes.

Like Hunt, Keats had acquired a Whig political vocabulary, a vocabulary founded on an analysis of the nation into three distinct orders: the monarchy, the aristocracy, and the people, but it was not possible for him to express his own place within the public world in the terms that this political vocabulary allowed him. Keats was ungrateful to Hunt, but Hunt remains the single most important influence on his poetry, because Hunt showed him the way out of his difficulty. Hunt showed him how to write a public poetry that derived its vigour not from the sentiments it expressed but from its style. Hunt showed him, that is, how to become a Cockney poet.

Morris Dickstein has proposed that Hunt's description of *Hyperion*'s 'transcendental cosmopolitics' should replace critical responses to the poem that confine attention to 'its epic ambitions, its sonorous impersonality, and the Miltonic "stationing" of its verse'. Dickstein suggests an analogy linking Saturn, the dying George III, and the deposed Napoleon. Alan J. Bewell notes that Keats associates his Titans with the art of Egypt, points out that Egyptian art was conventionally associated with tyrannical power and priestly mystery, and suggests an analogy between the action of Keats's poem and Napoleon's Egyptian campaign. A political allegory that allows Napoleon to be associated either with Hyperion and Saturn or with the Apollo who supersedes them seems unusually 'transcendental', and neither reading accommodates easily the pathos with which Keats invests the downfall of the Titans. Bewell recognizes such difficulties, and suggests that *Hyperion* espouses a 'political ideology', a Whig understanding of history as progress, only for Keats to find that this imposed on him a political language with which he was uncomfortable.[15] In its 'cosmopolitics', *Hyperion* remains incoherent: it is in its 'epic ambitions' that the poem vigorously places itself within the public world.

Keats seems not to have set about writing *Hyperion* in earnest until immediately after the attacks on *Endymion* by Lockhart and by Croker.[16] *Hyperion* is, in some sort, as Thomas Reed suggests,[17] a response to those attacks, a response at once defiant and submissive. Keats veers from Hunt to Milton, from couplets that risked 'wearying his readers with an immeasurable game of bouts-rimés' he turns to blank verse, and for the anarchically episodic structure of romance he substitutes the more regular narrative sequence of epic. In all this a wish to placate his hostile critics is evident enough. But Lockhart had also derided Keats's lack of title to the subject matter he claimed: he and Hunt 'write about Apollo, Pan, Nymphs, Muses, and Mysteries, as might be expected from persons of their education', from persons, that is, whose classical scholarship amounts to no more than 'a sort of vague idea, that the Greeks were a most tasteful people'. In writing *Hyperion*, Keats defiantly persists in claiming a right to appropriate the mythological subject matter from which, according to Lockhart, his educational deficiencies debarred him.

The plot of *Hyperion*, in which Saturn and the Titans are ousted, and Hyperion is forced to recognize the nobler music of Apollo, seems designed to express Keats's heady sense of his own irresistible genius. 'Byron, Scott, Southey, & Shelley think they are to lead the age', he once told Haydon, 'but ...', and Haydon's anxiety not to compromise his young friend's reputation for modesty led him to erase the rest of the sentence.[18] But Keats was given just as often to intense self-doubt, a sense of himself as having been forcibly removed from the 'strong identity', the 'real self' that would permit him to fulfil his ambitions, which is surely one reason why Saturn's overthrow only serves to secure his place within Keats's imaginative sympathies. It is easy to speak of these Keatsian characteristics as defining a personality, but it would be more accurate, as Levinson realizes, to recognize them as defining the social class to which Keats belonged. They are characteristics that inform the style more completely than the plot of *Hyperion*, and hence it is in its style, in its 'epic ambitions', that the poem makes its most forceful intervention in the public world.

More completely than any other of Keats's poems, *Hyperion* displays Keats's alternating reflexes, his capacity for 'in-feeling' and his concern with 'stationing'. He inhabits Hyperion's mouth, when the taste of incense sours to the 'savour of poisonous metal and brass sick', and he stations Thea, kneeling before Saturn; freezes her for a month in a single, mute posture of despair. So it is that the poem's characters are at once intimately possessed, and yet remain immeasurably remote. The first two books are dominated by dialogue,[19] in which the 'large utterance of the early Gods' is rendered into 'our feeble tongue'. Keats can afford gracefully to assume the modesty of the translator in the knowledge that he has so amply re-created 'that large utterance', but the apology works to alert the reader to a quality in the poem that aligns it with translation. It is as far as possible from Hunt's ideal of a 'free and idiomatic cast of language'. The poem displays to its reader the words from which it is made, offers them to be savoured as sounds, as actions in the mouth, as the 'ponderous syllables' of Enceladus, or the syllables that throb through Apollo's 'white, melodious throat'. We understand these words, and yet they retain a material opacity, like that of the 'hieroglyphics old' that have survived the loss of their 'import'. Hence, as in the very best translations, the poem seems to reconcile two languages, the comfortably familiar language of 'our feeble tongue' and another language that remains remote, and unaccommodated. It is through its style that the poem articulates Keats's understanding of his own place in the social structure, the 'neither/nor' place of a class that cannot claim, like Lockhart, the cultural attainments of the classically educated, and yet is unwilling to dispute a definition of culture that confines it to those who know Greek and Latin. But in *Hyperion* the plot and the style are at odds. The plot allies itself with an optimistic Whig view that understands history as a process in which one 'power' succeeds another in obedience to a benevolent 'eternal law', but the style gives voice to a social class that can take no part in such an evolutionary process.[20] It cannot achieve cultural power because it is defined by its aspiration towards it; it cannot arrive because it has its only being in becoming. In *Hyperion*, Keats generated a quite new kind of Cockney poetry, distinguished from Hunt's Cockney by its being not at all 'ridiculous'. In *Hyperion*, Keats had found a way 'to write fine things which cannot be laugh'd at in any way' (*Letters*, 2, p. 174), but he had not found a plot. Hence his decision to abandon the poem and begin work on *The Fall of Hyperion*.

In the revised poem, Keats turns, as Hunt had turned in *The Story of Rimini*, to Dante. It seems, from a modern perspective, grotesque that the Cockney poets should have nominated Dante as their ancestor, but it is less so than it seems. Hunt was drawn to a story in which desire is displaced from a book to the body, a story in which nature is a by-product of culture, and hence an appropriate story for a new kind of poetry which would take as its primary subject its own literariness. Keats seems to have been attracted by a poem that so transparently concerns itself with its own place within literary history. The Keats who represented himself as 'cowering under the Wings of great Poets' (*Letters*, 1, p. 239) would have responded immediately to Dante's Virgil, at once so protective and so overawing a presence. 'Those minute volumes of carey' (*Letters*, 1, p. 294) that Keats carried with him to Scotland in the summer of 1818 were to provide him with the clue that he needed to rework the material of *Hyperion* by including it as an episode within a new plot, the defining plot of Cockney poetry. It would no longer be a poem about Hyperion ousted by Apollo, but a poem in which Keats explored his own entitlement to write about the wars of the gods.

In *The Fall of Hyperion* much more directly than in its predecessor, Keats confronts his own cultural position. Lockhart had summoned up a comic vision of a nation suffering from a rhyming plague, 'Metromanie', a disease that has struck down farm-servants and unmarried ladies, footmen, governesses, and a young man 'bound apprentice some years ago to a worthy apothecary in town'. Keats's first response is moving in its simplicity:

> Who alive can say,
> 'Thou art no Poet – mayst not tell thy dreams'?
> (11–12)

Poetry is not the preserve of the privileged few, but available to 'every man', if only he 'had loved/And been well nurtured in his mother tongue'. The condition seems anodyne enough, until one remembers Lockhart's mockery of 'two Cockneys', one of whom 'confesses that he had never read the Greek Tragedians, and the other knows Homer only from Chapman'. The only 'breeding' that a poet needs is a breeding in the mother-tongue, and yet within the poem the maternal presence, the figure whose 'words/Could to a mother's soften', is a goddess called Moneta or Mnemosyne, a Muse as classical as even Lockhart could stipulate. The poem carefully places Keats in the 'neither/nor' position that defines the Cockney poet.

In the poem's first vision, the poet finds himself in a forest clearing, where a feast is spread on a mossy mound:

> Which, nearer seen, seemed refuse of a meal
> By angel tasted, or our Mother Eve...
> (30–1)

The poet standing amidst 'empty shells' and 'grape-stalks but half bare' forms a tableau that, since Bate, has functioned as the primal scene of poetic belatedness,[21] but, as Bate notes, Keats emphasizes the 'plenty' rather than the paucity of the 'remnants'. The poet has more than enough to eat and drink. The point, surely, is not at all the meagreness of the meal, but the undignified circumstances in which it is consumed. The poet's is precisely the position of the servant who gains entry to a costly banquet after the authentic guests have departed, and gluts himself on the rich remains of a meal to which he was not invited. The passage identifies the poet as an interloper. When he wakens from his sleep, the scene has changed, but not his role within it. The 'eternal domed monument' in which he finds himself is clearly a temple of culture. The bric-à-brac strewn at his feet, the 'draperies' and 'strange vessels', 'Robes, golden tongs, censor and chafing dish,/Girdles, and chains, and holy jewelleries', are items that suggest what Larkin calls 'the stuff up at the holy end', but more because of the reverence with which they are listed than the nature of the items themselves. The paraphernalia corresponds to the half-finished meal: it represents the detritus of a high culture, rich and enclosed, to which the poet has gained magical, guilty access. Moneta challenges him as a trespasser, as one attempting to 'usurp this height'.

K. K. Ruthven's observation that Moneta was, as Keats would have learned from Tooke's *Pantheon*, at once the supplier of 'wholesome counsel' and 'the goddess of money' has intrigued several recent critics, but, with the exception of Watkins, to oddly little effect.[22] The reason is, I suspect, that it has proved impossible to graft Ruthven's perception onto a view of Moneta that insists on representing her role within the poem as uncomplicatedly benign. The best antidote to such an assumption is to place side by side Moneta's remarks to the dreamer and Lockhart's remarks to the young Keats. Moneta accuses the poet of being 'a dreaming thing/A fever of thyself'. Lockhart had advised Keats that he was suffering from a 'disease', and belonged to a 'fanciful, dreaming' set. Lockhart describes a young man, stricken with a 'poetical mania' that has unfitted him for the 'useful profession' that his friends had destined him for, 'the career of medicine'. Moneta distinguishes between those who 'seek no wonder but the human face', and those like Keats whose activities are of no social utility:

> What benefit canst thou, or all thy tribe,
> To the great world?
>
> (167–8)

Lockhart offers his review as an astringent medicine that, if taken, will 'put the patient in a fair way of being cured'. The dreamer thanks Moneta for having 'medicined' him. Finally, Lockhart castigates the presumption of 'uneducated and flimsy striplings' such as Keats who dare to speak familiarly of their cultural superiors. The sonnet, 'Great spirits now on earth are sojourning', is singled out as a particularly egregious example of Keats's daring to place 'himself, and some others of the rising brood of Cockneys' on a level with 'the most classical of living English poets': 'Wordsworth and Hunt! what a juxtaposition!' Compare Moneta:

> Art thou not of the dreamer tribe?
> The poet and the dreamer are distinct,
> Diverse, sheer opposite, antipodes.
>
> (198–200)

Moneta's face, 'deathwards progressing / To no death', is itself a fit emblem of the notion of culture over which Lockhart claims guardianship, a notion that conceives culture as a condition of moribund immortality, as the spectral, unending afterlife of the dead civilizations of Greece and Rome, the essence of which is enclosed in the tomb-like chambers of Moneta's 'hollow brain', as in a mausoleum.

At this point, Ruthven's perception becomes crucial, because the forces that guard Lockhart's cultural precincts are, as Lockhart boasts, economic. He ends his review smugly prophesying that no bookseller will 'a second time venture £50 upon anything [Keats] can write'. In the months that Keats worked on *The Fall of Hyperion*, his true financial predicament seems to have been brought home to him for the first time. He began to cast about for some way of securing a competence: taking passage as a surgeon on an Indiaman, going to Edinburgh to qualify himself as a doctor, writing political articles 'for whoever will pay me' (*Letters*, 2, p. 176), and the figure of Lockhart presided over his difficulties. As he told his sister, he would 'try the fortune of [his] pen once more', and, should that fail, 'I have enough knowledge of my gallipots to ensure me an employment & maintenance' (*Letters*, 2, pp. 124–5).[23]

Moneta stares at Keats with blank, blind eyes, 'like two gold coins', as Ruthven has it, a ghastly embodiment of the defensive alliance between culture and economics that worked to deny Keats's right of settlement in the 'realms of gold'. But, as all the poem's critics have properly noted, Moneta's presence in the poem is monitory rather than minatory, her gaze benignant rather than baleful. She says hard words to the poet, too hard for many of the poem's critics,[24] but she is also 'kind' to him, her voice like a 'mother's', and the poet responds to her with grateful reverence. In the confrontation of the poet with Moneta Keats achieves his most complete expression of his cultural situation, for it accommodates fully both his capacity for reverence and his stinging sensitivity to ridicule. Keats's impulse is to keep the two responses apart, to maintain 'The pain alone; the joy alone; distinct'. He delights in fancying Shakespeare his 'Presider' (*Letters*, 1, p. 142), a cultural authority wholly different from the likes of Croker and Lockhart who preside over the reviews. Keats reverences 'genius', and genius is measured in inverse proportion to the taste of the 'literary world': 'Just so much as I am humbled by the genius above my grasp, am I exalted and look with hate and contempt upon the literary world' (*Letters*, 2, p. 144). But the distinction between 'genius' and the cultural institutions that accredit it is precarious, secured only by the passage of time. Keats's acutely erratic responses to his contemporaries, to Hunt and to

Wordsworth in particular, are controlled by conflicting needs to hail 'genius', and to maintain a lofty contempt for 'that most vulgar of all crowds the literary' (*Letters*, 2, p. 43). He writes a poetry that is impelled at once by a 'love of fame' (*Letters*, 2, p. 116), and a defiantly maintained indifference to literary success, and it is to the extent that this ambivalent stance 'venoms' the poetry that Keats's poems achieve their political importance. Jerome McGann has famously described Keats's 1820 volume as a self-conscious and determined attempt to 'dissolve social and political conflicts in the mediations of art and beauty'.[25] The evidence from both letters and poems establishes beyond possibility of argument Keats's passionate desire to find in the world of art a sphere independent of, and dissociated from, the corrupt spheres of power and of money, but just as clearly they record Keats's bitter recognition that the spheres are interlocked, near neighbours that there is no possibility of unperplexing.

Our classical education

Modern critics interested in the relationship between poetry and politics have constructed the brief period of Keats's poetic activity, the years from 1816 to 1819, as a single narrative that reaches its catastrophe in Manchester on 16 August 1819, at Peterloo. Hence the oddity that the question of the political significance of Keats's poems has been disputed most keenly in discussions of a single poem, 'To Autumn', a poem written just a month after the massacre.[26] The campaign that culminated at Peterloo had provoked a crisis of style. In these years Henry Hunt and Cobbett were involved in a determined attempt to wrest the radical leadership from the grasp of the radical Whigs, led by Burdett, and assume to themselves a quite different kind of leadership. Burdett and his associates, Kinnaird, Hobhouse, Byron, wielded political power by virtue of their wealth and birth, and chose to place that power at the service of the people. Hunt and Cobbett opposed them with a power secured only by popular support, by the mass readership of Cobbett's *Political Register*, and by the hundreds of thousands that Hunt could summon to his open-air meetings. Burdett spoke for the people in parliament: Hunt and Cobbett devised a technique of mass protest that entirely bypassed parliament, and in doing so they devised a new political language, the enduring monument of which is Cobbett's prose. It was a language designed not to address fellow parliamentarians or electors, not designed even to address the well-off radical London merchants who determined the outcome of elections at Westminster, but to speak directly to weavers, shoemakers, mill-hands.[27] Shelley responded with the composition of a group of poems, chief amongst them *The Mask of Anarchy*, in which he makes a conscious decision to essay a poetical style that would proclaim his solidarity with the Manchester demonstrators, a style that required him to repudiate his own literariness as a necessary condition for repudiating the class of which that literariness was a badge. Byron saw what was at issue as clearly as Shelley, but responded with passionate outrage that men such as Hunt and Cobbett should dare to dispute with the Whig aristocracy its claim to be the people's true leaders. He wrote angrily to Hobhouse when he heard that his friend planned to attend a dinner given in Henry Hunt's honour: 'Why our classical education alone... should teach us to trample on such unredeemed dirt.'[28] He transmuted his own responses to Peterloo, the Cato Street conspiracy and the Queen Caroline affair into the play *Marino Faliero*, and avoided the danger that he might be besmirched by intellectual contact with those lacking a proper education by his insistence on maintaining the rigid conventions of Italian classical drama.[29] Byron's and Shelley's responses to the political and stylistic crisis of 1819 could scarcely have been more divergent, and yet they have in common a certain theatricality. In Byron's case this is literally the case: not only does he turn to drama, but in the protracted agony that he suffered over the staging of *Marino Faliero* he contrived to rehearse the predicament of his Doge. Just as his hero was forced to capitulate to the necessity of entering into a conspiracy with plebeians that he despised, so the poet was forced to surrender to the humiliation of public representation, and place the success of his tragedy in the hands of the vulgar populace. Shelley's gesture, too, is theatrical, turning from *Prometheus Unbound*, which was characterized, in Mary's words, by an 'abstraction and delicacy of distinction' that was available only to minds as 'subtle and penetrating as his own' to the direct broadside ballad style of *The Mask of Anarchy*. Both Byron's classicism and Shelley's populism remain in their different ways feats of ventriloquism.

Their stylistic experiments serve to indicate a general awareness that by 1819 English politics had assumed a new character. The central political issues were no longer debated by individuals who differed in their views but shared a common language. Burdett and Cobbett both argued for a reform of parliament, but the antagonism between them was more implacable than that between, say, Burdett and Canning. They differed in the language that they used, and difference in language had superseded difference in policy as the critical indicator. Byron and Shelley, however much the latter might try to mend himself, shared the language common to those who had enjoyed a 'classical education'. This is why, of course, a Tory critic such as Lockhart could admire their poems despite his dislike of their politics, but find nothing in the poetry of Hunt and Keats that did not inspire him to contempt. His aesthetic sense could transcend difference of opinion, but could not rise above difference of class.

Keats's modern critics have been right to insist on restoring the political import of Keats's poems, but they have not been very much more successful in locating that import than Keats's reviewers, and for the same reason. The attempt has been to deduce from the poems a set of political opinions, to read 'To Autumn' as guiltily retreating from thoughts of the ill-fed weavers and mill-hands who assembled at Manchester into a visionary world of pastoral opulence, or, alternatively, to read the poem as incorporating a system of allusions to Peterloo which places Keats firmly 'on the liberal side of the question'. Such readings do not so much straitjacket the poems as dress them in a jacket remarkable for being so neatly reversible.[30] The political resonance of Keats's poems has its origin not in their opinions but in their style, which is to say, not in their liberalism but in their Cockneyism. It is through their style that the poems occupy the 'neither/nor' position that defined Keats's class, and it is the very indeterminacy of that particular social class, its unfixed medial position, that enables the poems to express the new politics of the years between 1816 and 1819, a politics that was characterized less by a conflict of opinion than a conflict between languages, between styles. Keats's poems do not take a side in that conflict, rather they accommodate it, and in doing so they expose more clearly than was possible for Byron or Shelley the politics of 'England in 1819'.

Notes

Introduction

1. Carl Woodring, *Politics in English Romantic Poetry* (Harvard University Press, Cambridge, Mass., 1970); F. M. Todd, *Politics and the Poet: A Study of Wordsworth* (Methuen, London, 1957); David Erdman, *Blake: Prophet against Empire: A Poet's Interpretation of the History of his Own Times* (Princeton University Press, Princeton, 1954); K. N. Cameron, *The Young Shelley: Genesis of a Radical* (Gollancz, London, 1951).
2. Amongst which I would cite Marjorie Levinson, *Wordsworth's Great Period Poems: Four Essays* (Cambridge University Press, Cambridge, 1986); David Simpson, *Wordsworth's Historical Imgaination: The Poetry of Displacement* (Methuen, London, 1987); Nicholas Roe, *Wordsworth and Coleridge; The Radical Years* (Clarendon Press, Oxford, 1988); Alan Liu, *Wordsworth: The Sense of History* (Stanford University Press, Stanford, 1989); Richard Bourke, *Romantic Discourse and Political Modernity* (Harvester Wheatsheaf, London, 1993).
3. Kelvin Everest, *Coleridge's Secret Ministry: The Context of the Conversation Poems 1795–1798* (Harvester, Brighton, 1979); Nigel Leask, *The Politics of Imagination in Coleridge's Critical Thought* (Macmillan, London, 1988); Malcolm Kelsall, *Byron's Politics* (Harvester, Brighton, 1987); Jerome Christensen, *Lord Byron's Strength: Romantic Writing and Commercial Society* (Johns Hopkins University Press, Baltimore, 1993); Paul Dawson, *The Unacknowledged Legislator: Shelley and Politics* (Clarendon Press, Oxford, 1980); Michael Scrivener, *Radical Shelley: The Philosophical Anarchism and Utopian Thought of Percy Bysshe Shelley* (Princeton University Press, Princeton, 1982).
4. See Jerome McGann's 1979 article, 'Keats and the Historical Method in Literary Criticism', reprinted in Jerome J. McGann, *The Beauty of Inflections: Literary Investigations in Historical Method and Theory* (Clarendon Press, Oxford, 1985); the special edition of *Studies in Romanticism*, 'Keats and Politics: A Forum', edited by Susan Wolfson, *SiR*, 25 (Summer 1986), pp. 171–229; Daniel P. Watkins, *Keats's Poetry and the Politics of the Imagination* (Associated University Presses, London and Toronto, 1989); Marjorie Levinson, *Keats's Life of Allegory: The Origins of a Style* (Oxford University Press, Oxford, 1989); *Keats And History*, ed. Nicholas Roe (Cambridge University Press, Cambridge, 1995) Nicholas Roe, *John Keats and the Culture of Dissent* (Clarendon Press, Oxford, 1997).
5. James Chandler, *England in 1819: The Politics of Literary Culture and the Case of Romantic Historicism* (University of Chicago Press, Chicago, 1998); Kenneth Johnston, *The Hidden Wordsworth: Poet, Lover, Rebel, Spy* (Norton, New York, 1998); Clifford Siskin, *The Work of Writing: Literature and Social Change in Britain 1700–1830* (Johns Hopkins University Press, Baltimore, 1998).
6. Marilyn Butler, *Romantics, Rebels, and Reactionaries: English Literature and its Background 1760–1830* (Oxford University Press, Oxford, 1982).

7   *Rethinking Historicism*, ed. Marjorie Levinson (Blackwell, Oxford, 1989), p. 4.
8   The exception here is the energetic attempt being made by a growing number of critics to rehabilitate the forgotten women poets of the period.
9   Jerome J. McGann, *The Romantic Ideology* (University of Chicago Press, Chicago, 1983).
10 Clifford Siskin, *The Historicity of Romantic Discourse* (Oxford University Press, New York and Oxford, 1988).
11 *Viewpoints: Poets in Conversation with John Haffenden* (Faber, London, 1981) p. 88.
12 William Hazlitt, 'Mr Wordsworth', in *The Spirit of the Age*.
13 David Simpson, *Romanticism, Nationalism, and the Revolt Against Theory* (University of Chicago Press, Chicago and London, 1993), p. 62.

Part One   Introduction – *Religious Musings*

1   *Collected Letters of Samuel Taylor Coleridge*, ed. Earl L. Griggs, 6 vols (Oxford University Press, Oxford, 1956–71), 1, p. 197. For versions of the same claim, see the letters to Poole and to Thelwall, pp. 203 and 205.
2   The fullest account of *Religious Musings* is offered by Ian Wylie, *Young Coleridge and the Philosophers of Nature* (Clarendon Press, Oxford, 1989), pp. 94–121. I am indebted to him.
3   Quoted in the *OED* entry under 'desultory'.
4   Quotations are from *The Poems of Samuel Taylor Coleridge*, ed. E. H. Coleridge (Oxford University Press, Oxford, 1912), but the text has been amended to that of 1796.
5   The first reference to *Religious Musings* seems to be in a letter to Southey of 29 December 1794: 'The Poem is in blank verse on the Nativity.' *Collected Letters of Samuel Taylor Coleridge*, 1, p. 147.
6   *Collected Letters of Samuel Taylor Coleridge*, 1, p. 162.
7   *Collected Letters of Samuel Taylor Coleridge*, 1, p. 187.
8   A note in the 1797 edition of the poem explains, 'This paragraph is intelligible to those, who, like the Author, believe and feel the sublime system of Berkeley; and the doctrine of the final Happiness of all men'.
9   *Collected Letters of Samuel Taylor Coleridge*, 2, p. 709.
10 Electricity, in particular lightning, had become through its association with Franklin the most powerful metaphor in these years expressing the process by which the current of revolutionary opinion passed between individuals and nations, and expressing too the confluence of philosophical and political opinion. Hence, in *Religious Musings* Coleridge pays his tribute to

> that blest triumph, when the patriot Sage
> Called the red lightnings from the o'er-rushing cloud
> And dashed the beateous terrors on the earth
> Smiling majestic.
> (234–7)

11 *Collected Letters of Samuel Taylor Coleridge*, 1, 207.

12 The manuscript jotting is quoted by Ian Wylie, *Young Coleridge and the Philosophers of Nature*, p. 61.
13 *Collected Letters of Samuel Taylor Coleridge*, 1, 147.
14 Don Cameron Allen, *The Harmonious Vision: Studies in Milton's Poetry* (enlarged edn, Johns Hopkins Press, Baltimore and London, 1970), p. 26.
15 For a somewhat different comparison of Milton's and Coleridge's treatment of time, see David Collings, 'Coleridge Beginning a Career: Desultory Authorship' in *Religious Musings*, *ELH*, 58 (1991), pp. 167–93.
16 On the revolutionary calendar see Simon Schama, *Citizens: A Chronicle of the French Revolution* (Alfred Knopf, New York, 1989), pp. 771–5.
17 *Collected Letters of Samuel Taylor Coleridge*, 3, p. 467.
18 Joseph Cottle, *Early Recollections; chiefly relating to the late Samuel Taylor Coleridge, during his long residence in Bristol*, (1837), 2, p. 52.
19 On *Religious Musings* as a rejection of Godwin, see Nicola Trott, 'The Coleridge Circle and the "Answer to Godwin"', *Review of English Studies*, 41(1990), 212–29. Coleridge spoke of Paine with open derision by 1796. See *Collected Letters of Samuel Taylor Coleridge*, 1, p. 197.
20 On Coleridge's Unitarianism, see H. W. Piper, 'Coleridge and the Unitarian Consensus' in *The Coleridge Connection: Essays for Thomas McFarland*, ed. Richard Gravil and Molly Lefebure (Macmillan, London, 1990), pp. 273–90.

Chapter 1: Erasmus Darwin: from the Bastille to Birmingham

1 *Collected Letters of Samuel Taylor Coleridge*, ed. Earl L. Griggs, 6 vols (Oxford University Press, Oxford, 1956–71), pp. 216 and 305.
2 Erasmus Darwin, *The Botanic Garden 1791* (Scolar Press, Menton, 1973) ed. Desmond King-Hele, p.v. All subsequent quotations are from this edition.
3 On Darwin's thought and its centrality, see Donald M. Hassler, 'Erasmus Darwin and Enlightenment Belief', *Enlightenment Essays*, 1 (1970), pp. 77–83.
4 Darwin is borrowing a metaphor that became enormously fashionable in the 1780s, prompting Turgot's famous epigram on Franklin: 'Eripuit Coelo Fulmen, Sceptrumque Tyrannis', and John Adams's sourer comment: 'It is universally believed in France that his electric wand has accomplished all this revolution.' See Simon Schama: *Citizens: A Chronicle of the French Revolution* (Penguin, Harmondsworth, 1989), pp. 42–6 for a brief account of the potency of this metaphor.
5 Samuel Taylor Coleridge, *Biographia Literaria*, 2 vols, ed. J. Shawcross (Clarendon Press, Oxford, 1907), 1, p. 54.
6 Maureen McNeil, 'The Scientific Muse: The Poetry of Erasmus Darwin' in *Languages of Nature: Critical Essays on Science and Literature*, ed. L. J. Jordanova (Rutgers University Press, New Brunswick 1986), pp. 159–203.
7 Karl Marx, *Grundrisse* (Penguin, Harmondsworth, 1979), p. 699.

8 Quoted in Neil McKendrick 'Josiah Wedgwood and Factory Discipline', *Historical Journal*, 4 (1961), 30–55, p. 34.
9 On Darwin's life, see Desmond King-Hele, *Erasmus Darwin* (Macmillan, London, 1963).
10 The Rev. T. J. Mathias publishing anonymously, *The Pursuits of Literature*, (T. Beckett, London, 1799) 1, 79–86, First Dialogue, first published 1794.
11 Richard Polwhele publishing anonymously, *The Unsex'd Females: A Poem Addressed to the Author of The Pursuits of Literature* (Cadell & Davies, London, 1798).
12 R. B. Rose, 'The Priestley Riots of 1791', *Past and Present*, 17 (November 1960), 68–88. E. P. Thompson, though working from Rose, is more inclined to credit Priestley's suspicion of ministerial complicity. See *The Making of the English Working Class* (Penguin, Harmondsworth, 1980), pp. 79–80.
13 Quoted in Neil McKendrick, 'Josiah Wedgwood and Factory Discipline'.
14 From a contemporary letter written by the Rev. J. Bartlam, quoted in R. B. Rose, 'The Priestley Riots of 1791'.
15 Quoted by R. B. Rose, 'The Priestley Riots of 1791'.
16 16 April, 23 April and 7 March 1798, *The Anti-Jacobin*, 2, 162–74, 200–5, and 274–80.
17 *The Anti-Jacobin*, 2 (1798), p. 280.
18 On Blake's relationship with Erasmus Darwin, see David Worrall, 'William Blake and Erasmus Darwin's Botanic Garden', *Bulletin of the New York Public Library*, 79 (1975), 397–417.

Chapter 2: William Blake and Revolutionary Prophecy

1 John Howard, 'An Audience for *The Marriage of Heaven and Hell*', *Blake Studies*, 3 (1970), 39–52.
2 David V. Erdman, *Blake: Prophet against Empire* (Princeton University Press, Princeton, 1954), p. 161.
3 Peter Ackroyd, *Blake* (Minerva, London, 1996), p. 100.
4 Robert Hindmarsh, *Rise and Progress of the New Jerusalem Church* (Hodson, London, 1861), p. 142.
5 David V. Erdman, *Blake: Prophet against Empire*, p. 160.
6 Michael Scrivener, 'A Swedenborgian Visionary and *The Marriage of Heaven and Hell*', *Blake An Illustrated Quarterly*, 21 (Winter, 1987–8), 102–4.
7 Jon Mee, 'The Radical Enthusiasm of Blake's *The Marriage of Heaven and Hell*', *British Journal for Eighteenth-Century Studies*, 14 (Spring, 1991), 51–60.
8 Mee is developing an argument first offered by Morton D. Paley in his 'William Blake, the Prince of the Hebrews, and the Woman Clothed with the Sun', in *William Blake: Essays in Honour of Sir Geoffrey Keynes*, ed. Morton D. Paley and Michael Philips (Clarendon Press, Oxford, 1973), pp. 260–93. On millenarian and apocalyptic currents of thought in the revolutionary period, see Clarke Garrett, *Respectable Folly: Millenarians and the French Revolution in France and England* (Johns Hopkins University Press, Baltimore, 1975).

9   On the proverbial tradition see John Villalobos, 'William Blake's "Proverbs of Hell" and the Tradition of Wisdom Literature', *Studies in Philology*, 87 (1990), 246–59.
10 On the Radical usurpation of the Tory jibe that 'the first Whig was the devil' see Peter A. Scock, '*The Marriage of Heaven and Hell*: Blake's Myth of Satan and its Cultural Matrix', *ELH*, 60 (1993), 441–65.
11 On Blake and Paine's reading of the Bible see Robert N. Essick, 'William Blake, Thomas Paine, and Biblical Revolution', *Studies in Romanticism*, 30 (1991), 189–212.
12 On Blake's illustrations, see David V. Erdman with Tom Dargan and Marleve Deverell-Van Meter, 'Reading the Illuminations of Blake's *Marriage of Heaven and Hell*', in *William Blake: Essays in Honour of Sir Geoffrey Keynes,* ed. Morton D. Paley and Michael Philips (Clarendon Press, Oxford, 1973), pp. 162–207.
13 Jon Mee, *Dangerous Enthusiasm: William Blake and the culture of radicalism in the 1790s* (Clarendon Press, Oxford, 1992), especially chapter 1.
14 Terence A. Hoagwood compares Priestley's dictum, 'powers of attraction and repulsion are necessary to its very being', *English Language Notes*, 15 (1978), 87–90.
15 Terence Allan Hoagwood, *Prophecy and the Philosophy of Mind: Tradition of Blake and Shelley* (University of Alabama Press, Alabama, 1985), p. 7.
16 Harold Bloom's reading, although he terms dialectical what I term contradictory, seems truer: 'Against the supernaturalist, Blake asserts the reality of the body as being all of the soul that the five senses can perceive. Against the naturalist, he asserts the unreality of the merely given body as against the imaginative body, rising through an increase in sensual fulfilment into a realization of its unfallen potential.' See 'Dialectics in *The Marriage of Heaven and Hell*', *PMLA*, 73 (1958), 501–4.
17 Joseph Priestley, *Institutes of Natural and Revealed Religion* (1772) in *The Theological and Miscellaneous Works of Joseph Priestley*, ed. J. T. Rutt, 12 vols (Hackney, 1816–31), 2, p. 370. On Priestley's apocalyptic writings, see Christopher Burdom, *The Apocalypse in England: Revelation Unravelling, 1700–1834* (Macmillan, London, 1997), pp. 112–14.

Chapter 3: The English Jacobins

1 *Blake: Complete Writings*, ed. Geoffrey Keynes (Oxford University Press, London, 1966), p. 383.
2 Even a prime ministerial mouthpiece. There is evidence that Pitt himself wrote the articles vigorously defending his own taxation policy.
3 9 July 1798, *The Anti-Jacobin or Weekly Examiner* (hereafter *AJ*) 2, 623–40.
4 The allusion is to Coleridge's poem 'To a Young Ass; Its Mother being tethered near it'.
5 *A J*, 1, 3–4.
6 T. J. Mathias, *The Pursuits of Literature: A Satirical Poem in Four Dialogues* (T. Beckett, London, 1798) p. 238.
7 The French Jacobins, of course, in this, too, more like the English Anti-Jacobins than their opponents, were conservative defenders of gender

difference, banning women from their club, and encouraging them to devote themselves to domestic duties rather than engage in politics.
8 Hannah More, *Strictures on the Modern System of Female Education*, 2 vols (T. Cadell, London, 1798), 1, p. 4.
9 *A J*, November 20, 1797, 1, pp. 31–4.
10 Quotations are taken from *The Poetical Works of Robert Southey*, 10 vols (Longman, London, 1837–8).
11 In 1796 the poem was published in 12 books, reduced in 1798 to ten by the extraction of *The Vision of the Maid of Orleans*.
12 *Critical Review*, 26 (August 1799), p. 475.
13 A point eloquently made by Stuart Curran, who argues that both *Joan of Arc* and *Gebir* reject the model of the Virgilian epic, and with it 'the value of an imperial mission and the warfare that sustains it'. In *Gebir*, Landor values 'the pastoral romance to which Gebir's brother Tamar gives his allegiance over the public imperialist duties of his epic hero'. See Stuart Curran, *Poetic Form and British Romanticism* (Oxford University Press, New York and Oxford, 1986), p. 168.
14 Stuart Curran writes: 'No reader of 1798 could miss the implications of a colonial power in Egypt, when Napoleon had just landed his armies and usurped the Mamaluke government' (*Poetic Form and British Romantic*, p. 168), but, as Simon Bainbridge points out, Napoleon's Egyptian expedition was known in England far too late in the year for Landor to have incorporated it into his poem. In June Napoleon's whereabouts remained a pregnant mystery. See Simon Bainbridge, *Napoleon and English Romanticism* (Cambridge University Press, Cambridge, 1985), p. 32.
15 In the second edition of *Gebir*, in 1803, Landor made in a note his recantation:

> Bonaparte might have been so, and in the beginning of his career it was argued that he would be. But unhappily he thinks, that to produce great changes, is to perform great actions: to annihilate antient freedom and to substitute new, to give republics a monarchical government, and the provinces of monarchs a republican one; in short, to overthrow by violence all the institutions, and to tear from the heart all the social habits of men, has been the tenor of his politics to the present hour.

16 Bainbridge argues that Landor places 'Napoleon in the pastoral tradition of his shepherd father, Tamar,' in order 'to represent Napoleon as the pastor who will lead his flock into the promised land', but even in 1798 such a representation was manifestly absurd, as Bainbridge goes some way towards admitting when he accepts that a more 'ironical' reading of the tribute to Napoleon would be possible (*Napoleon and English Romanticism*, p. 48).

Part Two   Introduction – *The Poet's Pilgrimage to Waterloo*

1 Howard Weinbrot, *Britannia's Issue: The Rise of British Literature from Dryden to Ossian* (Cambridge University Press, Cambridge, 1993).

2 Linda Colley, *Britons: Forging the Nation, 1707–1837* (Yale University Press, New Haven and London, 1992).
3 Philip Shaw, 'Commemorating Waterloo: Wordsworth, Southey, and "The Muses' Page of State"', *Romanticism*, 1.1 (1995), 50–67. See also Simon Bainbridge, '"To Sing It Rather Better": Byron, the Bards, and Waterloo', *Romanticism*, 1.1 (1995), 68–81.
4 Leigh Hunt, *The Descent of Liberty: A Mask* (Gale, Curtis & Fenner, London, 1815).

Chapter 4: Walter Scott and Anti-Gallican Minstrelsy

1 Scott included this ballad, that he believed to be an authentic work of the legendary Thomas of Ercildoun, together with his own continuation of it in the second volume of *Minstrelsy of the Scottish Border* (Cadell and Davies, London, 1802), from which quotations are taken.
2 Lukacs was the first critic to offer a powerful challenge to this view. Scott for him is the first historical novelist precisely because he was able to overcome 'the greatest obstacle to the understanding of history', which lay in 'the Enlightenment's conception of man's unalterable nature', Georg Lukacs, *The Historical Novel* (Merlin Press, London, 1962, first published 1933), p. 28. This view has become standard amongst Scott's critics, but Lukacs himself fails to sustain it, or rather he is able to sustain it only by introducing another category, the 'human', which he can represent as existing outside the historical process within which 'character' has its being. Hence, he is able both to recognize and to celebrate the 'human greatness' of Scott's characters (e.g. pp. 51, 56).
3 This and other examples are given by Edgar Johnson, *Sir Walter Scott: The Great Unknown* (Hamish Hamilton, London, 1970), 1, pp. 205–6. The extent of the freedom that Scott allowed himself in the transcription of ballads is discussed by his modern editor. See *Minstrelsy of the Scottish Border*, ed. T. F. Henderson, 4 vols (Oliver & Boyd, Edinburgh, 1932).
4 On the relationship between road-building and antiquarian research, see Stuart Piggott, *Ruins in a Landscape: Essays in Antiquarianism* (Edinburgh University Press, Edinburgh, 1976), 122–4. In Scotland, the Wade roads offered for the first time access by carriage to the Highlands. The Wade roads, it is important to note, were not built solely, nor even primarily, for commercial reasons, but to facilitate the garrisoning of the Highlands in the wake of the '45.
5 *The Complete Letters of Robert Burns*, ed. James A. Mackay (Alloway Publishing, Ayrshire, 1987), p. 55.
6 On this, see John Mullan, *Sentiment and Sociability: The Language of Feeling in the Eighteenth Century* (Clarendon Press, Oxford, 1988). The sentimental man, according to Mullan 'relies on feeling, indulges benevolence, and yearns for sociability', but his yearning is doomed to be unfulfilled, for the sentimental novel creates the man of feeling as 'a species only by being an exception – a simple soul in an unsentimental world', p. 146.
7 Harley, in Scott's favourite sentimental novel, *The Man of Feeling*, is typical of such novels in his benevolence, and typical, too, in his inability to explain

the principles that direct his generosity. When approached by an old man who excites pity by his poverty, but discourages the donor by being evidently roguish, Harley finds that 'Virtue held back his arm', but 'a younger sister of virtue's, not so severe' loosens his fingers, and he drops a shilling as alms, Henry Mackenzie, *The Man of Feeling*, ed. Brian Vickers (Oxford University Press, London, 1970), pp. 22–3.
8 J. G. Lockhart, *Memoirs of the Life of Sir Walter Scott* (Robert Cadell, Edinburgh, John Murray and Whitaker, London, 1837), 1, pp. 343 and 379–80.
9 *Memoirs of the Life of Sir Walter Scott*, 1, p. 67.
10 *Memoirs of the Life of Sir Walter Scott*, 1, pp. 381–2.
11 From Scott's own memoir of his early life, published in *Memoirs of the Life of Sir Walter Scott*, 1, p. 46.
12 Georg Lukacs, *The Historical Novel*, pp. 61–3. The necessary anachronism works to 'clarify and underline' the relationship between the past and the present.
13 *The Poems of Sir Walter Scott*, ed. J. Logie Robertson (Oxford University Press, Oxford, 1904), p. 53. Quotations from the poetry are taken from this edition.
14 *Memoirs of the Life of Sir Walter Scott*, 2, p. 24. The system of allusions is well explicated by Nancy Moore Goslee, *Scott the Rhymer* (University Press of Kentucky, Lexington, Kentucky, 1988), pp. 22–4. Goslee's is much the most authoritative and suggestive account of Scott's poetry yet published, and I am indebted to it.
15 *Poems of Sir Walter Scott*, 1.
16 Goslee usefully notes that these lines are spoken by the minstrel to 'his late seventeenth-century audience but also to Scott's own early nineteenth-century one. For both, though not for Deloraine, the abbey was in ruins', *Scott the Rhymer*, p. 34.
17 David Brown, *Walter Scott and the Historical Imagination* (Routledge & Kegan Paul, London, 1979), pp. 195–9. Brown argues for the decisive influence on Scott of the Scottish school of 'philosophical' history, to which he would have been introduced by Dugald Stewart, who lectured to him at university in Edinburgh. The seminal works of this school were Adam Smith's lectures delivered at Edinburgh University in the 1750s and 1760s, Adam Ferguson's *An Essay on the History of Civil Society* (1767), and John Millar's *Origin of Ranks* (1771). Scott's own *Essay on Chivalry*, first published in 1818, is itself sufficient to indicate his affiliation with this school.
18 Edgar Johnson, *Sir Walter Scott: The Great Unknown*, 1, p. 197.
19 *The Poems of Sir Walter Scott*, pp. 52–3.
20 *Memoirs of the Life of Sir Walter Scott*, 1, p. 243.
21 *Memoirs of the Life of Sir Walter Scott*, 1, p. 349.
22 *Memoirs of the Life of Sir Walter Scott*, 1, p. 258.
23 Edgar Johnson, *Sir Walter Scott: The Great Unknown*, 1, p. 212.
24 The unheroic nature of Marmion's criminality was noted disapprovingly even by reviewers who admired the poem and by Lockhart who thought *Marmion* Scott's greatest poetic achievement. It is an incongruity that continues to strike modern readers. Goslee, for example, notes 'the unchivalric nature of Marmion's crime – a crime that uses writing', *Scott the Rhymer*, p. 42.

25 Byron wrote on Scott's presentation copy of *The Giaour*, 'To the Monarch of Parnassus from one of his subjects', Edgar Johnson, *Sir Walter Scott: The Great Unknown*, 1, p. 462.
26 Scott's recognition of this may be deduced from his decision to publish at the very end of the third volume of *Minstrelsy of the Scottish Borders* his own 'War-Song of the Royal Edinburgh Light Dragoons':

> To horse! to horse! the standard flies,
>   The bugles sound the call;
>   The Gallic navy stems the seas,
>   The sound of battle's on the breeze,
>   Arouse ye, one and all!

27 *Memoirs of the Life of Sir Walter Scott*, 2, p. 155. Lockhart even claims that Jeffrey's lukewarm review of his friend's poem was prompted by his recognition that *Marmion* was the poem that 'first annouced him in that character': Scott 'had put the trumpet to his lips, and done his part, at least, to sustain the hope and resolution of his countrymen in that struggle from which it was the doctrine of the Edinburgh Review that no sane observer of the times could expect anything but ruin and degradation'. It is revealing of the manner in which war transforms the nature of ideological difference that, despite this, Lockhart can insist that 'feelings of political partisanship find no place in this poem'.
28 Edgar Johnson, *Sir Walter Scott, The Great Unknown*, 1, p. 102.
29 Lockhart records that it was the Tory, Lord Abercorn, who prompted Scott to add his eulogy of Fox. Abercorn may even have written the lines himself, *Memoirs of the Life of Sir Walter Scott*, 2, pp. 154–5.
30 Robert Crawford, *Devolving English Literature* (Clarendon Press, Oxford, 1992), pp. 16–44.
31 Edgar Johnson, *Sir Walter Scott: The Great Unknown*, 1, p. 262. One of Scott's concerns in *Rob Roy* is to trace through the developing relationship between Jarvie's Glasgow trading house and the large London house of the Osbaldistones the origin of this economic interdependence.
32 *Memoirs of the Life of Sir Walter Scott*, 2, pp. 110–11.
33 For a summary of these measures, see Bruce P. Lenman and John S. Gibson, *The Jacobite Threat – England, Scotland, Ireland, France: A Source Book* (Scottish Academic Press, Edinburgh, 1990), pp. 239–41.
34 On 14 October 1803, Scott wrote to George Ellis: 'God has left us entirely to our own means of defence, for we have not above one regiment of the line in all our ancient kingdom. In the meanwhile we are doing our best to prepare ourselves for a contest, which, perhaps, is not far distant', *The Letters of Sir Walter Scott*, ed. H. J. C. Grierson (Constable, London, 1932), 1, p. 204.
35 *Memoirs of the Life of Sir Walter Scott*, 2, pp. 71–2.
36 In his *Life of Napoleon Buonaparte*, Scott on several occasions implies the efficacy of the Napoleonic wars in realizing the idea of Britain, as when he remarks on the evident superiority in raw courage that the British soldier displays over his French counterpart: 'The Guards supplied by the city of London, may be contrasted with a regiment of Irish recruited among their

rich meadows, or a body of Scotch from their native wildernesses', but 'all are found to exhibit that species of dogged and desperate courage, which, without staying to measure force or calculate chances, rushes on the enemy as the bull dog upon the bear.' *The Prose Works of Sir Walter Scott* (Robert Cadell, Edinburgh; Whitaker, London, 1835), 12, p. 284.

Chapter 5: Wordsworth at War

1 All quotations from *Poems, 1807*, are taken from *Poems, in Two Volumes, and Other Poems, 1800–1807*, ed. Jared Curtis (Cornell University Press, Ithaca, New York, 1983). Most commentators have stressed the miscellaneous nature of the volumes, agreeing with Hartman: 'It would be wrong to treat this collection as a natural unity. It is, as the title indicates, a composite volume written over a number of years and with no single aim.' See Geoffrey H. Hartman, *Wordsworth's Poetry, 1787–1814* (Yale University Press, New Haven and London, 1964), p. 260. Jared Curtis has responded by pursuing the clue left by Wordsworth in his letter of 21 May 1807, to Lady Beaumont, *The Letters of William and Dorothy Wordsworth, 2, The Middle Years, Part 1, 1806–1811.* ed. de Selincourt, rev., Moorman (2nd edn, Clarendon Press, Oxford, 1969), 147. Hereafter *Letters 2*. Wordsworth claims that the 'Sonnets Dedicated to Liberty' 'collectively make a Poem on the subject of civil Liberty and national independence, which, either for simplicity of style or grandeur of moral sentiment, is, alas! likely to have few parallels in the Poetry of the present day'. Wordsworth goes on to defend the section entitled 'Moods of My Own Mind' against the charge that the poems are 'trifling' by arguing that, 'taken collectively', they 'fix the attention upon a subject eminently poetical, viz., the interest which objects in nature derive from the predominance of certain affections more or less permanent, more or less capable of salutary renewal in the mind of the being contemplating these objects'. Curtis extends Wordsworth's method to argue for the loose unity of other sections in the collection. See *Poems in Two Volumes, and Other Poems, 1800–1807*, pp. 35–9. See also Jared Curtis, *Wordsworth's Experiments with Tradition: The Lyric Poems of 1802* (Cornell University Press, Ithaca and London, 1971), pp. 30–5.
2 *The Prose Works of William Wordsworth*, 3 vols, ed. Owen and Smyser (Clarendon Press, Oxford, 1974), 1, 116. Hereafter *Prose*.
3 *The Letters of William and Dorothy Wordsworth: The Early Years, 1787–1805*, ed. de Selincourt, rev. Shaver (2nd edn, Clarendon Press, Oxford, 1967), pp. 313–15. Hereafter *Letters 1*.
4 See Richard Cronin, 'Walter Scott: The Mighty Minstrel of the Antigallican War', forthcoming in *ELH*.
5 The centrality of the traditional community of the Lakes in Wordsworth's political thought has been studied by Michael H. Friedman, *The Making of a Tory Humanist: William Wordsworth and the Idea of Community* (Columbia University Press, New York, 1979). Friedman also discusses the consequences for Wordsworth of his recognition that this community has not survived.
6 Theresa Kelley detects in Wordsworth's poetry of these years what she terms an 'aesthetics of containment', *Wordsworth's Revisionary Aesthetics*

(Cambridge University Press, Cambridge, 1988), pp. 137–69. After 1806, Kelley argues, Wordsworth elaborates an aesthetics in which 'the beautiful "wraps" the sublime by challenging its claim to exist outside time and outside society'. This new aesthetic is worked out, according to Kelley, in reaction against the 'sublime figure' of Napoleon.

7 Helen Darbishire describes the language of *Poems, 1807*, as 'no longer "the language spoken by men" but the richly reminiscent language of the poets. Spenser, Daniel, Ben Jonson, and above all Milton'. *Poems in Two Volumes*, ed. Helen Darbishire (Clarendon Press, Oxford, 1914), xxxix.

8 Helen Darbishire tabulates Wordsworth's metrical and stanzaic borrowing in an appendix to her edition of *Poems in Two Volumes 1807*, pp. 464–70.

9 See, for example the letter to George Beaumont of February 1808: 'The *People* would love the Poem of Peter Bell, but the *Public* (a very different Being) will never love it.' (*Letters*, 2, 194).

10 Curtis argues that the title of the first section, and the motto appended to it, were removed by the printer only because they appeared on the same page as the 'Advertisement' which Wordsworth was anxious to delete. He therefore restores them in his edition, though his reasoning has not convinced everybody. See for example *Wordsworth's Poems of 1807*, ed. A. L. Jones (Humanities Press International, Atlantic Highlands, NJ, 1987), xiii–xv.

11 It is true that F. M. Todd argues that, until 1808, when his interest was re-awakened by events in Spain, Wordsworth remained 'in that state of political indifference which had followed the death of his brother'. See F. M. Todd, *Politics and the Poet: A Study of Wordsworth* (Methuen, London, 1957), 136. But Todd's evidence suggests not an indifference to politics, but a disenchantment with both the two major political parties, and that is an attitude wholeheartedly maintained in *The Convention of Cintra*.

12 In her essay on the Immortality Ode, Marjorie Levinson argues vigorously that the rhetoric of the Ode works by incorporating a vocabulary that is weighted with a 'public symbolism' only in order to repudiate the public character of that symbolism. So, 'the Tree of Liberty' is emptied of its public meaning to become 'a Tree, of many one' but its former status is betrayed by 'the abrupt intrusion' of the image, and by 'the disproportionate emotion' that the poem invests in it. 'The historicity of the image' functions, for Levinson, as 'a return of the repressed'. See Marjorie Levinson, *Wordsworth's Great Period Poems: Four Essays* (Cambridge University Press, Cambridge, 1986), pp. 80–100. Abrams had distinguished between the public character of the odes of the 1790s and the 'spiritual character' of the lyric forms that succeeded them. In the later poems, Abrams suggests, history is transcended, whereas for Levinson it is repressed. The difference between the two critics remains inflectional rather than substantive. The persuasiveness of Levinson's case rests, I suspect, even though her argument does not rely on it, on its congruence with the view that after 1801, Wordsworth repressed his former adherence to revolutionary ideals and to the symbolism that embodied them. But even in *The Convention of Cintra* Wordsworth is prepared to declare his devotion to the tree of liberty:

> It is a common saying among those who profess to be lovers of civil liberty, and give themselves some credit for understanding it, – that, if a Nation be not free, it is mere dust in the balance whether the slavery be

bred at home, or comes from abroad; be of their own suffering, or of a stranger's imposing. They see little of the under-ground part of the tree of liberty, and know less of the nature of man, who can think thus. (*Prose*, 1, 322)

I argue that Wordsworth's subordination of the public to the private does not represent a retreat from politics but the ground on which he distinguishes 'English' from 'French' politics, in other words, that it is recognized as itself the articulation of a distinctive political position, and one that Wordsworth maintains and defends in a substantial part of *The Convention of Cintra*.

13 Quotations are drawn from reviews in the *Annual Review*, 6 1807, 521–9, the *Critical Review*, 7 August 1807, 399–403, and from Jeffrey's review in the *Edinburgh Review*, 11 October 1807, 214–31. Reviewers agreed in excepting the directly political poems from the charges brought against the collection as a whole.
14 *The Convention of Cintra* (1809), *Reply to 'Mathetes'* (in *The Friend*, 14 December 1809 and 4 January 1810), *Essays upon Epitaphs* (the first essay in *The Friend*, 22 February 1810, the second and third unprinted until 1876, but apparently written for *The Friend* in early 1810), the 'Introduction' to Wilkinson's *Select Views in Cumberland, Westmoreland, and Lancashire* (1810).
15 *Edinburgh Review*, 12 April 1808, 131–51.
16 In his review of *Poems*, 1807, Jeffrey had represented the final two lines of 'Ode to Duty' as nonsensical. Wordsworth responded by defiantly quoting the final stanza of the Ode as the conclusion to his *Reply to Mathetes*, but defensively prefacing his quotation with an explanation of the offending lines.
17 For an incisive discussion of these matters focused on 'Gipsies', see David Simpson, 'Criticism, Politics, and Style in Wordsworth's Poetry', *Critical Inquiry*, 11 (1984), 52–81.
18 Wordsworth revealed his sensitivity to Jeffrey's complaint by substituting, after 1820, a 'Turtle Shell' for the 'Household Tub'.
19 Compare Richard Bourke's reading of *Home at Grasmere*, in which he argues that a celebration of the vale's freedom from dependence on the world outside it releases the uncomfortable realization that the ideal status of the dale is secured not by its economy but by the imagination of the poet who surveys it. An ideal of economic self-subsistence yields to the ideal of a self-subsistent imagination. Richard Bourke, *Romantic Discourse and Political Modernity: Wordsworth, the Intellectual and Cultural Critique* (Harvester Wheatsheaf, London, 1993), 92–102.
20 Compare Alan Liu's reading of 'Composed Upon Westminster Bridge' which describes the sonnet as at once an example of 'topical poetry which talks *with* the nation *about* the nation's power', and a poem in which one can trace the story of how Wordsworth's ideology of nationhood 'shrunk to the ideology of the self'. Alan Liu, *Wordsworth: The Sense of History* (Stanford University Press, Stanford, California, 1989), 485.

Chapter 6: Mapping *Childe Harold I and II*

1 Carl Woodring, *Politics in English Romantic Poetry* (Harvard University Press, Cambridge, Mass., 1970), p. 156.

2 The fullest accounts of Byron's trip are given by William A. Borst, *Lord Byron's First Pilgrimage* (Yale University Press, New Haven, 1948), and by Leslie A. Marchand, *Byron: A Biography* (John Murray, London, 1957), 1, pp. 185–277.
3 *Byron's Letters and Journals*, ed. Leslie A. Marchand, 2 (John Murray, London, 1973), p. 198.
4 Ali Pasha's policy in the war years was directed by his ambition to secure one or more of the Ionian islands, and hence to establish himself in the Mediterranean. Corfu, because of its strategic importance, was the greatest prize. In 1806 Ali Pasha had tried to take the island from the Russians through direct military action, and had failed. Subsequently, he offered alliance to the British or to the French, whichever at the time seemed the more likely to be willing and able to cede to him an Ionian island. See Stefanaq Pollo and Apben Puto, *The History of Albania* (Routledge & Kegan Paul, London, 1981), pp. 100–1.
5 All quotations from *Childe Harold* are from the edition by Jerome J. McGann, *Lord Byron: The Complete Poetical Works*, vol. 2 (Clarendon Press, Oxford, 1980).
6 Croker's poem was described by its publisher, Murray, as having enjoyed a success greater 'than any short poem he knew'. Wellington's own acknowledgement of the poem was characteristically terse: 'I did not know a battle could be turned to anything so entertaining.' See the entry for Croker in the *Dictionary of National Biography*.
7 In his review of Croker's poem. See the *Quarterly Review*, 11 (1809), p. 426.
8 Byron acknowledges that Harold's farewell to England, 'his last Good Night', is modelled on 'Lord Maxwell's Good Night' in Scott's *Minstrelsy of the Scottish Border*. Recounting his entry into Tepaleen in a letter to his mother, Byron suggested she call to mind 'Scott's description of Branksome castle in his *Lay*', *Byron's Letters and Journals*, 1, p. 227. This helps to confirm what one would in any case have suspected, that Byron's response to the wild Albanians is directed by his sense of their similarity to the Highland clansmen and Border moss-troopers who feature in Scott's poems.
9 J. G. Lockhart, *Memoirs of the Life of Sir Walter Scott* (John Murray and Whitaker, London, 1837), 2, p. 155.
10 For example, Jeffrey praised Byron's poem by suggesting that of contemporary poets only Scott had a style 'equally strong and natural', *Edinburgh Review*, 38 (1812), p. 467.
11 Byron reveals in the 'Addition to the Preface' that first appeared in the fourth edition of the poem that this is a self-conscious tactic. He offers a somewhat facetious defence of his hero against the charge that he is '*unknightly*', and concludes:

> So much for chivalry. Burke need not have regretted that its days are over, though Maria Antoinette was quite as chaste as most of those in whose honours lances were shivered, and knights unhorsed.

12 *Quarterly Review*, 13 (1812), pp. 180–200, and *Edinburgh Review*, 38 (1812), pp. 466–77.
13 Jerome J. McGann, *Fiery Dust: Byron's Poetic Development* (University of Chicago Press, Chicago and London, 1968), pp. 53–4. McGann's brief

account of *Childe Harold* in his more recent *The Beauty of Inflections* (Clarendon Press, Oxford, 1985) indicates that his present position is much closer to my own in its insistence that in the first two cantos of *Childe Harold* there is no secure distinction between the public and the private: 'More than anything else this book says that the most personal and intimate aspects of an individual's life are closely involved with, and affected by, the social and political context in which the individual is placed', p. 261.

14 Lord Jocelyn's speech is reported in *The Times* for 8 January 1812.
15 *Quarterly Review*, 13 (1812), p. 151.
16 The glee of 'Stern Cobbett' when the Convention provided him with so stout a stick to beat the Ministry is recorded in a deleted stanza of *Childe Harold*. See *Lord Byron: The Complete Poetical Works*, 2, p. 20.
17 Robert F. Gleckner, *Byron and the Ruins of Paradise* (Johns Hopkins University Press, Baltimore, 1967), p. 65.
18 A useful survey of poems before *Childe Harold* in which English travellers express their resposes to Greece is given by Terence Spencer, *Fair Greece Sad Relic: Literary Philhellenism from Shakespeare to Byron* (Weidenfeld & Nicolson, London, 1954), pp. 247–94.
19 *The Works of Anna Laetitia Barbauld* (Taylor, London, 1825), 1, pp. 232–50. The poem was first published as a separate pamphlet in 1811.
20 The best account of the whole business is offered by William St Clair, *Lord Elgin and the Marbles* (Oxford University Press, London, 1967). St Clair points out that Elgin was a Tory fierce enough in his support for the war to have aroused the personal enmity of Napoleon, which may have added fuel to Byron's indignation at his activities.
21 *Edinburgh Review*, 36 (1811), p. 379.
22 *The British Critic*, 38 (1811), p. 522.
23 *Edinburgh Review*, 36 (1811), p. 391.
24 *Quarterly Review*, 7 (1812), pp. 309–13. Lucy Aikin, in the memoir prefixed to her collected edition of Mrs Barbauld's works, while admitting that a poem designed to give a check to 'national pride' could not have expected easy popularity, adds that only 'those thoroughly acquainted with the instincts of the hired assassin of reputation shooting from his coward ambush' could have anticipated that it would 'expose its author – its venerable and female author – to contumely and insult'. The reception of the poem persuaded Mrs Barbauld, she claims, to abandon publishing her poetry. See *The Works of Anna Laetitia Barbauld, pp. 1–1ii*.
25 *Quarterly Review*, 7 (March, 1812), pp. 151–9.
26 The best account of Byron's Whiggism is offered by Malcolm Kelsall, *Byron's Politics* (Harvester, Sussex, 1987), especially pp. 1–56.
27 Galt reports Byron as having said to Dallas as he left the Lords after making his maiden speech that 'he had, by his speech, given [him] the best advertisement for Childe Harold's Pilgrimage'. See John Galt, *The Life of Lord Byron* (Colburn & Bentley, London, 1830), p. 172.
28 Quoted by Marchand, *Byron: A Biography*, 1, pp. 292–3.
29 In his 'Addition to the Preface'.
30 Holland's enthusiasm prompted Byron to traduce him as 'Vulpes' in a stanza tactfully omitted from the published version of the poem. See *Lord Byron: The Complete Poetical Works*, 2, p. 42.

31 Whitbread's motion, for example, was defeated not by the Tories but by his fellow Whigs, whose leaders acted quickly to move next business, and hence to forestall the possibility of a divisive debate.
32 Quoted by Marchand, *Byron: A Biography*, 1, p. 335.
33 Pessimism concerning the prospects of ever bringing the war to a conclusion is apparent in many Whig parliamentary speeches in 1811 and early 1812, and evident too in Jeffrey's surveys of the international situation in the *Edinburgh*. But both Jeffrey and the Parliamentary Whigs are obviously embarrassed by their fear that their gloominess might be interpreted as a failure of patriotism. Leigh Hunt could, and did, allow himself to be more explicit. Early in 1812, he wrote:

> there is nothing at all in the present aspect of Spanish affairs to do away with the impression made upon calm spectators of its condition, and so often repeated in this Paper, – that Spain, after proving what it might have done had its spirit met with early and proper encouragement, will be conquered by the lingering corruptions of its upper orders, their divisions, their timidity, and their utter worthlessness', *The Examiner*, 214 (2 February 1812), p. 72.

34 Byron wrote on Scott's presentation copy of *The Giaour*, 'To the Monarch of Parnassus from one of his subjects'. See Edgar Johnson, *Sir Walter Scott: The Great Unknown* (Hamish Hamilton, London, 1970), 1, p. 462.
35 *The Poems of Sir Walter Scott* (Oxford University Press, Oxford, 1904), pp. 380–1.

Part Three   Introduction – *Peter Bell the Third*

1 *The Life and Correspondence of Robert Southey*, vol. 4, ed. Rev. C. C. Southey (London, 1860), 360.
2 *The Letters of John Keats*, vol. 2, ed. H. J. Rollins (Cambridge University Press, Cambridge, 1958), 180.
3 *The Examiner*, no. 608 (22 August 1819), 530.
4 *Blackwood's Edinburgh Magazine*, 5 (September 1819), 639–42.
5 See the lead article entitled 'State of the Country', *Edinburgh Review*, 32 (October 1819), 293–309.
6 *The Examiner*, no. 610 (5 September 1819), 561–2. See also the leading article, 'More Absurdities of the Courier Respecting the Trades of the Reformers etc.', in no. 614 (3 October 1819), where Hunt vitiates his earnest insistence on the dignity and utility of trade by repeating his jibes at Gifford and the proprietor of the *Courier*.
7 See, for example, *The Examiner*, no. 603 (18 July 1819), 460–1, and the reports of the trial and execution of Robert Dean, no. 588 (4 April 1819), 212, and no. 591 (25 April 1819), 259–61. Dean, upset because his addresses had been refused by a young lady, had taken his revenge by cutting the throat not of the woman who had rejected him, but of a four-year-old girl who had nothing to do with the matter. It had occurred to him that the

soul of the woman who had offended him might not be in a fit state for Heaven, whereas he was assured of the innocence of the child. Hunt, somewhat wildly, suggests that Dean's mode of reasoning is an instance of the corrupting power of Methodism.
8   Halevy and E. P. Thompson have both argued that Methodism was the most powerful force inhibiting revolution in the first two decades of the nineteenth century. More recently, their thesis has been challenged by a number of historians who have succeeded in demonstrating that the Methodist leadership was ineffective in its attempts to control the political activities of its membership. See, for example, D. Hempton, *Methodism and Politics in British Society 1750–1830* (Hutchinson, London, 1984). But even if Hempton is correct, it remains the case that the authority of a popular orator such as Henry Hunt could be maintained only in competition with the Methodist preachers.
9   *The Letters of Percy Bysshe Shelley*, 2, 134–5.
10 *The Journal of Mary Shelley*, 124.
11 Michael Scrivener has detected in the poem a 'social snobbery' that is exposed in aristocratic 'sneers' and 'jibes' at the merely bourgeois. See *Radical Shelley: The Philosophical Anarchism and Utopian Thought of Percy Byshhe Shelley* (Princeton University Press, Princeton, 1982), pp. 218–24.
12 On Shelley's distrust of the comic, see Timothy Webb, 'Shelley and the Ambivalence of Laughter', *Essays and Studies* (1992), *Percy Bysshe Shelley: Bicentenary Essays*, ed. Kelvin Everest, 43–62.
13 On Castle's activities, see E. P. Thompson, *The Making of the English Working Classes*, 2nd edn (Penguin, Harmondsworth, 1980), pp. 534, 537–9, and 693–6.
14 *The Letters of Percy Bysshe Shelley*, 2, 135.
15 The stanza was first published by F. W. Bateson, 'Shelley on Wordsworth: Two Unpublished Stanzas from *Peter Bell the Third*', *Essays in Criticism*, 17 (1967), 125–9. Bateson wonders whether the stanza might indicate that Shelley shared his own suspicions concerning the relationship between William and Dorothy, but this seems wholly unlikely.
16 *Quarterly Review*, 18 (January 1818), 328. A further proof of how far Peter Bell has, by this point, become a type of the poet rather than a satire on Wordsworth is that Shelley believed this review, in fact the work of John Taylor Coleridge, to have been written by Southey.
17 James Chandler, *England in 1819: The Politics of Literary Culture and the Case of Romantic Historicism* (Chicago: Chicago University Press, 1998).

Chapter 7: Asleep in Italy: Byron and Shelley in 1819

1   The quotation from *Le Cosmopolite, ou le Citoyen du Monde* that Byron chose as the epigraph to *Childe Harold I and II*.
2   *Byron's Letters and Journals*, ed. Leslie A. Marchand, 12 vols (John Murray, London, 1973–82), 7, p. 17. All references to Byron's letters are to this edition.
3   The joke associates the Cato Street conspirators with the Utican Cato, Utica being the place of his suicide. Thistlewood's plot, Byron rightly suggests, was suicidal.

4 Samuel Bamford, *Passages in the Life of a Radical* (London: MacGibbon & Kee, 1967, first pubd 1844), 23.
5 *Byron's Bulldog: The Letters of John Cam Hobhouse to Lord Byron*, ed. Peter W. Graham (Ohio State University Press, Columbus, 1984), p. 284.
6 *Byron's Bulldog*, p. 281.
7 *Byron's Bulldog*, 290–3. Byron's defence, that he had intended Murray to show the squib only to Hobhouse, is disingenuous. The satirical verses that he was in the habit of enclosing in his letters to Murray were Byron's means of commenting on topical matters and were clearly intended for circulation. Hobhouse's relationship with Byron was a matter of political importance. In his first attempt to win the Westminster seat he had been attacked for his association with the licentious poet. To be publicly disowned by that same poet during the second campaign must have been irksome. It should at least be considered how far Hobhouse's and Kinnaird's advice against publishing *Don Juan* was weighted by their awareness of the damage that the poem might do to their own political chances.
8 See for example Erdman's essay in *Shelley and His Circle*, vol. 3, ed. Kenneth Neill Cameron (Harvard University Press, Cambridge, Mass., and Oxford University Press, London, 1970), pp. 282–323, and Andrew Rutherford, *Byron: A Critical Study* (Oliver & Boyd, Edinburgh and London, 1961), p. 187.
9 In his letter to Hobhouse of 29 March 1820, Byron passes almost immediately from 'such infamous scoundrels as Hunt and Burdett' to 'the blackguards' who have attacked Pope (7. 62–3).
10 William Hazlitt, 'Pope, Lord Byron, and Mr Bowles', *The Complete Works of William Hazlitt*, ed. P. P. Howe (J. M. Dent, London and Toronto, 1933), 19, 62–84.
11 Charles Robinson subtitles the chapter in which he describes this period, 'Shelley and Byron differing more than ever on politics, drama, morality and Keats', *Shelley and Byron: The Snake and Eagle Wreathed in Fight* (Johns Hopkins University Press, Baltimore and London, 1976), p. 138.
12 *The Letters of Percy Bysshe Shelley*, ed. F. L. Jones (Clarendon Press, Oxford, 1964), 2, 99, 120. All subsequent references to Shelley's letters are to this edition.
13 Hazlitt, who was peculiarly sensitive to social distinctions, defines the gentleman thus: 'It must be evident that he looks and does as he likes, without any restraint, confusion, or awkwardness. He is in fact master of his own person, as the professor of any art or science is of a particular instrument; he directs it to what use he intends', *The Complete Works of William Hazlitt*, 12, 209–10.
14 In this letter Shelley describes Cobbett as 'a fine umnopoios', that is, hymnwriter, or, more exactly, minstrel or balladeer. He and Peacock were fond of sharing little Grecian whimsies, but, like Byron's reference to the 'Utican conspirators', this seems remarkably flimsy, as if Shelley's immediate response when praising Cobbett was to invoke the classical education that separated him from Cobbett and that Cobbett famously despised.
15 Cobbett was consistently denounced in *The Examiner* until the summer of 1819, when there is a sudden change of tone. For example, Hunt rebuts the argument that the lower orders were too ignorant to be allowed to vote by appealing to the educative power of Cobbett's writings. On 5 September

1819, he wrote of Cobbett, 'with all our dislike of him on some accounts, he is at once the most powerful as well as popular political writer now living'. See *The Examiner*, no. 610, 561–2.
16 Kenneth Neill Cameron, 'Shelley, Cobbett, and the National Debt', *Journal of English and Germanic Philology*, 42 (1943), 197–209.
17 Quotations from 'A Philosophical View of Reform' are taken from *Shelley's Prose: The Trumpet of a Prophecy*, ed. David Lee Clark (University of New Mexico Press, Albuquerque, 1954).
18 *Shelley and His Circle*, 6, ed. Donald H. Reiman (Harvard University Press, Cambridge, Mass., 1973), p. 954.
19 So much so, that Robert Elliston carefully censored the script of the play before applying for a licence for public performance. See Thomas L. Aston, 'The Censorship of Byron's *Marino Faliero*', *Huntingdon Library Quarterly*, 26 (1962), 27–44.
20 Richard Lansdown is entirely persuasive in his argument that for all Byron's claims to be rejecting the Shakespearean tradition, Shakespeare continues to influence him more deeply than any other dramatist, and persuasive, too, in nominating *Julius Caesar* as the play that exerted a primary influence on *Marino Faliero*, but Lansdown surely underestimates the importance both of Byron's superficial and his more fundamental divergences from Shakespeare. See Richard Lansdown, *Byron's Historical Dramas* (Clarendon Press, Oxford, 1992), pp. 102–39.
21 The classic account of this episode is David V. Erdman, 'Byron's Stage Fright: the History of his Ambition and Fear of Writing for the Stage', *ELH*, 6 (1939), pp. 219–43,
22 Steven Jones, *Shelley's Satire: Violence, Exhortation, and Authority* (Northern Illinois University Press, DeKalb, 1994), pp. 94–123. See also Michael Henry Scrivener, *Radical Shelley: The Philosophical Anarchism and Utopian Thought of Percy Bysshe Shelley* (Princeton University Press, Princeton, NJ, 1982), pp. 198–210.
23 The further implication is that the Spenceans and the Cabinet were, to all intents and purposes, indistinguishable, for the revolutionary plan had, it seems, been hatched not by Thistlewood, but by John Castle, who was an *agent provocateur* in the pay of Sidmouth, the Home Secretary. See E. P. Thompson, *The Making of the English Working Class* (Penguin, Harmondsworth, 1980, first edition 1963), p. 693. It is a point that Shelley makes economically in two lines of *Peter Bell the Third*: 'There was a Castles, and a Canning,/A Cobbett and a Castlereagh.' Jerome Christensen has offered a 'Girardian' reading of *Marino Faliero*, in which the Doge's insurrection is represented as 'homeopathic', an enterprise through which Faliero does not threaten but secures the authority of the state by offering himself as scapegoat, *Lord Byron's Strength: Romantic Writing and Commercial Society* (John Hopkins University Press, Baltimore and London, 1993), pp. 258–75. But, as Byron's and Shelley's responses to the Cato Street conspiracy indicate, the politics of 1819 and 1820 permitted no other than a Girardian reading. All attempts to challenge state power served only to strengthen it.
24 Steven E. Jones, *Shelley's Satire*, p. 99, and Percy Bysshe Shelley, *Poems and Prose*, ed. Timothy Webb (J. M. Dent, London, 1995), pp. 470–3. Jones also

compares Hone's and Cruikshank's *The Political House that Jack Built* with its *Parody*, pp. 97–8.
25. William Godwin, *Enquiry Concerning Political Justice* (Penguin, Harmondsworth, 1976), p. 643.

Chapter 8: Leigh Hunt, Keats and the Politics of Cockney Poetry

1. Current interest in the political significance of Keats's poems originated with Jerome McGann's 1979 article, 'Keats and the Historical Method in Literary Criticism', reprinted in Jerome J. McGann, *The Beauty of Inflections: Literary Investigations in Historical Method and Theory* (Clarendon Press, Oxford, 1985), was developed in a special edition of *Studies in Romanticism*, 'Keats and Politics: A Forum', edited by Susan Wolfson, *SiR*, 25 (Summer 1986), 171–229, and culminated in two book-length studies and a volume of essays: Daniel P. Watkins, *Keats's Poetry and the Politics of the Imagination* (Associated University Presses, London and Toronto, 1989), Marjorie Levinson, *Keats's Life of Allegory: The Origins of a Style* (Oxford University Press, Oxford and New York, 1989), *Keats and History*, ed. Nicholas Roe (Cambridge University Press, Cambridge, 1995), *John Keats and the Culture of Dissent* (Clarendon Press, Oxford, 1997). Jeffrey N. Cox's fine study *Poetry and Politics in the Cockney School: Keats, Shelley, Hunt and Their Circle* (Cambridge University Press, New York, 1998) was published too late, unfortunately, to have influenced this chapter.
2. *The Letters of John Keats*, ed. Hyder Edward Rollins (Cambridge University Press, Cambridge, 1958), 2, p. 244 hereafter *Letters*.
3. *Keats: The Critical Heritage*, ed. G. M. Matthews (Routledge & Kegan Paul, London, 1971), p. 2.
4. Walter Jackson Bate, *John Keats* (Harvard University Press, Cambridge, Mass., 1963), p. 366.
5. Vincent Newey makes the strongest possible case for the political import of the poem, offering it as 'a critique of society', but even in this reading it does not appear to be a critique either powerful or pointed. See Vincent Newey, 'Keats, history and the poets' in *Keats and History*, ed. Nicholas Roe, pp. 165–93, 168–9.
6. William Keach, 'Cockney Couplets: Keats and the Politics of Style', *SiR*, 25 (Summer 1986), 182–96.
7. Hunt continued to tinker with the poem until 1844. Quotations are taken from the first edition, *The Story of Rimini* (John Murray, London, 1816). In this edition the lines are not numbered.
8. Hunt presumably derives his word from the verb, 'jaunce', which describes the prancing of a horse, but 'jauntiness' already carried its modern sense.
9. J. G. Lockhart, signing himself 'Z', 'The Cockney School of Poetry', *Blackwood's Edinburgh Magazine*, 2 (November, 1817), 194–201.
10. In both poems the husband detects the crime when the wife speaks endearments to her lover in her sleep.
11. *The Complete Works of William Hazlitt*, ed. P. P. Howe (J. M. Dent, London and Toronto, 1931), 12, p. 208.

12 See Walter Jackson Bate, *The Stylistic Development of John Keats* (Modern Language Association, New York, 1945).
13 Bamford published his first volume of verse, *The Weaver Boy*, in 1819. Keats seems to have been irked that Bamford was, like Keats, given the advantage of Hunt's benevolent patronage in *The Examiner*.
14 Marjorie Levinson, *Keats's Life of Allegory: The Origins of a Style*, p. 5.
15 Morris Dickstein, 'Keats and Politics', and Alan Bewell, 'The Political Implication of Keats's Classicist Aesthetics', *SiR*, 25 (Summer, 1986), 175–81 and 220–9. Bewell's conclusion, that 'Keats's inability to speak in an assured political voice' represents an identification with those whose political voice had been silenced', is less convincing. It comes close to taking Keats for a 'weaver boy'.
16 J. G. Lockhart, signing himself 'Z', 'The Cockney School of Poetry', no. IV, *Blackwood's Edinburgh Magazine*, 2 (August, 1818), 194–201, and J. W. Croker, unsigned review, *Quarterly Review*, 19 (April 1818, although this issue was, in fact, published in September), 204–8.
17 Thomas A. Reed, 'Keats and the Gregarious Advance of Intellect in *Hyperion*, *ELH*, 55 (1988), 195–232, p. 195. The fullest and most suggestive account of Keats's response to his critics as embodied in his poetry is offered by Andrew Bennett, *Keats, Narrative and Audience: The Posthumous Life of Writing* (Cambridge University Press, Cambridge, 1994) to which I am indebted.
18 Walter Jackson Bate, *John Keats*, p. 131.
19 Bate notes that 58 per cent of the lines in the first two books consist of dialogue, *John Keats*, p. 391.
20 Michael O'Neill shares my suspicion of the poem's inability 'to believe full-bloodedly in a liberal, optimistic version of history', but would rather deny that this failure is 'class-motivated'. For him, it is a product of Keats's dawning recognition of the inevitable difference between imaginative and political value. See Michael O'Neill, '"When this warm scribe my hand": writing and history *in Hyperion* and *The Fall of Hyperion'*, in *Keats and History*, ed. Nicholas Roe, pp. 143–64.
21 Walter Jackson Bate, *John Keats*, p. 590. Bate extended and generalized his belief that Keats suffered from a sense of his own belatedness in his *The Burden of the Past*, which Bloom acknowledges as supplying the germ of *The Anxiety of Influence*, and its successors.
22 K. K. Ruthven, 'Keats's *Dea Moneta*', *Studies in Romanticism*, 15 (1976), 445–59. Levinson comments that Ruthven 'does not do very much in a critical vein with his mythographic findings', only to agree that 'there's not a great deal to do'. She goes on to use Ruthven's perception in her discussion of *Lamia*, not *The Fall of Hyperion*, *Keats's Life of Allegory: The Origins of a Style*, p. 257. Watkins is unique in insisting on the complexity of Moneta's dialogue with the poet, a dialogue in which the poet is 'belittled and maligned while at the same time being rewarded', and allowing that recognition to control his response to the poem. My difference with Watkins is that, in the end, he reads the poem as an allegory in which Moneta is the embodiment of the 'market place' that is the governing power of Keats's world. The market place values poetry only as a 'product' that functions to absorb the contradictions inherent in a capitalist society and to 'soothe

the frustrations of the alienated'. Such a reading grants Keats a stable, ironic understanding of the naivety of the poet, establishing him as the authoritative analyst of his own cultural and historical predicament. See Daniel P. Watkins, *Keats's Poetry and the Politics of the Imagination*, pp. 156–76.
23. Compare Lockhart: 'It is a better and wiser thing to be a starved apothecary than a starved poet; so back to the shop Mr John, back to "plasters, pills, and ointment boxes," &c.'
24. Bate, for example, insists that lines 187–210, the lines in which Moneta denies the poet's title to the name of poet, should not be regarded as a part of the poem on the sole authority of a single memorandum by Woodhouse: 'Keats seems to have intended to erase this and the next twenty-one lines' (Walter Jackson Bate, *John Keats*, pp. 599–600). But it is easy to understand Woodhouse's response as an attempt to save his friend from supplying, even after his death, ammunition of the kind that hostile critics had shown themselves so ready to use. Woodhouse would have had bitter memories of the critical response to the Preface to *Endymion*. Stillinger seems right to argue that Woodhouse's note has the status of a critical conjecture rather than a record of an authorial decision. See Jack Stillinger, *The Text of Keats's Poems* (Harvard University Press, Cambridge, Mass., 1974), p. 262.
25. Jerome J. McGann, *The Beauty of Inflections: Literary Investigations in Historical Method and Theory*, p. 53.
26. See Geoffrey Hartman, 'Poem And Ideology: A study of Keats's "To Autumn"', in *The Fate of Reading and Other Essays* (Chicago: Chicago University Press, 1975), pp. 124–46; Jerome McGann, *The Beauty of Inflections: Literary Investigations in Historical Method and Theory*, pp. 48–65; William Keach, 'Cockney Couplets: Keats and the Politics of Style', *SiR*, 25 (Summer, 1986), 192–6; Nicolas Roe, 'Keats's Commonwealth', in *Keats and History*, ed. Nicholas Roe, pp. 194–211.
27. In 1819 Cobbett published an English grammar, addressed to 'Young Persons', and 'more especially' to 'Soldiers, Sailors, Apprentices and Ploughboys'. Cobbett's design is to challenge the monopoly of literacy claimed by those who had enjoyed a classical education, and hence to challenge the monopoly of political power to which, they claimed, their education entitled them. On Cobbett's *Grammar*, see Olivia Smith, *The Politics of Language 1791–1819* (Clarendon Press, Oxford, 1984), pp. 239–48.
28. *Byron's Letters and Journals*, ed. Marchand, 7, p. 81.
29. On the topicality of *Marino Faliero*, see Malcolm Kelsall, *Byron's Politics* (Harvester, Brighton, 1987), pp. 89–109.
30. Another example of this is Susan Wolfson's contrast between Shaw's appreciation of Keats's attack on the 'avaricious capitalism' of Isabella's brothers and John Scott's distaste for Keats's 'schoolboy vituperation of trade and traders'. It is clear to me that Scott is offended not, as Wolfson would have it, by a proto-Marxist radicalism, but by what he takes to be an affected, genteel contempt for trade and traders. See Wolfson's 'Introduction' to 'Keats and Politics: A Forum', *SiR*, 25 (Summer, 1986), 171–4. Again, one finds that the same passage offers itself to a reversible political understanding.

Index

Abrams, M. H., 1, 4, 5, 9, 11
Ackroyd, Peter, 203
Aikin, Lucy, 213
Allen, Don Cameron, 25, 202
Althusser, Louis, 8
Anacreon, 74
Analytical Review, 4, 63
Annual Review, 211
Arnold, Matthew, 4, 9, 11
Aston, Thomas L., 217
Austen, Jane, 6, 11, 102

Bage, Robert, 3
Bailey, Benjamin, 181–2
Bainbridge, Simon, 205, 206
Ballantyne, James, 94
Bamford, Samuel, 159, 189, 219
Barbauld, Anna Laetitia, 29, 137–8, 140
Bate, Walter Jackson, 194, 218, 219, 220
Bateson, F. W., 215
Beaumarchais, Pierre, 36
Beaumont, Lady, 119
Bedford, Duke of, 62–3
Bennett, Andrew, 219
Bentham, Jeremy, 166
Bewell, Alan J., 191, 219
Birmingham, 27–41 *passim*, 49
Blair, Anthony, 14
Blackwood's Edinburgh Magazine, 147–8, 181, 187–8, 195–6
Blake, William, 1, 3, 4, 29, 44, 77
 Ahania, 61; *Fertilization of Egypt*, 30, 55–6; *French Revolution* 56; *Los*, 61; *Marriage of Heaven and Hell*, 4, 7, 17, 48–60, 61;
 Songs of Innocence and Experience, 49, 56; *Urizen*, 61
Bloom, Harold, 6, 204
Borst, William A., 212
Boucher, François, 30
Bourke, Richard, 200, 211

Bowles, William Lisle, 11
Bridgewater, Duke of, 32, 38
Brindley, James, 32, 33, 38, 41
British Critic, 139–40
Brooks, Cleanth, 1
Brothers, Richard, 52, 58–9
Brougham, Lord Henry Peter, 149, 159
Brown, David, 99, 207
Bryant, Sir Arthur, 85–6
Buceleuch, family of, 96–7
Burdett, Sir Francis, 148, 157–62 *passim*, 177, 182, 190, 197, 198
Burdom, Christopher, 204
Burke, Edmund, 15, 21, 62, 132
Burns, Robert, 94–5
Butler, Marilyn, 2, 5, 9, 11–16 *passim*, 200
Byron, George Gordon Lord, 1, 2, 4, 6, 8, 14, 17–18, 55, 99, 103, 154, 156–63, 198–9
 Childe Harold, 85, 90–1, 103, 128–44;
 Don Juan, 157, 179; *Marino Faliero*, 162, 166–74, 198; *Parisina*, 187; *Sardanapalus*, 163; *The Two Foscari*, 169

Calvert, Raisley, 127
Cameron, K. N., 1, 200, 217
Canning, George, 46–7, 62–4, 65, 82, 198
The New Morality, 62–4, 68, 72–3
Carey, Robert, 93
Carlile, Richard, 149–50, 162
Caroline, Queen, 156, 159, 162, 166
Cartwright, Major John, 158
Castle, John, 152, 217
Castlereagh, Lord, 152, 160, 174
Cato Street Conspiracy, 157–8, 162
Chandler, James, 1, 13, 155, 200, 215
Chaucer, Geoffrey, 114, 186
Christensen, Jerome, 1, 200, 217
Clarkson, Thomas, 89

221

Clinton, William Jefferson, 14
Cloots, Anacharsis, 18
Cobbet, William, 15, 148, 152, 158–66 *passim*, 177, 182, 188, 197, 198, 216–17, 220
Coleridge, John Taylor, 215
Coleridge, Samuel Taylor, 1, 6, 10, 14, 15–16, 39, 63, 70
  The Ancient Mariner, 72; *Christabel*, 98; *Fears in Solitude*, 72–3; *France: an Ode*, 73, *Osorio* (later entitled *Remorse*), 69–70: *Religious Musings*, 21–8; *The Watchman*, 22, 25; 'To a Young Ass', 63
Colley, Linda, 85, 206
Collings, David, 202
Constable, George, 35
Cornwall, Barry, 3
Cottle, Joseph, 22, 27, 202
Courier, 61, 63, 149
Cowley, Abraham, 39
Crabbe, George, 122
Crawford, Robert, 104, 208
Crewe, Emma, 30, 36
Critical Review, 63, 205, 211
Croker, John Wilson, 130, 135, 136, 140–1, 191, 212
Cronin, Richard, 209
Cruikshank, George, 175
Curran Stuart, 205
Curtis, Jared, 209, 210

Daily Star, 63
Damer, Mrs, 36
Dante, 193
Darbishire, Helen, 210
Darwin, Erasmus, 3, 9, 16–17, 48, 50, 51, 57, 63
  The Botanic Garden, 29–47; *The Temple of Nature*, 47; *Zoonomia*, 38
Dawson, Paul, 1, 200
Delaney, Mrs, 33, 36
De Man, Paul, 4
De Quincey, Thomas, 77
Derrida, Jacques, 171
Devonshire, Duchess of, 143
Dickstein, Morris, 191, 219

Dilke, Charles, 181
Dryden, John, 101
Dupuis, Charles, 3

Edgeworth, Maria, 104
Edinburgh, 94, 100, 103, 146
Edinburgh Review, 31, 107, 121, 139, 141, 148, 211, 214
Eldon, Lord, 174
Elgin, Lord, 139
Ellis, George, 62, 99, 132, 141
Erdman, David, 1, 50, 200, 203, 204, 215, 217
Erskine, Thomas, 63
Essick, Robert N., 204
Everest, Kelvin, 1, 200
Examiner, The, 148–50, 162, 164, 182–3, 188, 214, 216–17

Fabre, Philippe, 26
Ferguson, Adam, 207
Fielding, Henry, 151
Fitzgerald, Lord Edward, 62
Foucault, Michel, 11
Fox, Charles James, 61, 62, 101, 103–4, 111, 116–17, 125, 157–9, 182
Franklin, Benjamin, 27, 33–4, 45
French, Mrs, 36
Frere, John Hookham, 46–7, 62, 65, 82
Friedman, Michael H., 209
Fuseli, Henry, 29, 30, 33, 35–6

Galt, John, 213
Garrett, Clarke, 203
George III, 34–5, 75, 77
George IV, formerly the Prince Regent, 86, 175
Gibson, John S., 208
Gifford, William, 62, 82, 149, 173
Gillray, James, 62–4
Glasgow, 107
Gleckner, Robert, 136, 213
Godwin, William, 28, 29, 54, 56, 63, 70–1, 72, 166
Goldsmith, Oliver, 121
Goslee, Nancy Moore, 207
Gray, Thomas, 32
Grenville, Lord George, 140
Grey, Lord, 142–3

Halévy, Élie, 215
Hardy, Thomas, 23
Harrowby, Earl of, 157
Hartley, David, 23, 25, 27
Hartman, Geoffrey, 12–13, 15, 209, 220
Hassler, Donald M., 202
Haydon, Benjamin, 191
Hazlitt, William, 15, 108–9, 161, 166, 187–8, 216
Hegel, G. W. F., 5–6, 96
Heine, Heinrich, 6
Hempton, D., 215
Henderson, T. F., 206
Henry V, 67
Henry VIII, 93
Hill, Geoffrey, 12–3, 15
Hindmarsh, Robert, 48, 49–50, 203
Hoagwood, Terence A., 204
Hobhouse, John Cam, 156–61 *passim*, 216
Holbach, P. H. D. d', 56–7
Holland, Lord, 142, 157
Hopkins, G. M., 13
Howard, John, 48, 50, 203
Hunt Henry, 18, 147–8, 158–9, 177, 179, 182, 188, 197
Hunt, Leigh, 18, 147–51, 162, 166, 181–3, 189–91, 193, 196
The Descent of Liberty, 16–17, 88–9
The Story of Rimini, 183–8, 193

Indicator, The, 182

Jeffrey, Francis, 106, 120, 121–3, 125, 132, 134–5, 139–41, 208, 211, 212
Jocelyn, Lord, 132
Johnson, Edgar, 100, 206, 208
Johnson, Joseph, 17, 29–31, 48, 50, 52
Johnston, Kenneth, 1, 200
Jones, A. L. 210
Jones, Miss, 38
Jones, Stephen, 175, 217–18

Kauffman, Angelica, 36
Keach, William, 182, 218, 220
Keats, John, 1, 4, 18, 147, 154, 161–2, 181–2

Endymion, 181; *The Fall of Hyperion*, 193–6; *Hyperion*, 189, 191–3; *Isabella*, 181, 189; 'La Belle Dame Sans Merci' 7; *Lamia*, 189; 'On First Looking into Chapman's Homer', 189–90; 'To Autumn', 199
Kelley, Theresa, 209–10
Kelsall, Malcolm, 1, 2, 200, 213, 220
King-Hele, Desmond, 203
Kinniard Douglas, 156, 158

Lamb, Charles, 63
Lamb, George, 158
Landor, Walter Savage, 17
  Birth of Poesy, 74–5; *Gebir*, 74–87
Lansdown, Richard, 217
Larkin, Philip, 194
Leask, Nigel, 1, 200
Lenman, Bruce P., 208
Le Pluche, Abbé, 36
Levinson, Marjorie, 1, 2, 3, 189–90, 200, 201, 211–12, 218, 219
Linnaeus, 29, 37
Liu, Alan, 200, 211
Lockhart, J. G., 95–6, 99, 103, 187–8, 191, 193–6, 207, 208, 220
Lloyd Charles, 63
Edmund Oliver, 70–2
London Corresponding Society, 62, 70
Longman, William, 95
'Loves of the Triangles, The', 46–7
Louis XVI, 36, 43, 63, 77
Lukacs, Georg, 96, 98–9, 206, 207
Lyttelton, George, Lord, 122

Mackenzie, Henry, 206–7
Malmesbury, Lord, 61
Malthus, Thomas, 80
Marchand, Leslie, 212, 213, 214, 215
Marino, Gian Battista, 39
Marx, Karl, 6, 41, 202
Mason, William, 223
Matthews, Geoffrey, 181–2
Mathias, T. J., 42–3, 62, 65
McAdam, Thomas, 94
McGann, Jerome, 1, 4, 5–9, 12, 16, 132, 141, 197, 200, 212–13, 218, 220

McKendrick, Neil, 203
McNeil, Maureen, 40–1, 202
Mee, Jon, 52–3, 56, 58 203, 204
Methodism, 149–50, 152
Michelangelo, 56, 114
Mill, John Stuart, 11
Millar, John, 207
Millar, William, 105
Milton, John, 25–7, 101, 114–15, 127, 190
Montrose, Earl of, 115
Moore, Sir John, 140
Moore, Thomas, 150
More, Hannah, 65
Morning Chronicle, 51–2, 61, 63
Morning Post, 61, 160
Mullan, John, 206
Murray, John, 105, 140–1, 160, 161, 212

Napoleon, 63, 80, 85–144 *passim*
Nelson, Horatio, 18, 118, 136
Newey, Vincent, 218
Newton, Isaac, 23, 27, 30
North, Mrs, 36

O'Coigley, Daniel, 62
O'Connor, Arthur, 63
O'Neill, Michael, 13, 219
Oxford, Lady, 65

Paine, Thomas, 15, 28, 29, 45, 48, 50–60 *passim*, 63
Paley, Morton D., 203
Peacock, Thomas Love, 62, 164
Peckham, Morse, 5–6
Peel, Robert, 156, 157, 159
Peterloo Massacre, 147–9, 154, 174–9 *passim*, 199
Piggott, Stuart, 206
Piper, H. W., 202
Pitt, William, 23–4, 47, 61–2, 67, 75, 77, 101–4 *passim*, 119
Political Register, 164, 197
Pollo, Stefanaq, 212
Polwhele, Richard, 42–3
Poole, Thomas, 24
Pope, Alexander, 122, 153, 161–2
Portland, Duke of, 33
Portland Vase, 30, 32, 33

Preston, Thomas, 175
Priestley, Joseph, 17, 23–9 *passim*, 35–6, 44–5, 49–50, 57–9, 63
Proud, Joseph, 49
Pursuits of Literature, The, 42–3, 62, 65
Puto, Apben, 212

Quarterly Review, 133, 140–1, 149, 154, 160, 181, 191, 212

Reed, Thomas, 191, 219
Reeves, Clara, 74
Reiman, Donald, 165
Reynolds, John Hamilton, 149, 181
Reynolds, Sir Joshua, 168
Robinson, Charles, 215
Roe, Nicholas, 1, 200, 218, 220
Rose R. B., 44–5, 203
Rose, William Stewart, 101
Rousseau, Jean-Jacques, 36, 63
Rutherford, Andrew, 215
Ruthven, K. K., 195–6, 219

Saint-Just, Louis Antoine, 15, 54
Sappho, 74
Schama, Simon, 202
Scock, Peter A., 204
Scott, John, 220
Scott, Walter, 92–109, 111, 131–2
'The Field of Waterloo' 86; *The Heart of Midlothian*, 108; *The Lady of the Lake*, 100; *The Lay of the Last Minstrel*, 85, 96–100, 104, 106, 111; *Life of Napoleon Bonaparte*, 208–9: *Marmion*, 100–8, 131–2; *Minstrelsy of the Scottish Borders*, 92–7, 208; *The Talisman*, 104; *A Vision of Don Roderick*, 131, 139–40; *Waverley*, 104, 108
Scrivener, Michel, 1, 51–2, 200, 203, 215, 217
Shakespeare, William, 171–2
Shaw, Philip, 86–7, 206
Shelley, Harriet, 154, 163
Shelley, Mary, 154
Shelley, P. B., 4, 14, 17–18, 50, 79, 163–5, 197–9

Shelley – *continued*
  Adonais, 153; *Alastor*, 4; *Charles I*, 11; *The Mask of Anarchy*, 162, 166, 174–80, 197–8; 'Mont Blanc', 11, *Peter Bell the Third*, 147–55, 179; 'A Philosophical View of Reform'; 164–6; *Prometheus Unbound*, 163, 176, 178; *Queen Mab*, 7, 163, 174; *The Triumph of Life*, 174
Shenstone, William, 101
Sidmouth, Lord, 174–5
Sidney, Algernon, 114, 190
Sidney, Sir Philip, 8, 114
Simpson, David, 15–16, 200, 201, 211
Siskin, Clifford, 1, 9–11, 12, 200, 201
Skene, James, 100
Smith, Adam, 207
Smith, Olivia, 220
Smollett, Tobias, 194
Southey, Robert, 17, 63, 64, 147, 150
  Joan of Arc, 65–8, 72, *The Poet's Pilgrimage to Waterloo*, 85–91
Spa Field Riot, 175
Spencer, Terence, 213
Spenser, Edmund, 101, 114
Spinoza, Baruch, 25
Stafford, John, 175–6
St Clair, William, 213
Sterne, Laurence, 95
Stewart, Dugald, 207
Stillinger, Jack, 220
Surrey, Earl of, 93
Swift, Jonathan, 53, 56

Tennyson, Alfred, 103
Thelwall, John, 23, 26, 62
Thistlewood, Arthur, 157–8, 175
Thompson, E. P., 203, 215, 217
Times, The, 147
Todd, F. M., 1, 200, 210
Tooke, Horne, 23, 62, 63
Trott, Nicola, 202

Unsex'd Females, The, 42–3

Vendler, Helen, 13
Villalobos, John, 204
Volney, Constantin, 36, 50–1, 52

Watkins, Daniel, 1, 195, 200, 218, 219–20
Watson, Dr James, 175
Watt, James, 44
Watt, James, Jr, 46
Waugh, Evelyn, 14
Webb, Timothy, 175–6, 215
Webster, Thomas, 52, 58
Wedgwood, Josiah, 3, 30, 33, 38, 40–1, 44, 46
Weinbrot, Howard, 85, 205
Wellington, Duke of (Arthur Wellesley), 86, 118, 212
Wesley, John, 150, 152
Westminster Elections, 158–60
Whitbread, Samuel, 63, 142
Wilson, John (Christopher North), 119, 147
Wolfson, Susan, 2, 200, 218, 220
Wollstonecraft, Mary, 29, 42–3, 48, 63, 72, 154
Woodring, Carl, 1, 2, 128, 200, 211
Wordsworth, William, 1, 3, 4, 9, 10, 13, 14, 15, 86, 109, 110–27, 149–53, 185–6, 197
  The Borderers, 69–79; *Descriptive Sketches*, 56; *The Excursion*, 124; *Lyrical Ballads*, 4, 7, 11, 16, 18, 73, 110–11, 114–15, 121, 185–6; *Peter Bell*, 149–50; *Poems in Two Volumes*, 110–27; *The Prelude*, 11, 149–50; *The Ruined Cottage*, 67
Worrall, David, 203
Wren, Sir Christopher, 24
Wright, John, 52, 58
Wylie, Ian, 201, 202